MW01096594

Strategic Media Relations in the Age of Information

An Evidence-Based Approach

Dustin W. Supa
Boston University

Lynn M. Zoch
Radford University

New York   Oxford
OXFORD UNIVERSITY PRESS

Oxford University Press is a department of the University of Oxford.
It furthers the University's objective of excellence in research, scholarship,
and education by publishing worldwide. Oxford is a registered trade mark of
Oxford University Press in the UK and certain other countries.

Published in the United States of America by Oxford University Press
198 Madison Avenue, New York, NY 10016, United States of America.

Library of Congress Cataloging-in-Publication Data

Names: Supa, Dustin W., author. | Zoch, Lynn M., author.
Title: Strategic media relations in the age of information : an
    evidence-based approach / Dustin W. Supa, Boston University, Lynn M.
    Zoch, Radford University.
Description: First edition. | New York : Oxford University Press, [2021] |
    Includes bibliographical references and index.
Identifiers: LCCN 2019028868 (print) | LCCN 2019028869 (ebook) | ISBN
    9780190844271 (paperback) | ISBN 9780190844288 (ebook)
Subjects: LCSH: Public relations. | Communication. | Mass media.
Classification: LCC HD59 .S79 2021 (print) | LCC HD59 (ebook) | DDC
    659.2—dc23
LC record available at https://lccn.loc.gov/2019028868
LC ebook record available at https://lccn.loc.gov/2019028869

To our families.
Without their patience and amazing ability
to be ignored for long periods of time
this book would not have been written.

TABLE OF CONTENTS

PREFACE

This book offers an evidence-based perspective on the modern practice of media relations, primarily focusing on the development and strategic execution of a media relations program for a variety of organizations. It is targeted to students in advanced courses in public relations or communications, and to entry and midlevel public relations and media relations practitioners. Even with that being the case, we have written it with the knowledge that many colleges and universities don't have room in the curriculum for a stand-alone media relations course. Therefore, it has been reviewed by colleagues across the country who teach media relations in a variety of courses and ways, and who have suggested ways to adapt the book for a wide variety of public relations courses.

We decided to take on this project because a lot of questions concerning the value of media relations in the modern information environment have been raised over the past few years. In an era when organizations can reach their audiences directly via social media, the importance of traditional media relations is constantly being challenged. Yet, in a recent *PR Week* study, 84% of practitioners were optimistic about the future of media relations—if the practitioner can adapt to the modern media environment. That same study revealed that 74% of practitioners have already altered their approach to media relations. In this book, we will look at some of those adaptations for media relations and explore the knowledge that is needed to practice in the modern environment.

What this book is not is a public relations writing text. We leave that task for others, and for courses with that focus. Our purpose and plan is to use research and practice to support our contention that using media relations can and should be a strategic process for a practitioner and an organization. To that end we have grounded the book in history, theory, and empirical research studies about the practice of media relations and the relationship between practitioners and their main audience—journalists.

We have presented the information in the book in four sections. The first section introduces media relations and provides an overview of key concepts. It also includes the importance of media relations in a modern world and a short history of media relations. Section 2 provides the strategic grounding for the practice of media relations, including an overview of theories useful to the practice, how to think strategically about audiences, relationships with journalists, and ethical guiding principles. Section 3 contains chapters that focus on the execution of a media relations program. The chapters include how to assess newsworthiness; managing goals objectives, strategies, and expectations from organizations and journalists; tactics used within a strategic media relations plan; and proactive measurement and evaluation. Section 4 addresses ways in which a strategic media relations program can be applied to various fields and to diverse audiences. We also provide a final chapter that is comprised of four case studies for further strategic thinking and discussion.

AUTHOR BIOS

Dustin W. Supa, PhD

Dr. Supa is senior associate dean and associate professor of public relations at the College of Communication at Boston University. He previously directed the public relations sequence and taught at Ball State University. He is a member of the Arthur W. Page Society and is the current head of the public relations division of Association for Education in Journalism and Mass Communication (AEJMC). Dr. Supa serves on the advisory board for the International Public Relations Research Conference and the International History of Public Relations Conference, and on the editorial boards of *Public Relations Review* and the *Journal of Public Relations Research*. Supa has a master's in public relations and a doctoral degree in mass communication from the University of Miami, where he was an advisee of his coauthor. Prior to earning his PhD, he worked in multiple areas of public relations, including agency, nonprofit, and governmental public affairs. Supa continues to serve as an industry consultant and has been invited to lecture nationally and internationally.

Dr. Supa has authored or coauthored nearly two dozen peer-reviewed articles, more than 40 conference papers, and five book chapters. He is the editor of *The World of Communication—The Human Storyteller*. He and his coauthors have received top paper awards for their research on media relations and corporate communication, and he was recently honored for his contributions to research in the field of the history of public relations.

Lynn M. Zoch, PhD

Dr. Zoch is Emerita Professor of public relations at Radford University in Virginia, where she formerly served as the founding Director of the School of Communication. She previously taught at the University of South Carolina where she served as director of the School of Journalism and Mass Communication's master's degree programs and sequence head for the advertising and public relations programs; the University of Miami where she taught and mentored her coauthor; and the University of West Florida. She teaches across the public relations curriculum, as well as strategic communications, organizational communication, research methods, training and development, and pedagogy, primarily at the upper-undergraduate and graduate levels. Zoch has master's and doctoral degrees from Syracuse University in public relations management and public communication, respectively, and an undergraduate degree from St. Lawrence University. Prior to receiving her PhD and starting her teaching career, she worked in nonprofit, educational, and association public relations.

Her research interests all involve the intersection of research and theory with the practice of public relations, and include media relations, nonprofit public relations, and organizational legitimacy. She is the author of numerous articles and book chapters and has presented her work nationally and internationally. In 2019, Zoch was awarded the Institute for Public Relations Pathfinder Award for the impact of her research contributions to the profession of public relations. She is active in the public relations division of the Association for Education in Journalism and Mass Communication (AEJMC) and serves the Public Relations Society of America (PRSA) as a reviewer for the Certificate in Education for Public Relations (CEPR).

ACKNOWLEDGMENTS

Throughout the writing of this book, our goal has been to provide a means for students and practitioners to elevate their thinking about media relations and to consider it a strategic program rather than a tactical activity. At the same time, we tried to support that thinking with useful tactics and suggestions for how they might be incorporated into the strategic plan. We have not spared media relations from criticism, nor denied its problems. But, at the end, we feel optimistic for its future, as practitioners of today and tomorrow learn to adapt to the new technologies and media world that awaits them.

As with all projects such as this, we could not have completed this book without the cooperation and help of colleagues, friends and former students. We want to thank Melissa Brown, Sarah Dasher, Marianne Eisenmann, Mike Fernandez, Karen Freberg, Michael Holley, Matt Kelly, Ray Kotcher, Tina McCorkindale, Janet Morrissey, and Jonathan Withington for their thoughtful and timely commentary—from a professional viewpoint—about our subject areas. We also thank Professor Jim O'Rourke from the Fanning Center for Business Communication, and his students in the Mendoza College of Business at the University of Notre Dame for not only sharing their case studies with us but allowing us to adapt them to a media relations viewpoint.

Two of our, now former, students helped us with our research and indexing: Breyuana Smith at Radford University and Audrey Sun at Boston University. In addition, our appreciation goes out to the people at Oxford University Press who got us started on this path and helped us along the way: Toni Magyar, former editor; Keith Chasse, current editor; Alyssa Quinones, assistant editor; Brad Rau, production project manager; and Marne Evans, copy editor.

Our sincere thanks are also extended to the reviewers of this text. They include: Brad Van Alstyne, *Dominican University of California;* Matt Charles, *University of Virginia;* William L. Cowen IV, *Villanova University;* James Devitt, *New York University;* Francine Edwards, *Delaware State University;* Betsy Emmons, *Samford University;* Darrick Evensen, *Cardiff University;* Catherine Foster, *Canisius College;* Tamara L. Gillis, *Elizabethtown College;*

Randy Hines, *University of North Georgia;* Ann D. Jabro, *Robert Morris University;* Kelly McBride, *York College of Pennsylvania;* Alexandra Merceron, *Columbia University;* Cayce Myers, *Virginia Tech;* Margaret C. Ritsch, *Texas Christian University;* Cathy Rogers, *Loyola University New Orleans;* Kirsten Ruby, *University of Illinois;* Amy Shanler, *Boston University;* Jessalynn Strauss, *Elon University;* Anne E. Stuart, *Lasell College;* Matthew S. VanDyke, *University of Alabama;* Christopher Wilson, *Brigham Young University;* Margot Winick, *University of Miami;* and, Brenda Wrigley, *Curry College.*

1 WHAT DOES IT MEAN TO PRACTICE MEDIA RELATIONS?

Media relations, broken down into its most basic components, is a fairly simple proposition. In fact, those wishing to garner journalists' attention for an organization only need to follow three simple steps; one—find the story, two—find an audience, and three—tell the story to the audience. However, if media relations were really that simple, there wouldn't be a need for this book, nor for the wide variety of seminars, webinars, journal articles, how-to guides, blog posts, and checklists focused on what makes an organization's media relations successful.

But where do the complexities lie, and what are the aspects of media relations that make it one of the most practiced yet least understood areas of public relations? What are the challenges that create the need for so many pundits and training experts? The goal of this book is to explore those aspects of media relations that create confusion and challenge, allowing the reader to discover or rediscover areas that can be particularly problematic for an organization of any type. Ultimately, we hope the reader will become a more conscientious media relations practitioner who understands the dynamics of this deceptively simple field.

While our initial three steps seem simple enough—and they are!—each contains complexities that communicators who practice effective media relations must deal with to serve the organization they represent in the best ways possible. Throughout the book, we'll explore and break down each of these three areas—find the story, find the audience, and tell the story to the audience—until we have a strong understanding of each, so that by the end of this text, media relations really can become a simple three-step process.

The first step in our journey to becoming an effective media relations practitioner is to know what questions we need to ask. Let's explore our three steps to identify some of the complexities each has.

1. **Find the story.** Whenever the media relations practitioner wants to share news, the first step is to identify what the news is for the organization for which you're working. This may be somewhat simple for an organization that creates new products for which there is already a built-in audience—something that people are willing to line up for a week in advance. Likewise, finding stories is easy for an organization whose decisions might have an immediate impact on the economy, or for an organization that has information that people not only care about but actively seek out.

   For the majority of media relations practitioners, however, finding stories isn't nearly as easy, and the option of simply announcing a press conference will not yield a roomful of journalists eager to ask questions and find their own unique angle to report the news. Rather, the media relations practitioner is often relied upon to act as the initial journalist. This involves identifying a possible story idea, envisioning what it could become, and then following that idea through to execution. This can truly be an exercise in creativity. Take for example the situation where a business owner would like to have the celebration of his company's tenth anniversary in business covered by a media outlet. In a small community with a weekly newspaper this might be considered news, but in a large urban area with a 24/7 news cycle, there could be any number of businesses celebrating an anniversary, or a promotion, or some small accomplishment. How does one story stand out from another? In other words, how does the media relations practitioner find the story that garners attention when there are so many competing stories? Creativity is certainly needed, but as important is a deep understanding of what news means to journalists. The practitioner also needs a grasp both of journalists as audiences themselves and of media processes. The position also involves a high level of organizational knowledge—and maybe, a second dash of creativity. In other words, finding the story may not be as simple as we would like it to be, but after reading this book, you'll come away with the tools you need to find a potential news story for any organization.

2. **Find the audience.** This part, too, seems simple enough—our audience is whomever we want to tell the story to, and in the case of media relations, our audience is the journalist. Beyond that, though, it gets a little more complicated. Unlike the local community, the state or local government, investors, customers, or any other of the targeted groups

your organization reaches out to directly, if your audience is a journalist, chances are it is because you want them to tell a story to *their* particular medium's audience. But what if your customers don't get their news from the same media outlets as your investors or your employees, your suppliers, your donors . . . well, you see the problem. The media relations practitioner may see the journalist as the audience, but each journalist—or media outlet—also has an audience. Gone are the days of there being only three broadcast outlets and maybe a handful of radio stations and a newspaper or two. Now, our media audience options include broadcast, cable, radio, satellite radio, magazines, and the Internet, where there are literally billions of audiences. So maybe finding the audience isn't so simple, but after finishing this book, you'll be able to break down your audiences into manageable and identifiable chunks.

3. **Tell the story.** If you've managed to find a story and have narrowed down your audience, then it stands to reason that it should be fairly easy to tell your story to your chosen journalists. This may seem especially true once you've determined which media to target to effectively share your story; the best way to package your story—who to quote, when to use a graphic, how long the story needs to be, and how to frame the information; when and how to send the information; the list goes on. This part of media relations is generally considered the actual *media relations* part, and is the focus of many of the aforementioned training webinars and seminars. As such, this book won't focus a lot on the tactics of media relations, such as writing press releases or producing video clips that are easily used by media outlets; but we will examine ways in which you will be able to best maximize tactics to become an effective practitioner of media relations.

So media relations may not be so simple after all—and we still haven't addressed how our three steps fit into the overall communication strategy for an organization, or how to best evaluate the effectiveness of our media relations efforts. Nor have we discussed how to best build relationships with journalists or touched on the many other factors that may impact our efforts—and would surely impact our long-term success. You now know that media relations, as a practical concept, isn't simple, but we haven't necessarily addressed what it *is* yet.

Defining Media Relations

Media relations is the planned, purposeful and strategic relationship between a practitioner working on behalf of an organization and a journalist working on behalf of a media outlet.[1] By using this as our starting definition, we emphasize the necessity that media relations be part of an overall communications plan for an organization. However, there are a lot of misperceptions about media relations out there, so let's address some of those and start to differentiate between those who practice effective media relations, and those who do not.

What Media Relations Does Not Mean

Media Relations Is Not Publicity

Have you ever seen someone on a street holding a sign telling you about a sale at a store—or maybe a sign for an open house? That's a good example of publicity. Or maybe you've seen a vehicle decorated like an energy drink staffed by a team of college "interns" handing out free samples, or a televised weigh-in the day before a title boxing match, or movie stars appearing on talk shows before a new movie premieres—these are all examples of publicity as well. Publicity can be an integral part of the marketing mix to get information out to people about a product, service, or organization in a variety of ways. Perhaps you're familiar with the term "publicity stunt," an event designed to attract the attention of the media—we'll talk more about these later. The difference between "publicity" and "media relations" hasn't always been so clear, but let's just say, in the modern professional communication environment, the difference between the two is vast. Publicity is designed to gain attention once; media relations is a sustained effort to form a relationship. Publicity is generally one-way communication, whereas media relations relies on two-way communication. Publicity relies on emotional appeals, whereas media relations often involves a more cognitive approach. And while both are valuable—media relations and publicity are not the same.

Media Relations Is Not Public Relations

Researchers Thomasina Shaw and Candace White called media relations "the tip of the public relations iceberg . . . it's most visible part."[2] But we also know that two thirds of an iceberg lies below the surface of the water. The same goes for public relations. While many people view media relations as the essential part of public relations, it is in fact only one of the many functions that a comprehensive public relations program should include. However, with nearly 80% of public relations practitioners reporting that media relations is something they do on a daily basis, it is certainly an important part of public relations practice. For many, the idea that public relations and media relations are the same likely stems from the history of the field—as the fledgling public relations industry was often populated—and still is to some degree—with former journalists who were tasked with using their skills to produce news stories for their employers. Moving forward, it is most important to know that media relations is an important aspect of public relations, but that a comprehensive public relations program includes many facets that do not necessarily include media relations.

Media Relations Is Not Media Training

Learning to become an effective organizational spokesperson is an important skill for many media relations professionals, organizational leaders, government officials, and others who are called on to talk with media representatives. We've all seen examples of spokespersons who got flustered in front of a camera or reacted poorly to an unexpected question from a journalist. And, undoubtedly, a poor performance during an interview or press conference can be disastrous for an organization. However, training to be an effective and dynamic spokesperson is different from training in media relations. Just as media relations is an aspect of a comprehensive public relations program, media training is one aspect of an effective media relations program.

Not Everyone Is Capable of Conducting a Media Relations Campaign

There is a popular perception, primarily among non-communication professionals, that practically anyone can work in the public relations field. This idea is likely fed by many of the portrayals in popular culture of public relations professionals being party planners or social butterflies—or worse. However, the idea that anyone is capable of working in public relations or media relations isn't entirely off base, much in the same way that anyone is capable of building a house or working as a medical doctor: All that is needed is the willingness to put in the time and effort necessary to develop, learn, and practice all of the skills required to become a truly effective practitioner. Just as we wouldn't say someone who is qualified to apply a bandage to a paper cut should be able to perform surgery, we wouldn't say someone capable of making a phone call or sending an email is qualified to conduct a media relations campaign. A broad range of skills are needed to work as an effective media relations practitioner and there is a wide gap between mastering basic skills and mastering effective campaign management. Unlike medicine, though, media relations does not require a specific degree or a special license—thus allowing anyone with a phone and a computer to test the waters. But just as people generally avoid unlicensed doctors, they should likewise avoid untrained media relations practitioners who either haven't received some type of formal (college degree with internships) or informal (working on the job and learning from mentors) education.

Social Media Has Not Made Media Relations Obsolete

This is another popular misconception. That is, the traditional media no longer have the influence or reach to maximize the media relations practitioner's time or effort, and they would be better served by communicating directly to their intended audience via social media. New communication channels have certainly caused enormous change in the information landscape, not only in terms of what's possible but also in how people receive—and prefer to receive—their information. But to indicate that the evolving communication landscape has caused media relations to become obsolete is incorrect for two reasons. First, the traditional media continue to play a major role as both an agenda builder for news and as an important source of credible information for many in their audiences. These two functions are important for the media relations practitioner as well, and we will explore them further in later chapters. Second, and more importantly, media relations includes social media. The most trusted influencers in social media are often accurately considered journalists, and therefore media relations necessarily includes establishing relationships with these people as well. In fact, the same rules often apply when establishing relationships with "social media journalists" as they do with traditional journalists; only the communication vehicles change. So while social media may not fit into an ultratraditional media relations definition, it certainly is included as part of a modern media relations campaign.

So we now know what media relations does not mean, but we've not yet addressed the bigger question: What is media relations, and why is an understanding of how to do it effectively so important to organizations? We've already defined it as the planned, purposeful, and strategic relationship between a public relations professional and a journalist, so let's break down that concept to begin to figure out what it means to practice effective media relations.

What Does It Mean to Practice Media Relations?

First of all, effective media relations is *planned*. This indicates that effective media relations is proactive; but does not necessarily mean it requires proactive outreach to journalists, though in some cases it does. Rather, the planned aspect of media relations refers to being prepared to address journalists' inquiries, assigning responsibility for the management of the individual aspects of a media relations campaign, and establishing some form of evaluation for both media relations efforts and media exposure—whether good or bad. Planning is an integral part of an effective media relations program, no matter what type of program an organization decides to pursue. Next, we will look at different ways of approaching media relations and various types of campaigns.

Effective media relations must also be *purposeful*. It is safe to say that every organization should utilize media relations, but not every organization's media relations needs are the same, nor should they be. Each organization must approach media relations in a way that makes sense for its own goals. There are two basic types of media relations programs, proactive and reactive, each of which serves a specific purpose depending on the organization. Each of these types can be effective, but each also has an ineffective extreme—thus creating four main typologies of media relations practice.

Proactive

This type of media relations program is used by an organization that is seeking to receive media coverage at regular intervals and is taking the steps necessary to do so. Practitioners who are involved in this type of media relations actively seek media coverage by building relationships with journalists, identifying and crafting news ideas and stories, and serving as a resource for journalists seeking information about the organization. Proactive media relations might also include efforts to ensure that information available on both static and social organizational websites is journalist friendly, as well as training and preparing organizational leaders for media appearances. It also involves working to establish the organization as a leader in its field, and therefore becoming a trustworthy source for media representatives. The effective proactive media relations practitioner also seeks to establish a way of measuring and evaluating media relations efforts—which we'll discuss more in Chapter 13. Overall, the proactive media relations program seeks to establish strategic relationships with key journalistic audiences for the purpose of garnering a steady flow of positive media mentions.

Hitchhiker

The negative extreme of the proactive media relations program is characterized by the "hitchhiker" media relations campaign. In this style of campaign, media relations practitioners focus on creating as many opportunities for the organization in the media as possible, without regard to creating strategic relationships with journalists, or focusing on specific audiences. For example, the hitchhiker media relations practitioner might send out several hundred—or thousand—pitches or press releases each week, working under the idea that with enough outreach, there are bound to be media that will publish the information—and, in turn, there is likely to be some change in audience awareness. The hitchhiker practitioner is not necessarily focused on measurement and evaluation of the effectiveness of their efforts but is highly focused on *clip counting* to showcase the "success" of their efforts. In this way, the hitchhiker practitioner is focused primarily on information dissemination, and generally does very little with regard to other media relations activities.

Reactive

The effective reactive media relations program constantly monitors media to track issues and trends and prepares the organization to respond to media queries. Reactive media relations campaigns are often utilized by organizations that either do not often have novel information to share, or whose news could be considered controversial. The reactive media relations campaign type is characterized by a lack of outreach to journalists with regard to story ideas or other types of output, but it is not necessarily a *passive* media relations program. A reactive campaign might also be paired with other professional communication tools, such as advertising or marketing, to best leverage the communication mix without maximizing budgets. Although there is a lack of outreach to journalists, there is a substantial amount of planning and monitoring that occurs, as well as relationship building with journalists so that the organization can be an effective resource for media outlets.

Passive

The negative extreme of reactive media relations programs is the passive program. The passive media relations program generally comes from an organization that not only does not participate in outreach to journalists but also does not react to journalists' queries. The passive media relations program is not the equivalent of having no media relations program (though any organization without a media relations program could also be considered passive), because the passive media relations program consciously avoids media coverage, and actually takes action to *avoid* media mentions. The passive program is characterized by an organization whose management either feels it does not need media coverage, does not have the budget for a media relations program, or in some way mistrusts the concept of media relations. Passive media relations organizations might not use other forms of professional communication, or they might use them in some limited fashion. These organizations are often very small in size, or are so highly specialized in their products or services that very few people outside of a particular industry would know of their existence.

It should be noted that some organizations use a combination of proactive and reactive media relations campaigns depending on immediate needs and the goals of the organization. For example, an organization that produces tangible products might use a proactive campaign for new product releases but otherwise uses a reactive program. Or a nonprofit may use a proactive campaign as part of an annual fundraiser, but otherwise it does not actively seek out media attention. A combination of media relations campaigns might be the most effective for an organization, particularly in terms of time and budget considerations, but each organization must determine which type of campaign will be most beneficial, particularly in terms of the overall organizational goals or overall communication strategy.

This brings us to the final aspect of our media relations definition, that effective media relations is *strategic*. This means that media relations efforts should fit into both the organization's communication goals, and its overall goals. Many textbooks and articles cite the concept of *excellent* public relations as coming from an organization in which the organization's chief communicator has a seat at the management table, or at least some involvement in the executive decision-making of an organization. If it is the case that public relations is involved with organizational decision-making, then media relations as a function of public relations is also part of that process. In a case where public relations is not part of the management of the organization, or where the organization outsources its media relations to a third party—such as a public relations agency—then it is incumbent upon the media relations practitioners to ensure their activities are in line with the organization's goals.

The second aspect of strategy that is important to effective media relations is that media relations practitioners must be deliberate in their use of information subsidies—press releases, pitches, media alerts, and so forth—not only in their judicious use but also in how they are used to communicate with specific journalistic audiences. "Strategic" in this sense means media relations practitioners must be aware of which journalists—and journalists' audiences—are most likely to have an interest in a piece of information, how to best manage sharing—or pitching—or not sharing information, knowing when to use proactive or reactive strategies, and how to integrate media relations activities into overall business objectives. The final aspect of effective media relations is to have a plan for monitoring and evaluating media relations efforts as well as their results.

The last part of our definition refers to a *relationship* between public relations practitioners working on behalf of an organization and a journalist. It should be noted the term "organization" is used because of the varying types of businesses, nonprofits, educational institutions, entertainers, healthcare facilities, and governmental and nongovernmental organizations that use media relations. Media relations is not just for corporations, nor is it the sole property of public relations agencies or firms. While each type of organization may use slightly different tactics and campaign types, this book hopes to serve as a resource to all media relations practitioners, regardless of the type of organization they represent.

The most important concept of the final part of our definition is that of the *relationship*. The word "relationship" can have various meanings, but in this case, we are referring to sharing information, a mutual understanding of each other's objectives and limitations, and some form of reciprocal benefit. The meaning here is also indicative of a process that occurs over time, that it requires the investment of resources, and that it must be initiated by one of the parties involved. Ideally, the role of relationship initiator falls on the effective media relations practitioner. We will explore more about the relationship between a media relations practitioner and a journalist in Chapter 4, but for now we need to view the relationship between an organization and journalists as the most integral aspect of determining whether the media relations program can be deemed effective or not.

Professional Commentary

Sarah Dasher
Strategic Communications Consultant, Cisco

I was initially drawn to professional communication through a blend of being naturally curious and loving to write. The guidelines foundational to quality research and reporting, as well as the art of the written word have served me well in my career as a corporate communicator. But regardless of how illuminating and creative one's content might be, it doesn't matter to an employer if that content lands to . . . crickets. Sure, what you communicate on behalf of an organization should be precise, but *how* you communicate it has never been more crucial.

Agency- and corporate-side PR pros must incorporate outcome-driven strategy to successfully get their messages heard by the right audience at the right time. Without thoughtful planning, you're just another voice, sending your words out into the already noisy ether. The convenient paradox is that the technological revolution that's made the world so loud also empowers savvy communicators with the digital tools not just to reach people but to activate them toward organizational objectives.

A good journalist is likely to be uncomfortable with such a statement within the context of media relations. Given the importance of the Fourth Estate, they should be. It's the media's role to question authenticity, but that doesn't make all PR folks flacks or our tactics inherently insincere. Pick an ethically sound organization to work for and you'll sleep fine at night knowing professional communicators are just as vital to information dissemination as the media are. It has been critical for me to embrace that concept in my career, especially as we increasingly leverage forensic-like data tracking and analysis to guide our messages and actions.

The sharpest communicators push past merely keeping media lists up to date. We are paying attention to who the end user readers/viewers/listeners are in each channel and what they care about. We also track and identify, at a granular level, exactly which publications and media personnel align best with achieving specific outcomes.

Plunk a stack of earned media placements on an executive's desk and you're likely to get a "so what?" response unless you can quantify what all those mentions ultimately do for the organization's mission. Gaining a 360-degree understanding of your employer's business and using data and technology to precisely map your media planning to it empowers communicators to act with confidence, measure success, and adjust course accordingly.

The usefulness of tech tools of course extends past the planning phase. Communication and media professionals alike continue to be asked to produce greater results with smaller budgets. Web-based media events are an excellent way to problem solve for that and they're certainly not limited to press conferences. You can double down on returns for an employee or client event through webcasting. Then you triple down with all the multimedia content by repackaging bite-sized output for ongoing social reach.

Every organization has so many compelling stories that beg to be told, and given today's split-second news cycle, lack of demand is not an issue. All too often, internal awareness is half the battle in being able to connect the media to those great storytelling moments.

It is your responsibility to proactively network within the organization and the ecosystem sustaining it so you can spot the stories that shape and inform your communication strategies. You also have to nurture trust-based relationships with key media influencers. One-on-one communication is more traditionally associated with our marketing brethren, but I think it's the most undervalued resource we have for building and keeping media relationships.

I used to jokingly refer to myself as the "information octopus" sitting at the center of the organization with tentacles reaching out into all aspects of the business and beyond. It is, honestly, still the best visual analogy I can use to describe a lot of what it is that I do.

Sarah Dasher Biography

Sarah Dasher is a communications professional with more than 15 years of experience, including leadership roles as the marketing and communications director for preeminent behavioral healthcare system Willingway. She also provided leadership as the southeastern research manager for Jones Lang LaSalle, a *Fortune* 500 professional services firm specializing in real estate and investment management. Dasher recently completed a midcareer master's degree in public relations at Boston University's College of Communication and holds a BA in journalism from the University of Georgia's Grady College. Currently, Sarah is a strategic communications consultant for Cisco's global platform.

Why Are We Concerned With Effective Media Relations?

Thus far, we have tried to showcase some of the differences between effective media relations and media relations practices that are less than optimal for an organization. But a very important question remains: Why are we concerned with media relations at all?

Media relations provides multiple benefits for an organization. Each organization that engages in media relations can have slightly different reasons for doing so but, in general, the benefits of a media relations program fall into one of the following categories.

Media Relations Creates Awareness

Whether your organization is brand new or has been around for a long time, media coverage helps to build awareness of either a new product or service, a slight change or update in the organization, or any other news that an organization wants the public to know about. Certainly garnering media coverage is not the only way of accomplishing this, but it is one way that media relations helps to serve an organization's goals.

Media Relations Creates Information Credibility

Surely any organization can set up a social media account or website to deliver information to audiences, but that information is still coming from an obviously biased source. And while there are many times that an organization should share information directly, having information disseminated by a third party that is considered unbiased is valuable for an organization. Consider advertising, for example: An organization can clearly communicate a message through *paid media*; they have nearly complete control over what is put into the message, when it is run, and sometimes, even who will see it. But the audience's perception of the message is that it has been paid for and that it is meant to create some awareness. Consider the difference between an advertisement that is paid for, and a media placement, which is considered *earned media*. In earned media, a message is disseminated not because its placement was paid for but rather because a third party—the media outlet—considers the information true and worthy of being considered news. The perception of the message by an audience is therefore different, and it will potentially resonate more with those who view the message.

Media Relations Is Cost-Effective

One of the biggest advantages of an organization engaging in media relations is the cost-effectiveness, particularly when compared to other means of communication. A single person can conduct an effective media relations campaign—although more should certainly run a larger campaign—and the tools required to do so are minimal. The cost of an advertising campaign, on the other hand, can be substantial, particularly if it is a national campaign. While the cost of conducting a media relations campaign is certainly higher than doing nothing at all, the benefit for many organizations far outweighs the costs.

Effective Media Relations Can Mitigate Crises

Strong relationships with journalists will not prevent a crisis from being covered in the media—nor should it—but having a preexisting relationship with journalists covering a crisis might mean that you will at least have the opportunity to comment or present your organization's view before the outlet publishes the story. Crisis mitigation should not necessarily be a primary goal for conducting a media relations campaign, but it certainly can be a benefit.

Sustained Media Relations Can Impact Audience Attitudes

A single media placement, while valuable, does not in the end do much for changing attitudes among audience members. However, a sustained media relations effort, which results in multiple media placements over time, can have a strong impact on audience perceptions. Effective media relations can create and foster perceptions about an organization, and practitioners who supply information of legitimate news interest have the opportunity to impact the attitudes of not only the journalists but also their audiences.

Media Relations Lets You Tell the Story of an Organization

The main purpose of media relations is that it allows an organization to share information that would otherwise go unnoticed. An effective media relations campaign allows for an organization to create and maintain a presence in the minds of audiences, whether they are consumers, investors, employees, or any other audience. Effectively using media relations allows an organization to better position itself within the business community, and within society at large.

Media relations provides many benefits to an organization; and a greater understanding of the history, theory, and strategic practices of the processes involved in crafting an effective media relations campaign provides great benefit to the practitioner. Our goal for you, the reader, after completing this book, is that you will have a deeper understanding of those processes, and you will also be able to apply research-based findings to the crafting of a media relations campaign. It is our hope that any student of media relations—whether they be in a classroom or on the job—will be able to learn to be a better media relations practitioner, thus advancing not only an organization but the public relations field as well.

The Plan Moving Forward

There are a lot of books, websites, blogs, and speakers focused on the topic of media relations, and many of them provide excellent examples of how to execute the daily tactics of creating and fostering relationships with journalists. We will look at some of the best practices for these tactics later, but our objective is to examine those tactics through the lens of strategy. Our plan for this book is to take the approach that media relations is a strategic aspect of an organization's public relations, and we will examine the elements of that strategy in each chapter.

As we progress in our understanding of media relations, we will move from the historical beginnings of the field through the modern-day practice, with a special emphasis on understanding how to best create, foster, and maintain an effective relationship between an organization and the media. We will also examine some broader topics like ethics and measurement so that we can help our readers understand how these more general public relations topics apply to media relations strategy.

In the end, our goal is that the reader will become a more informed practitioner of media relations, one who understands not only *how* to practice media relations but also *why* we seek to practice it strategically—as part of an overall public relations and organizational plan. At the conclusion of the book, readers will be able to use their knowledge to establish relationships with journalists, share information with constituents via the media, and measure the impact of that information for their organization. This will leave the reader with the ability to bring greater value to their media relations programs, and to their organizations.

Key Concepts

Media relations is a *strategic* endeavor of public relations that seeks to establish *relationships* between journalists and organizations. That process should be *planned and purposeful*. Effective media relations can create multiple benefits for organizations, though there is seldom a "one-size-fits-all" approach. Media relations is not simply gaining publicity for an organization or speaking to journalists during an interview. It is, instead, a part of an organization's long-term approach to managing its relationships, reputation, and place in the eyes of the public.

Challenge Case

The following challenge is presented in two parts and is designed to make you think critically about media relations. Read the challenge and ask yourself if you've faced a similar situation. How did you approach it then—and how might you approach it now?

> SITUATION 1: You are working on the new account acquisitions team for your full-service agency. The partner in charge has just handed you an RFP—request for proposal—for a midsized company with five offices spread

geographically across the country. They are seeking public relations representation and want the agency to also handle social media, but the scope of work indicates they are not interested in traditional—broadcast, print—media. The partner in charge wants you to put together the business-pitch proposal and wants you to include traditional media relations as part of the overall strategy. How will you convince the client in your written presentation that media relations should be included as part of their outreach strategy?

SITUATION 2: You are again working on the acquisitions team, but this time you have a face-to-face meeting with a potential client, a local business with only two locations in the same metro area. They are asking you to create a national buzz about their brand and have advised you that they want to appear in as many media outlets as possible, with a heavy focus on national media. They are expecting to appear in all types of media, including social. How will you convince your potential client that a more strategic approach to their media relations strategy will be of more benefit to their business goals?

REFERENCES

1. Supa, D. W., & Zoch, L. M. (2009). Maximizing media relations through a better understanding of the public relations–journalist relationship: A quantitative analysis of changes over the past 23 years. *Public Relations Journal, 3*(4).
2. Shaw, T., & White, C. (2004). Public relations and journalism educators' perceptions of media relations. *Public Relations Review, 30*(4), 493–502.

2 MEDIA RELATIONS IN THE ERA OF INFORMATION

In Chapter 1, we examined a definition of media relations that highlights the importance of being purposeful and strategic in any media relations effort. In this chapter, we will look at other types of communication and how media relations fits into an organization's overall communication strategy.

This is also a good place to talk about the importance of media relations. And although it may be surprising to read in a book solely focused on media relations as a topic, media relations is not always the best tool for every organization, or for every purpose. Effective practitioners learn to understand when media relations will provide the greatest benefit and when it will not. Let's use an example from outside of professional communication. Let's say you drive to work every day on the highway because it should get you to your office in the least amount of time with the fewest number of turns. Now let's say that there is an accident on the highway, causing a delay of an hour or more. Should you still take the highway—or might it be faster to take a back road, or even public transportation? Being a good communicator means keeping your options open to other possibilities. And while media relations is very often an effective tool for an organization, it isn't the only one.

Unlike our highway example, various communication strategies are not an either/or proposition. In fact, many organizations use multiple means of dissemination to best tell their stories. In this chapter, we will examine how media relations works in conjunction with other information channels; we will highlight when it might be the best option, and also when it likely is not.

The Marketplace of Information

Of all the products traded in societies, perhaps none is more valued or more impactful than information. We know that information is everywhere, but just how ubiquitous is it and, in turn, does the availability of information diminish its impact? It was fewer than fifty years ago when newscaster Walter Cronkite, in his closing remarks on the *CBS Evening News*, said that "it seems more certain than ever that the bloody experience of Vietnam is to end in a stalemate"—a remark which popularly was equated with the idea that America could not win in Vietnam. And in 1968, when only three newscasts were available—of which CBS was the most popular—the statement resonated with a great deal of impact across the country. Of course, news was more difficult to come by in those days. The Internet only existed in an army lab computer and the closest thing the public had to a mobile phone was a CB radio. Radio and newspapers were the predominant forms of information dissemination, but they were primarily focused on local and regional news. The national reach of programs like *CBS Evening News*, with their focus on news from across both the country and the world represented, for most people, their exposure to information from around the globe.

Today, very few media personalities, or media outlets, have the ability to inform such a large segment of the U.S. population as Cronkite, or *CBS Evening News* did at that time. There are, perhaps, a few exceptions. Oprah Winfrey at the height of her popularity could, in a single segment of her daytime show, create enough awareness of a product or brand to catapult it to success. Of course, the front page of the *New York Times* or the *Wall Street Journal*—and a few other major newspapers—still have considerable power in terms of information dissemination, as do the nightly network newscasts and national morning shows. But in terms of the ability to inform the majority of the population in a single message, such a vehicle doesn't really exist today, at least in the form it used to.

This does not mean the traditional mass media has lost its power to inform people; what individual media outlets have lost is their singular power to control the flow of information on a particular topic. This has happened for several reasons, and has taken place over a period of time, although such change has been expedited greatly by the rise of social media and by the increasing amount of time people spend interacting with media on a daily basis. Some of the major changes are highlighted here.

>**Growth of television.** While entire volumes can be—and have been—written on the impact of the growth of television, our discussion here is mainly concerned with the amount of programming available via the

increase in channel options. In the United States, we've grown from three broadcast networks to more than a thousand available channels across broadcast and cable. A 2014 Nielsen[1] report said that Americans receive, on average, 189 channels in their homes, with the data showing consumers receive approximately 10 more channels each year.

Rise of the Internet. In 1991, there was one page available on the World Wide Web. A December 2018 Netcraft[2] survey indicated there are now more than 1.6 billion active websites.

Newspapers. Most major cities at one point had one or two newspapers. While the industry is clearly in decline, there are still more than twelve hundred newspapers in the United States alone. This does not include their online presence. Even though the number of physical newspapers has been in a fairly steady decline over the past 20 years, the content produced has seemingly increased. The *Washington Post* produces about 500 articles each day across its paper and website, the *New York Times* averages around 230, and the *Wall Street Journal* approximately 240.

Social media. It is estimated that nearly 78% of Americans have at least one social media profile.[3] That equals nearly 250 million people. And while active users tend to vary from month to month and from platform to platform, the Global Web Index[4] indicates that Facebook tops the list with 42% of profiles being active, while most other platforms have from 8–24% in terms of active profiles. So even though not everyone who has a profile is active, there are still significant numbers of people garnering information from social media platforms.

This is obviously not an exhaustive list of changes in the media landscape but does represent some of the most significant changes that have occurred in the last 40 to 50 years for media relations practitioners. The important question here, though, is what do these changes mean for media relations? First, they tell us that over the course of a career, an effective media relations practitioner needs to be adaptable; that the communication channels we used in the past to tell stories may not now be the best for our particular needs. The changes also show us that the competition for attention has increased substantially. We can no longer rely on a single placement, or just a handful of relationships with journalists. But perhaps most important, changes in the media landscape mean that more outlets than ever need information to create content. This is where the media relations professional can truly have an impact.

However, examining changes in the media landscape only gives us half the picture. We also need to examine what changes have occurred in how consumers engage with and use the media. A 2015 report indicated that we spend more than eight hours a day consuming media content. And while television remains the highest percentage of that (around three hours a day), the Internet is following closely at two hours, and the report predicts it will soon surpass television. In fact, the report indicates that from 2010 to 2015, there was a 105% increase in Internet engagement, while consumption of nearly every other media category dropped during the same time frame.[5]

If we look at content production and media consumption, a picture begins to emerge. Outlets are producing increasingly more content, and people are consuming that content at a faster pace. While some theorists are concerned with which of the two is behind the wheel of the information explosion, for the media relations practitioner, the only thing that matters is that *people are looking for content and the media relations practitioner has the means to provide it.*

But content varies greatly. Most media relations practitioners are not going to be concerned with much of the content people are looking for, whether it is videos of smiling cats, last night's lottery numbers or, the most popular, adult content. But people also search for *news*. In fact, a 2018 Pew Research Center survey[6] showed that 96% of American adults get news online.

The reports noted above also drew some conclusions regarding the sources people seek out and trust. The majority of respondents showed the highest level of trust in traditional news outlets, no matter how they accessed the information. The respondents indicated they had the least trust in the news they obtained from social media. Likely this also explains why 61% of the study's respondents preferred to hear news directly from news organizations, rather than from a secondhand source.

So again, we're left with wondering what this all means for the media relations practitioner. The most obvious takeaway is actually good news for traditional news outlets. While people do get their news from a variety of sources, the traditional news outlet still reigns in terms of trust and preference by consumers. The data also show that when it comes to seeking news online, whether via news alerts sent to their phones or news aggregate sites—Google News, Yahoo, and others—most consumers still say they have the highest trust in the traditional news organizations. As more of these traditional organizations—networks and newspapers—transition to providing more multiplatform content, it stands to reason that traditional outlets will remain at the forefront of consumers' news preferences.

But changes in how, and where, consumers seek content have necessitated a change in how organizations share their information with publics. Clearly media relations, the sharing of an organization's information with journalists who, in turn, use that information to produce content, still is a vital component of any organization's communication strategy. It is not the only way though, and in the next section, we will explore other ways in which organizations can disseminate their information.

Paid, Owned, Shared, and Earned Media

An organization's media options can be viewed generally from four perspectives: *paid, owned, shared*, and *earned*. For an organization to maximize its relationship with all its stakeholders, its communicators must think strategically about how to use each of these tools to distribute information to intended audiences. In use, each perspective often benefits from the others, though in some cases only one of them is needed at a particular time. In this section, we will review the four types of organizational communication methods individually, and then explore how each might be used on its own or in concert with the others.

Paid

Most commonly, paid communication refers to advertising which is the paid placement of messages on behalf of an organization. It is one of the two types of external communication that give an organization nearly total control of its message—with some limitations that are regulated by various agencies. In addition, it is the only communication method where an organization can exert control over the time and place audiences will view—or hear—the intended message. For these reasons, advertising has long been an important component of organizational communication.

Advertising is fairly overt—most people are able to recognize advertising when they see it. Certainly, when we listen to the radio or watch television, we can easily recognize the difference between the medium's program content and its advertising. Similarly, when examining print or online media, we can usually recognize the difference between the content on the page and an advertisement, similar to the way we can recognize the difference between a highway sign indicating route numbers and a billboard. However, not all paid placement is as clearly discernable from the content around it. Examples of this include *advertorials,* or advertising designed to look like the print content around it; *product placement,* which is paying to have products featured prominently within content such as television shows or movies; *sponsorship,* which is an event or program that has been underwritten by an organization and where that organization might be featured in the title or associated in some other way within the event; and there is *paid inline linking,* where a particular product or industry is mentioned in an online article containing a hyperlink to a particular product or specific external site.

Advertising has long been a fixture of communication. In fact, the excavation of Pompeii revealed nearly perfectly preserved walls that featured advertising for various political candidates. The main purpose of advertising is to create awareness of something. Its secondary purpose is often to create a feeling associated with what is being advertised, whether that feeling is a desire to purchase, to donate, or to support. The ultimate goal is to convince the reader or viewer to act in some way. Usually this is done using a persuasive element that might include an appeal to logic, fear, or humor, or through propaganda techniques, such as power words, testimonials, or "everyone else does it" approaches.

Owned

Owned media refers to the communication platforms that are controlled by an organization. Most often, this includes the organization's website, newsletters, corporate-owned magazines, annual reports, mailers, brochures, and the like. Owned media is used for a variety of purposes, though it is most often directed toward *internal publics,* such as employees, volunteers, shareholders, or toward targeted *external publics,* where consumers or donors, for example, are the primary audience. Owned media is valuable because an organization usually has an attentive audience and total control of the message. For example, it may not be acceptable to claim an organization is "the best" in an advertisement—unless it can be empirically proven, of course—yet it is acceptable to use the term "best" on a platform owned by the organization. Increasingly, however, organizations are recognizing the value and role of owned media to external audiences, such as journalists. A prime example of this is the online media room—or online newsroom—section of an organization's website.

Your authors conducted research on online media rooms from 2005 to 2014, examining the *Fortune* Global top 50 companies and how they used their online portals for journalists, and more specifically, how those organizations changed over time. When we started, we noticed that some of the organizations required journalists to register for access, while others simply had a list of links to their press releases. Very few organizations were using the Internet to its fullest capabilities—relative to the 2005 time of the study. When we looked again in 2009, nearly all the organizations were using online media rooms without the necessity of registration, and many had incorporated materials such as executive biographies, earnings reports, photos, and a variety of other elements. In 2014, when we began to look again, we saw that every organization was using their online media room to engage not only with journalists but with any visitor seeking information. In fact, the wholesale change in organizations' use of online media rooms was so ubiquitous, conducting additional analysis didn't make sense.[7] Organizations, it seems, had learned the value of their owned media and were capitalizing on it.

Like paid media, such owned media are valuable components of an organization's communication toolbox. Its primary goal is to inform audiences, but it might also be used to reinforce behavior—such as to purchase again, donate again, invest more, and so forth. As such, a variety of message strategies can be used, including some of those that might be employed in paid messaging. Modern approaches to owned media also allow messages to be tailored (or seemingly tailored) to individuals. An example might be an email generated by a nonprofit organization to encourage a previous donor to donate once again. If the individual previously donated online, there is likely sufficient information available to send a personalized email containing at least the individual's name. It is also possible, depending on the software the organization used, that enough information was collected to include material of potential interest to them.

Shared

Did you notice in the previous section that we did not mention an organization's social media sites as owned media? While social media sites do have many of the components of owned media, they are also distinctively different, enough so that they are categorized differently. Shared media is meant for distribution to a wider audience than owned media is: Not only is it *directed* to the population at large but that wide audience is welcome to *contribute* to the message stream (Type I). In addition, the intent of shared media is often to have the audience help *distribute* the message (Type II). In this way, shared media spans the boundary between owned media and grassroots messaging.

Type I shared media would include an organization's social media sites, particularly ones that invite audience feedback and interaction. This type of shared media is nearly always overt, in that the social media channel clearly belongs to the organization. Organizations are increasingly using their social media to interact with audiences, whether to answer customer complaints, respond to journalists' inquiries, or to share products and promotions. Likewise, audiences are becoming accustomed to interacting with organizations via social media and are often using social media to interact publicly. A recent example includes actress Emilie de Ravin, who took to Twitter in the summer of 2016 to "request" an American Airlines employee be terminated following de Ravin's accusation of assault by the employee.

However, not all Type I shared media is necessarily negative for an organization. Organizations are often liked, retweeted, followed, friended, and/or pinned for a variety of positive reasons, and organizations use these interactions to help build community. These communities, in turn, might become a mechanism that the organization can use as brand ambassadors. Organizations might also use shared media to more quickly and directly share information with their audiences. In 2013, for example, the Securities and Exchange Commission (SEC) started to allow corporations to release their earnings statements via social media, as long as investors were notified. Shared media continues to gain acceptance as a legitimate form of communication and will likely continue to do so even more as time goes on.

Unlike Type I shared media, which is primarily interactive over a shared social platform, Type II shared media focuses on the message. One term that is often associated with Type II is "content marketing," which is the production of messages designed to be distributed to audiences, and then shared by those audiences with their contacts. When online video was first introduced, the term "viral" became prevalent to describe how information—in this case videos—was shared. The goal of content marketing is to create dynamic and interesting information that shares the story of an organization, and—organizational communicators hope—causes a behavioral reaction. That reaction might be for audiences to become engaged, purchase, donate, or something else. However, content marketing might also be used to influence attitude. For example, an organization could create online content that shows how committed the organization is to a social cause. If the content positively reflects on an organization and the consumer perceives that the organization is "doing good" for society, then that consumer might be more likely to engage in a behavior with that organization.

Organizations have been participating in Type II shared behavior for many years, but the heavy adoption rate of social media, and the speed at which information is created and then shared, has brought the idea of content marketing to the forefront. Instead of simply creating content for a local community, organizations now have the ability to create content that can be shared worldwide—including with journalists—in a very short time.

However, one of the main differences between Type I and Type II shared media is the transparency of communication. In Type I, the communicator, or in this example, the owner whose page is on the platform, is clearly identified. In Type II, those responsible for producing the message content may not be as clear. While certainly not always the case, it is entirely possible that the organization that produces the Type II content is not identified, thus allowing audiences to focus on the message contained in the content, rather than on its originator. Organizations and audiences should be careful to maintain transparency, a concept we will discuss fully in Chapter 6.

Earned

This type of media is the result of organizational action taken to garner coverage by outside media. Media relations, if successful, falls into this category. Persons (usually public relations personnel) working on behalf of an organization, bring information of interest to journalists, who then potentially cover the organizational news in their respective media outlets. However, an organization might gain earned media in other ways as well. For example, the Dove Campaign for Real Beauty started as an advertising—*paid*—campaign that blossomed into an online movement—*shared*—that has garnered significant news coverage—*earned*. Not all earned media is necessarily positive, though. An organization in crisis that is laying off hundreds of employees is likely to "earn" some media coverage of their troubles. In the next section, we will explore the advantages of *positive* earned media.

This book is about media relations and is therefore all about earning media coverage—hopefully the kind your organization is looking for and not the negative kind. We will spend the remainder of the text discussing all of the elements that go into an effectively planned media relations campaign. But it is important to note that media relations often works best if done in concert with the other types of media—paid, owned, and shared. To that end, organizations that seek to maximize their relationships with multiple audiences are wise to use all of the communication tools at their disposal. Similarly, a wise communicator knows an organization's goals and is able to adapt to using different means of information dissemination.

Professional Commentary

Ray Kotcher
Retired CEO and Chairman, Ketchum

The public relations profession is going through a period of profound change. Much of the change is being driven by technology, and as technology evolves, as the authors of this text point out, it has a direct impact on media delivery systems and how people interact with the media.

Similarly, technology is driving secular changes in news and journalism. People are consuming content at breakneck speed and news organizations are racing to fill the demand. Journalists are time constrained and resource challenged. While these changes in news and journalism create a greater demand for the content we provide in our media relations work, other disciplines also see an opportunity and are racing to fulfill the need.

There are, of course, other forces impacting today's PR world: As our colleague, Professor Gary Sheffer observes, pervasive risk in the operating environment is creating complex communication challenges. The intense worldwide regulatory scrutiny of companies such as Google and Facebook— Mark Zuckerberg, Facebook's CEO and chairman, addressed just that in his company's April 24, 2019 earnings call—are just two of thousands of such examples of companies strategizing, communicating, and acting in today's global, high-risk environment.

Rapid disruption is another. Think Amazon.

Closer to our world of PR is the rapidly growing sophistication and application of artificial intelligence (AI) to communications.

As the authors point out, we are living and working in an attention economy: Today media is real time. And that bodes well for us. Public relations (PR) grew out of a need to participate in both agenda setting and news making in real time. But today's PR professional needs to deal with more than just the gatekeepers of the traditional media brands. Today, as the authors note, citizen and corporate publishers can go directly to specific end users of information. They can microtarget, narrowcast. Media also is becoming an experience—gaming for example.

In this newly complex media ecosystem, organizations are using every asset to break through: They are applying sophisticated data and analytics; communicating via multiple and varied channels and platforms; making use of new and reconstituted technologies—the martech stack, for example; creating compelling narratives and content; video; animation; and gaming. Organizations are in a battle to win the information wars. They are in an arms race.

And today, organizations are taking a hard look at the human assets they develop and embed in their own organizations versus the resources they contract externally. As *PRWeek* reported in its 2019 agency business report, clients are increasingly "in-housing." This, of course, is impacting the agency world.

To this point and the larger point of this chapter—though it is too early in our data collection to deem this statistically valid—early returns from the second annual, 2019 Boston University (BU)/*PRWeek* Bellwether Survey indicate that client companies are responding that they are keeping media relations in-house. Yet, agencies say that their clients are outsourcing this to them. This suggests that media relations is becoming hyperspecialized with each subspecialty requiring specific professionals with deep, distinctive knowledge and unique expertise and skill sets, and that the work is going to these super specialists, wherever they might be. This dynamic certainly will be explored in depth when all of this year's survey results are in, thoroughly analyzed, and interpreted.

That said, in last year's 2018 BU/*PRWeek* Bellwether Survey (believed to be one of the largest studies ever undertaken on the state of the PR industry) the data were clear: Organizations are looking for efficiencies and ways to reduce duplication of effort. In that 2018 survey, respondents using a low-to-high scale of 1 to 5 scored the importance of finding efficiencies in the PR/communication and marketing functions both at 4.1. A prime example is Procter & Gamble (P&G), which is trimming and reallocating its spending.

(Continued)

If recent financial results are an indicator, this restructuring is resulting in stronger sales and increased productivity.

As the 2018 BU/*PRWeek* study also showed us, the integration of PR and marketing is one of the specific places where efficiencies are being sought. Sixty percent of our respondents said that their organizations are now integrated.

So, in an era of integration, for PR to continue to succeed we need to understand the marketing vocabulary and to apply marketing tools to our work. Yet on our 5-point scale, the importance of understanding and applying paid media to the work of PR scored just 3.7 among PR/Comms professionals; paid content, 3.8; and media buying, 3.3.

Perhaps most concerning is how the PR/Comms respondents viewed the application of new technologies—Artificial Intelligence 3.7; Augmented Reality 3.2; and Virtual Reality 3.2—on the same 5-point scale. It behooves us to learn more about paid content and the marketing world, though there is growing evidence to suggest that PR professionals now are rapidly mastering these skills. This will be another important area for analysis and interpretation once the 2019 BU/*PRWeek* survey data are in.

All of that said, and to the point of this chapter, PR brings great strategic advantages, and a unique skill set to the mix—particularly the potent tools of media relations. They are the competency out of which our discipline was born. Earned media is the outcome. A well-executed media relations effort earns credibility. It is at the root of public relations and fundamental to most every PR strategy.

Indeed, in my experience as global Chair and CEO of the large international PR firm Ketchum, clients always wanted to know that the firm had relationships with traditional media outlets—national, local, and vertical. But, of course, they also knew that traditional media relations most often works best if done in concert with other types of media—the potency of traditionally earned media multiplied by social—and vice versa.

Referring again to the 2018 Boston University/*PRWeek* Survey, when we asked how important media relations is to today's practice of public relations, it was rated as highly important at 4.3. And when we asked how important it is for the next generation of PR professionals to master earned media as a future skill, the answer came back as 4.4.

So, whether one looks back to the origins of contemporary public relations or looks to our future, despite today's profound changes, there is little doubt that the historical and fundamental advantage of public relations— credible media earned through excellence in media relations—is more relevant than ever. What has brought us to today can serve as a sustainable advantage for generations of practitioners to come.

Ray Kotcher Biography

Ray Kotcher is Professor of the Practice of Public Relations at Boston University's College of Communication. Prior to that, he spent more than 30 years at Ketchum. From 2000 to 2016, he served as the agency's CEO and then chairman. Kotcher believes in service to the industry and its practitioners—particularly those just embarking on a career in public relations. He regularly hosts a widely viewed national webcast for the Public Relations Student Society America (PRSSA), Life After College. It features interviews with industry leaders who provide advice for students making the transition from academia to professional life.

Kotcher is a recipient of the PRSA's Gold Anvil and IPR's Hamilton Medal. In 2016, he was inducted into the Page Society Hall of Fame. He also is a member of both the *PR News* and ICCO Halls of Fame and is a recipient of *The Holmes Report* Individual Achievement Sabre Award. Ray is a member of PRSA's College of Fellows and is a distinguished alum of both Boston University and its College of Communication. In 2018 he was named a Living Legend by the Plank Center.

Why Are We So Concerned With Media Relations—or Earned Media?

While all media have advantages and disadvantages, this book is concerned with media relations, or the traditional aspect of earned media. But in an era of increased technology and ease of communication directly with audiences, why should we be concerned with earned media? After all, by utilizing media relations we are giving up control over the final message that will reach our audiences; we don't control when or where the message will appear; and for all we know, the journalist may even say something negative about our organization. It seems we would be much better served using message platforms that we can control.

And that's why we rely so much on earned media.

Did you miss it? Remember in Chapter 1 when we talked about building relationships with the media? Two of the most important aspects of organizational communication are trust and credibility. If we, as an organization, put out messages to our audiences telling them how wonderful we are, how likely are those audiences to believe it? Recall that earlier we looked at a study that stated 61% of respondents would rather hear about news from a news source rather than from a secondary source. In the case of that study, secondary sources referred to seeing a news article on a news aggregate site or through social media. There was no mention of comparing news sources to organizational sources. Why? Likely for the same reason that if a stranger tells you something, you are less likely to believe it than if one of your closest friends told you the same thing. Source credibility is one of the key components of human communication. We ascribe a higher level of credibility to those we trust than to those we don't. And for all the talk about media bias and diminishing trust of the news media, they remain one of the most trusted sources of information across all platforms.

We know that news organizations are relying less and less on their traditional formats and turning much of their attention to increasing the number of their readers—viewers, listeners—via online platforms. Print, as it turns out, isn't "dead," it is slowly reinventing itself and manifesting itself differently. The same goes for television and magazines. For example, if we look at the most followed Twitter accounts in the world, mixed in among the scores of celebrities are traditional news outlets such as CNN—17th and 29th, the *New York Times*—23rd, ESPN—37th and 41st, the BBC—30th and 73rd, the *Economist*—82nd, and Reuters—93rd.[8] If you only look at followers in the United States, Twitter feed rankings of traditional news outlets are even higher, and the list includes individual journalists as well. When we look at other social media, we see a similar trend; people tend to put their trust for information in the hands of traditional news outlets, no matter the method of information dissemination.

Earned media is a way for media relations practitioners to "borrow" some of that trust and credibility for their own information. The public is less likely to pay attention to, or trust, information that comes directly from an organization; earned media allows for organizations to have their voices heard and trusted. While all the media types are valuable to an organizational communicator, only earned media has the ability create an atmosphere of perceived credibility of information to the public. As such, it is considered the most valued. However, the ability to borrow the credibility of a news outlet, such as occurs in media relations, is not a loan the media makes to just any information. This is why it is earned and not given.

The Value of Media Relations to an Organization

Clearly, the main value of media relations to an organization is in the way in which an organization garners earned media. While establishing credibility and third-party endorsement of the value of your organization's information is certainly the main benefit for an organization, media relations can offer additional value as well.

Media relations, as we will continue to discuss throughout this book, is all about establishing relationships between a public relations practitioner and a journalist. Those relationships really are the foundation for the benefits that are the result of media relations to an organization. The ability to establish relationships is integral to nearly all aspects of an organization's communication, whether with the media, consumers, investors, donors, regulators . . . just about every audience upon whom the success or failure of an organization depends.

While we would all like to believe that our organization is capable of creating a dialogic, or two-way, relationship with each of our key audiences, the reality—and result—of the number of available hours in a day makes this impossible. Instead, we often rely on a series of one-way interactions, which much of the time means we have to rely less on relationships and more on ensuring that our audiences are receiving information. This information often becomes the groundwork for our organization's reputation among our audiences. As such, one of the key value-added benefits of media relations is the *ability to establish a positive reputation among our audiences.* The more—positive—earned media an organization garners, the more likely the same organization will be perceived in a favorable light.

Another key benefit media relations has for an organization is based on the effective and positive relationships it creates with journalists. Assuming media relations is done well, journalists should, over time, seek information about an organization from these organizational experts—us. After all, research has shown that journalists tend to trust the media relations practitioners they know, and inherently distrust those that they don't. What does this mean for the organization? It can have a lot of positive benefits. Perhaps you are involved with an organization that employs a large number of people, and there is a rumor that major layoffs are coming. An organization with effective media relationships might get a phone call asking if the rumors are true, an organization without such relationships might wake up to see their company name on the front page of a newspaper announcing the layoffs. *Effective relationships with journalists, then, may help to mitigate crises,* or at least allow for an organization to be part of the conversation. While this should not be the first goal of media relations, and certainly we hope your organization never goes through a major crisis, it is a very real and tangible benefit to the work being done through building relationships with media professionals.

Perhaps the most important aspect of effective media relations is that it allows for organizations to help in the *agenda-building* process. Cobb, Ross, and Ross[9] have defined two types of agenda: The *public* agenda, which consists of topics that have a high level of public interest; and the *formal* agenda, which consists of topics that policy makers are actively considering. For media relations, we might consider the formal agenda to be those topics that media are actively covering, which in turn, will often help to create the public agenda. As such, effective media relations can impact both the formal agenda of the media and subsequently the public agenda, thus helping to achieve organizational goals.

Key Concepts

Changes in the media landscape have had a significant impact on how information is disseminated. While new platforms have changed the look of media, the power and pervasiveness of information has had a profound impact on many peoples' lives. Media relations is one way for organizations to bring their message to the forefront, and the practice of media relations allows for those voices to be heard. While not the only tool available, media relations is often considered the best way for organizations to garner credible coverage, and to contribute to the marketplace of information.

Challenge Case

The following is a checklist to ensure effective media relations; it comes from David R. Yale's 1993 book, *The Publicity Handbook*. Based on what you've read over the first two chapters of this text, and on what you know about information dissemination in the modern marketplace, how might you change—or not change—each of the suggestions to fit modern media relations?

1. Have you included a prestamped reply card with your mailed publicity material so you can get feedback?
2. Does the fax service you're considering use a mainframe computer?
3. Have you asked the journalists you work with closely if they subscribe to an electronic mail service—and if that's how they want you to deliver your publicity material?
4. Is all your publicity material on 8½-by-11-inch paper?
5. Are you mailing all your publicity material with first-class postage?
6. Are you being straightforward about your organization or business? Have you given journalists a complete picture?

REFERENCES

1. Nielsen Reports. (2014, May 6). Changing channels: Americans view just 17 channels despite record number to choose from. https://www.nielsen.com/us/en/insights/article/2014/changing-channels-americans-view-just-17-channels-despite-record-number-to-choose-from/
2. Netcraft. (2019 January). December 2018 web server survey. Retrieved from https://news.netcraft.com/archives/2018/
3. Statista. (2019, March 18). Percentage of U.S. population with a social media profile from 2008 to 2019. Retrieved from https://www.statista.com/statistics/273476/percentage-of-us-population-with-a-social-network-profile/
4. Global Web Index. (n.d.). The latest social media trends to know in social media 2019. Retrieved from https://www.globalwebindex.com/reports/social
5. Pew Research Center. (8 October 2015). Social media usage: 2005–2015. Retrieved from http://www.pewinternet.org/2015/10/08/social-networking-usage-2005-2015/

6. Pew Research Center. (17 July 2018). Use of mobile devices for new continues to grow, outpacing desktops and laptops. Retrieved from http://www.pewresearch.org/fact-tank/2018/07/17/use-of-mobile-devices-for-news-continues-to-grow-outpacing-desktops-and-laptops/

7. Supa, D. W., & Zoch, L. M. (2010 August). *Has the use of online media rooms to create a dialogue with journalists changed in global corporations? Comparing 2004 to 2009.* Conference paper presented at AEJMC Annual Conference, Denver, CO.

8. Twitter: Most followers. Friend or Follow. (n.d.). Retrieved from https://friendor-follow.com/twitter/most-followers/

9. Cobb, R., Ross, J.-K., & Ross, M. H. (1976). Agenda building as a comparative political process. *American Political Science Association*, 70(1), 126–38. doi: 10.2307/1960328

3 THEORY IN MEDIA RELATIONS

We have all probably read, or at least heard of, Kurt Lewin's quote, "there is nothing more practical than a good theory." Lewin (1890–1947), sometimes called the father of modern social psychology, also wrote, "if you want to truly understand something, try to change it," a concept we'll come back to later in this chapter. As we appear to be on a roll with quotes, here's one more to start off our discussion. These words are attributed to the German socialist philosopher and collaborator of Karl Marx, Friedrich Engels (1820–1895). He wrote: "An ounce of action is worth a ton of theory."

These statements provide three seemingly conflicting ideas concerning the importance of theory, a topic that is a focus of this chapter. In our case, we will be referring to the importance of theory to media relations. But *are* these opinions conflicting, or do they simply come from different viewpoints? In this chapter we will make the argument that a good theory is a useful one, and if used strategically, that theory will improve our ability to successfully perform our jobs to the benefit of our organizations. We will also discuss how we developed the expectations management theory for media relations, and how, in trying to change the practice for the better, we have come to understand it better. Even Engels's seemingly antitheory quote can be used as a building block in developing a theory that communicators will find helpful.

Although the term "theory" can seem intimidating and a bit too academic for many people, a theory is a fairly straightforward concept. Theories, and their predecessors, *models*, provide in as simple a way as possible an abstract understanding of a process.[1] In our case we will primarily be discussing communication theories and models— because media relations is part of public relations, and public relations is a communication process. A theory attempts to provide an abstract understanding because the goal is to not just describe a single event or process but rather all events and processes that are similar.

A good media relations theory, therefore, should shed light on all instances where strategic media relations is taking place, not just media relations in one specific situation.

What Makes a Theory a "Good" Theory?

The Goal of a Theory Is to Explain

In public relations (PR), of which media relations is a part, we try to connect PR with other concepts—such as personal communication, organizational structure, and social media—and to explain the relationships that exist between the two. The same is true with communication theories in general, or journalism theories, or persuasion theories, and so on, within any of the communication fields. It is also true of useful theories that come from the disciplines of psychology, sociology, or education, all of which can be useful to communicators.

The Best Theories Make Connections

The best theories work by providing explanatory links. How is A related to B? Why is A related to B? What in A is related to what in B? And, also, where and when do these relationships occur? For example, in media relations we might wonder how an email pitch is related to a journalist deciding to go with the idea we are proposing. Why is this pitch being picked up while dozens that were sent before it have not been used? What is it about this pitch? Is it the story itself? The way it was written in the email? Is it related to the current needs of the journalist? Does this journalist look for something in a pitch that we don't know about?

Even more difficult to discover are the questions of where and when these relationships occur. Do stories about our organization only get picked up by local media, and never go national? Does that have to do with our organization itself? Do we not understand the different needs of a national outlet? Why does some of what we write quickly make it into a media outlet when other pieces never make it at all?

A "Good" Theory Will Help Make Those Connections for Us

A good theory can be *applied* within our everyday activities. It will be based on dozens or even hundreds of "actions"—but definitely more than "an ounce" (see the Engels quote mentioned earlier). And a good theory will be adjusted and tweaked as new information comes in from research or through experiences of professionals. A good theory is a living theory, not a static one.

Why Theory Is Important to Media Relations

Most people, even those who work in the field, think of media relations as a tactical and practical part of the public relations function. Very seldom, in our experiences, have we talked with someone who thinks about theories as they conduct their daily media relations activities. Media relations professionals are more likely to operate the way they do because of their own backgrounds. Some of us were journalists prior to coming to media relations and we do things in certain ways because that's the way we would have wanted a media relations person to approach us when we were working in that field. Some of us learned our media relations skills in the classroom; others were "trained" on the job by the person we replaced or by another coworker. Still others have always used the same approach and just don't give a lot of thought to it.

The use of theories is important to those of us in media relations because they can help us do our jobs better. Theories that last more than a year or two in scholarly or academic or practical work before they fade into the background endure because they are useful: They explain how to do something better, or clarify why something happens the way it happens in a particular situation.

Theories have a variety of purposes according to Stephen Littlejohn,[2] the author of one of the best-selling and most highly used books about communication theories. The functions of a theory that connect the most to those of us practicing media relations are that they:

1. **Organize and summarize knowledge.** Very seldom does a researcher or scholar just one day "dream up" a theory. Generally, especially when you're dealing with a theory that will stand the test of time and turn out to be useful to those applying it, a lot of research goes into a particular phenomenon. This all happens before introducing the theory to the world. Such a phenomenon relating to media relations might be how to successfully relay your message to the media. An effective theory organizes, pulls together—and sometimes simplifies—a lot of information that was gathered to develop the theory.

2. **Focus observation on particular items.** Earlier we talked about explanatory links within a theory. A useful theory can relate one thing to another in a way that is clear and reproducible in practice. For example, learning how to write a successful email pitch could be a matter of focusing on particular items that are important to journalists. Sometimes it just takes a lot of focus on the items of interest—such as identifying what journalists look for in a story or in a story idea—and then working with what you have learned. For instance, being able to define what makes something newsworthy; pinpointing the kind of issues a particular journalist likes to write about; or even knowing a journalist's preferred method of receiving information, might be other approaches to consider.

3. **Predict**. A useful theory will predict what will happen in a certain situation. For instance, a theory we will talk about later in this chapter, the two-step flow of communication theory, predicts that most people get their information from what are called *opinion leaders*, rather than directly from the media. Research using this theory has shown time and again that this is the case. If you are conducting media relations, this is useful information because it allows you to target not only a journalist or producer but also opinion leaders for your ultimate targeted audience, who are likely to consume a particular medium. Identifying your final audience as well as those people your audience considers opinion leaders then becomes the job.

4. **Clarify**. Sometimes we observe something but don't totally understand what is going on. A useful theory can help us to understand observed relationships and to interpret events. Suppose you find that your outreach to the local city newspaper generally results in the acceptance of your stories for publication, whereas the stories you have pitched or sent to the large out-of-town newspaper has resulted in nothing but wasted time on your part because the reporters seem to have no interest in what you are sending them. What is happening? Although there are several theories that might explain what is going on, the theory of rhetorical sensitivity might provide one answer. This is a theory that tells us it is important to *adapt our message to the audience*. It is likely that reporters in the larger nearby city are not interested in the same topics as those who work more locally. This means that to be successful you'll have to do better research to determine what is of interest or concern to different reporters in those different types of outlets.

5. **Help us control events**. A useful theory can even go so far as to establish norms of how to do our jobs effectively, so we'll be successful. For example, we might notice in our workplace that some media relations practitioners have better "luck" getting information about our organization accepted by the media than do others. The expectations management theory discussed later in this chapter might be able to clarify why this takes place by explaining how relationships with the media can be successfully developed by media relations practitioners.

Theories That Help Structure Media Relations

Most of the theories that are useful to those of us in media relations come from the various fields within the overarching discipline of communication—especially journalism and interpersonal communication. Psychology has also contributed several theories that add to our understanding of how best to be successful in our work. As with many interactions, the process of communication is often looked at contextually, meaning we have to ask: What is the context of the communication that is or will be taking place? For those of us involved in the practice or study of media relations, that context is *the planned, purposeful, and strategic relationship between a practitioner working on behalf of an organization and a journalist working on behalf of a media outlet.*

Although some readers might argue there are many theories beyond those included here that potentially could be considered of importance to media relations, we have chosen the theories—and models—we, and others, have used again and again in our practice and in our research, and that we cover in our media relations classes. The theories we will discuss briefly in this section, though originally developed for other purposes, can help us be more successful media relations professionals if they are used to support our outreach to journalists.

Two-Step Flow Theory

One of the earliest media theories, two-step flow, was developed in the 1940s during a period of great interest in the effects of mass communication on people. Developers of the theory found that mass media had less of a direct effect on people than most at the time had supposed. They also discovered the effects media had were more complicated than had been suspected. These early researchers found that personal influence had as great, if not greater, influence on people than did the media. This personal influence is the second step in the two-step flow of the theory.

According to this theory, ideas flow from the mass media to *opinion leaders*, and then on to everyone else. **Opinion leaders** are people who pay more attention to the media than do the rest of us. As well, they tend to be especially well educated about certain issues. A person you consider an opinion leader has more influence on your opinions than do the media, because you view them as trustworthy and knowledgeable about specific issues that are relevant to you. You also believe that person has no reason to "trick" people or force a certain belief onto others. Critics of this theory consider it no longer valid because it was developed at a time when few people had access to the mass media, and now that everyone has constant access if they wish it, it no longer applies.[3]

Those of us in media relations might argue with that criticism, however. The importance of opinion leaders or *thought leaders*, as they are sometimes called, has only *increased* in the era of social media, and 24/7 connectivity to the many available forms of media. Reaching out to influential bloggers, for example, is now as important as reaching out to the traditional media—sometimes more so. Depending on your organization's purpose or product, being mentioned in a prominent blog could be essential to your success simply because that blogger—opinion leader—has thousands of followers who believe in what the person says and then act on it.

Agenda Setting and Agenda Building

Agenda setting is also one of the theories that comes from study of the media; it was developed by McCombs and Shaw[4] to attempt to explain the importance of news media in forming public opinion. Their focus at first was strictly on politics. How does what the media report affect people's opinions about candidates and the issues inherent in every political campaign? Over time, researchers have studied agenda setting in terms of a variety of issues. Most studies have found that agenda setting not only tells people what to think about but it also informs them of how to interpret the issue being considered. Some have called these two different ways of viewing the theory. One way is *passive* agenda setting—the media doesn't tell you *what* to think, it tells you what to think *about*. The other way is *active* agenda setting—the media, by the way the topic is presented in a specific medium, *do* tell you what to think about.

Whether or not you believe agenda setting is passive or active, those who study the theory believe there are several reasons why agenda setting works for media audiences. Those reasons have also been called **priming** by media researchers.[5] Priming involves the amount of space or time that various media give to an issue or topic. That repetition alerts the audience that the topic is important by giving them a context every time the issue is raised. It allows the audience to better understand the issue because it is presented to them repeatedly and in small chunks. Each of these activities by the media is something that media relations professionals need to be aware of because they will help you to identify an issue or topic that is trending and that will become focal to the people who see it repeatedly:

- Journalists and other information disseminators must be selective in reporting the news because they don't have time or space for everything;
- They must choose not only what to report but *how* to report it;
- Media signal their audiences about what news items are most important;
- These signals include the frequency with which a story is repeated; the prominence with which a story is displayed—for example, front page of a newspaper, or lead-in story for a television or radio broadcast; the length or time allotted for the story; and how the story is framed. (See discussion of framing that follows.)

For media relations professionals, it is not really media agenda setting that we need to discuss and think about but rather the question of who sets the agenda for the media.[6] This question of what we call **agenda building** has been around almost as long as has the agenda-setting theory. If media are setting the public's agenda, who, then, is setting the agenda for the media? If understood, the agenda-building model ought to make media relations practitioners ask themselves, "Why shouldn't we be involved in that?"

Agenda building is a complicated, dynamic, and shared process. The media, the public, and in some cases public officials or organizations, all influence each other, and at the same time are influenced by each other.

As a media relations practitioner, if you read or see or hear something from the media that has a relationship in *any way* to your organization, wouldn't you try to figure out how to relate your organization to that topic in such a way that the media will be interested? Perhaps your organization has or is developing a solution to the problem. Perhaps you have someone working in your organization who has studied the issue and can connect it to the local community. Whatever the connection, you want to help build the media's agenda as it relates to the issue, problem, or topic in a way that gets your organization's point of view "out there." Materials submitted to media outlets by media relations practitioners *do* influence and become part of media coverage; therefore, media relations is involved in building the media agenda.[7] And you want to be proactive about it, rather than allow the topic to get away from you in a direction that could be negative for your organization.

Framing Theory

Some scholars refer to **framing** as a theory, and some refer to it as a concept within agenda setting. Whereas agenda setting and priming are involved in putting an issue or topic in the forefront of the audience's awareness, framing affects how audiences think about a topic by focusing on some of its specific attributes to the detriment of others.

According to Scheufele and Tewksbury, framing "is based on the assumption that how an issue is characterized in reports can have influence on how it is understood by audiences."[8] Hallahan noted there are two types of framing that are prevalent in news coverage: **episodic** and **thematic**. "Episodic framing involves storytelling from the perspective of people and individual events,"[9] and this is the type of framing media relations professionals use regularly, even if they don't recognize it as such. Thematic framing tells the story of the issue or problem from a societal rather than individual or event perspective and tends to use abstract rather than specific concepts.

"Frames select or call attention to particular aspects of the reality described," wrote Entman in 1993, "which logically means that frames simultaneously direct attention away from other aspects."[10] Zoch and Molleda used the metaphor of a window frame when describing how framing works in media relations. The message framer has the choice of what points or aspects are to be emphasized in the message, just as a carpenter can emphasize a particular view through a window by where he or she frames, or places, the window. If the window had been framed on a different wall, the view would be different, just as the message of a story would be different if other aspects were emphasized.[11]

A frame can also be an idea, focus, or central storyline that organizes the events related to an issue or problem or even a simple feature story. It provides the reader or viewer with what the writer wants to be recognized as the overall meaning of the piece.[12] As the media relations professional working with media outlets to attempt to get the point of view of your organization out into the public for discussion, it is essential for you to focus attention on the language of the story. It is also essential to clearly define the issue under consideration, or the problem being discussed, so there are no misunderstandings. The use of common strategies such as slogans and mottos, descriptions, metaphors, examples, interpretations, and visual images also help to more clearly frame the issue or problem from the writer's perspective.

As framing can be considered a subset of agenda setting and agenda building, the next two areas of discussion flow logically from framing and work hand in hand with it.

Source Credibility and Information Subsidies

Source credibility is a concept that goes back to ancient Greece and Aristotle's *Rhetoric* in which he discussed persuasion and what it takes to influence your audience. Aristotle believed that to be convincing, a speaker had to bring three methods of persuasion to an audience: ethos, logos, and pathos. Pathos is emotion, logos is logic, and **ethos** is the credibility a communicator brings to the audience, even when that audience is a single journalist. In media relations, credibility means that the audience—the journalist in this case—has trust in the authority and the honesty of the source. The speaker or writer is seen as experienced and knowledgeable about the topic or issue at hand. Whether you, the professional, are the communicator, or that communicator is someone you recommend to a journalist because that person has expertise on a specific topic—say, a financial expert or a scientist—being recognized as credible is essential. That need for credibility holds true for not only the source, but also for your organization, and for the continuing relationship with the journalist.

A theory that developed around the concept of source credibility is the elaboration likelihood model (ELM).[13] It states that whether an audience perceives a source or communicator to have positive of negative credibility serves as a cue through which receivers—audiences—make quick judgments about whether or not to believe a message. A number of researchers have developed scales that can be used to determine if an individual sees a source as being credible. This has helped scholars determine what makes up the concept of credibility.[14]

What is important for us, within the framework of media relations, is to make sure both we, and the people we recommend as sources, are considered to be credible. The two main aspects to this credibility are *expertise* and *trustworthiness*. In Chapters 5 and 7 we will discuss what it takes for you to develop that credibility among the journalists with whom you work.

A credible source is one way we provide **information subsidies** to media outlets. The generation of information by media relations practitioners not only helps an organization get out information about its products and services and its points of view to the media for potential dissemination but also facilitates the newsgathering process of these same media outlets. Media organizations save the time, staff, and money it would take to produce information when they receive already-prepared information from organizational communicators. In the world of media relations, information is a commodity, both a product and a service, because it has value to those who provide it as well as to those who use it. Turk wrote "sources who make information quickly and inexpensively available to journalists through . . . 'information subsides' increase the likelihood that the information will be consumed by journalists and used in media content."[15]

The value of an information subsidy to the media is based on several items. They may include how indiscernible your organization's self-interest is, how well framed the message is, how credible the sources are, how diverse the competing information available to the reporter is, how newsworthy the information provided is, and how thorough and accurate the information provided is. Anything the media relations professional can do to speed up and cut down on a reporter's work will increase acceptance of the information subsidy, as long as you, the practitioner, are considered credible by the recipient.

Cumulative Effects Theory

This theory, developed by political scientist Elisabeth Noelle-Neumann, indicates that while the media does not have an immediate effect on its audience, it does have a cumulative, lasting effect over time. What this theory suggests for media relations practitioners is that we must get the same message out multiple times for it to have an effect on the final audience we are trying to reach. That might mean getting the same message out over a period of time in the same publication, or it might mean getting the message out at the same time in multiple media.

Only you will know what will work best because by the time you make the decision you will have carefully researched and identified the ultimate audiences you're trying to reach and the media they consume. If your choice is to communicate once through multiple media, each information subsidy must be framed to suit the needs of each different medium and the journalists you'll be targeting. That means considering the focus of the medium as well as whether it is print, broadcast, or Web. These considerations will be discussed in Chapter 10.

Social Exchange Theory

This theory is a major theoretical perspective in sociology and has been extensively studied in psychology and anthropology as well as in microeconomics. For those of us who work in media relations, it has a direct connection to the need to build relationships with the journalists with whom we work. **Social exchange theory** can be viewed as providing an economic metaphor to relationships. Self-interest and interdependence are concepts central to social exchange.[16] Therefore, the theory's basic principles are that humans in social situations realize their interdependence, and in such situations strive to act in ways that might improve their self-interest. For the media relations practitioner, that self-interest is the need to gain media coverage for the organization for which you work. For the journalist, self-interest involves gathering information of potential interest to readers or viewers to fill the ever-expanding news hole. As those of you reading this know by now, these self-interests are interdependent, as each professional relies on the other to reach their goals.

Social exchange theory also has some assumptions that make it work well in a media relations context. As explained by Chibucos and Leite in their book about social exchange in families, social exchange theory operates first on the assumption that those involved are generally rational and are able to calculate the costs and benefits in social exchanges. Because of these calculations, use of this theory generally involves decision-making. Second, social exchange theory builds on the assumption that those involved are rationally trying to maximize benefits to be gained from the situation, especially in terms of meeting their professional needs. Third, exchanges that produce payoffs or rewards for the individuals involved lead to creating patterns of social interactions.[17] For any media relations professional working with journalists over time, this is an important step.

Finally, social exchange theory assumes that individuals are goal oriented, and the process of exchange is taking place in a freely competitive social system. Because of the competitive nature of social systems, power in social exchanges lies with those individuals who possess greater resources that provide an advantage in the social exchange.[18] In the case of media relations, that power and advantage lie in holding the most-useful information or news.

Having the ability to frame information accurately and strategically, being a credible source, and providing timely information subsidies gives a great power advantage to a media relations professional working in a competitive media environment.

Relationship Management Paradigm

The concept of organizations managing their relationships with their publics and constituents has been discussed in public relations for the past 30 years. But it wasn't until a study by Broom, Casey, and Ritchey in 1997 that the field of public relations had a model of relationship management. The failure of scholars to develop theory in that area was caused by the lack of a clear definition of the central concept: There is no commonly used definition of "*relationships*," no matter what field you look at, and there are many that involve relationships. "Interpersonal relations, family relations, group dynamics, labor–management relations, counselor–client psychotherapy relations, organizational studies, and international relations are but a few of the many domains of theory and practice based upon understanding and observation of relationships."[19]

Although focused on relationships between organizations and their constituents rather than on relationships between journalists and media relations professionals, Broom, Casey, and Ritchey make some excellent points about the importance of relationships that can be easily transferred to our specific needs. While not mentioning social exchange theory, some of their conclusions were:

- The formation of relationships occurs when parties have perceptions and expectations of each other [and] when one or both parties need resources from the other;
- Relationships consist of . . . linkages through which the parties in relationships pursue and service their interdependent needs;
- Relationships are the dynamic results of the exchanges and reciprocity that manifest themselves as the relationships develop and evolve; and
- Relationship formation and maintenance represents a process of mutual adaptation.[20]

In 2000, Toth, another public relations scholar, added to these ideas by developing a concept of **interpersonal influence** (rather than personal influence).[21] By citing Simon, an early author on public relations, Toth places the needs of media relations squarely in the center of her argument. Toth wrote:

An example of how public relations was performed because of interpersonal communication comes from Simon, who cast public relations work with the media as the "buffer zone, the no man's land in which public relations practitioners so often find themselves in trying to establish and maintain credibility."[22]

Simon argued that public relations people could not accomplish their objectives without credibility and trust, individual elements [that could be attributed] to what the individual did interpersonally to reach specific goals.[23]

Toth asserts the focus in these relationships needs to be on the *communication* between those involved rather than the management aspect, and states, "the end goal of interpersonal communication is to establish and maintain successful relationships."[24] She emphasizes the interpersonal nature of relationships, and the give and take that must occur for such relationships to succeed, as well as the importance of the parties' *perceptions* of each other. We discuss the perceptions journalists and media relations practitioners have of each other in Chapter 5.

The balanced communication discussed by Toth indicates successful relationship management is built on a give and take between the parties, and it mirrors several of the concepts discussed by Broom, Casey, and Ritchey in their model, as well as concepts in social exchange theory. This balanced view of the journalist–media relations practitioner relationship is continued in the expectation management theory, discussed at the end of this chapter.

Theories of Media Relations

As we have discussed thus far, theories that are useful to those of us who work in media relations primarily come from other fields within communication. To date, the only theory that has been proposed that focuses directly and specifically on the practice of strategic media relations is the expectation management theory. And even that theory is only in development; all of its constructs, or concepts, have not yet been tested by other researchers.

Prior to this theory, researchers undertook two attempts to envision a strategic view of media relations. The first attempt, by Zoch and Molleda in 2006, presented an overall model of media relations. It clearly sets out a process a communicator can undertake to achieve strategic media relations and looks at what should happen within an organization prior to any sort of media relations taking place. It does not focus directly on the media relations relationship building as discussed and explained throughout this book.

Work by Shoemaker and Reese, who set forth internal and external influences on journalists, underpinned the second attempt to envision media relations as a systematic process.[25] Pang used their earlier work to develop an exploratory model of media relations by indicating how practitioners can respond to these influences on journalism.

Model of Media Relations

The model proposed by Zoch and Molleda is mainly intraorganizational. What that means is it addresses what takes place within an organization as the media relations communicator prepares to initiate contact with a media representative. The only reference to the *media relations process* is when the model indicates the communicator should "provide news media" with the prepared information.

This model was built on the framework of three interconnected and useful theories, or paradigms as the authors call them—agenda-setting, framing, and information subsidies. The authors explain that, prior to their 2006 chapter published in *Public Relations Theory II*, they had been unable to easily find any theory-based underpinnings to media relations, and, so, set out to create a theoretical framework for what they too saw as a strategic process. They wrote, "We describe it as an active process in which the public relations practitioner has, at the least, a modicum of control over the message she wishes to reach the public, its timing, the source of that information, and the effect on the media agenda of the issue presented."[26]

The authors clearly indicated the purpose of the model was to point out the internal steps in the process of preparing framed information subsidies for consumption outside of the organization, primarily focused toward the media. (See Figure 3.1.)

The model starts with information management and issues tracking within the context of a particular organization and emphasizes that the need for an information subsidy can be caused by any number of occurrences, initiated either internally or externally. The communicator must gather information about the issue or situation, and produce a carefully framed—to the organization's point of view—information subsidy that uses traditional news values as discussed in Chapter 7. The media relations communicator provides a news subsidy to the media and is prepared to clarify or follow-up with the media as necessary. The authors make a point of bringing up the likelihood of competing sources of information that may differ from that provided by the organization, and that the media relations person must be prepared and knowledgeable about those too. The last step in the model is to evaluate the process and outcome to improve future media relations efforts.

Although of great use to an entry- or midlevel media relations practitioner, the authors indicate the model was developed to map out what needs to be done when management decides an information subsidy is called for. They write that the model "could be applied in the day-to-day production of framed information subsidies, the attempt by the media relations practitioner to participate in building the news media agenda, and ultimately inclusion on the public's agenda of issues."[27]

Journalist-Centric Media Relations Model

Pang's 2010 exploratory model is grounded in previous literature about the relationship between journalists and media relations practitioners, as well as on

Proactive *information management* and issues tracking entail:
- Direct communication with organizational sources;
- Identify management positions regarding current or potential issues.

Need to generate an *information subsidy* starts the process:
1. Actions or operations will affect a public.
2. A public reacts before the organization, which failed in tracking an issue/crisis.
3. A real-world event produces consequences for the organization.
4. The news media reports an issue that involves the organization and publics.

Proceed with the internal/external *newsgathering* process:
- *Internal*: Use information file/intranet–website/organizational sources.
- *External*: Use professional/industry associations, opinion leaders, experts, etc.
  - Identify/seek authorization to express organizational viewpoint/position statement.
  - Produce information subsidy using traditional news values.
  - Include organizational viewpoint through framing.

Provide news media, interest/grassroots groups with subsidized information:
- Be ready/available with framed viewpoint for clarification/further inquiries from the news media.
- Monitor news media and audiences' responses/reactions.
- Follow up responses/possible generation of a sequence of information subsidies.
- Pay attention to competing sources—the more competing sources, the more difficult it is to be heard.

***Evaluate* the process and outcome to improve the media relations' efforts.**
- Be sure to assess final interpretations/reactions of affected publics regarding organizational viewpoint.

FIGURE 3.1 A Model of Media Relations

the premise that media relations practitioners can best practice systematically by making it clear they understand the needs of, and pressures imposed on, journalists. Unlike the earlier Zoch and Molleda model, this model is primarily externally driven, and is based on three propositions:

1. Practitioners must engage in proactive media relations, rather than always trying to keep a low profile,
2. Practitioners must take the responsibility of cultivating good relationships with journalists, as journalists value relationships, and
3. The onus is on the practitioner to understand how journalists operate within their environment, not on the journalist to understand the needs of the practitioner.[28]

Pang believes that the negative viewpoint of journalists toward media relations communicators is based on lengthy historical roots that tell them that not only do practitioners not understand what journalists want, but we don't understand the work of journalists nor do we understand what media relations truly is about.

As noted above, Pang's 2010 model uses the work of Shoemaker and Reese, who wrote about how journalists work and the pressures that affect them. The model then tells us how practitioners can adapt to those pressures to conduct media relations in a systematic manner. Too many media relations communicators still see their jobs as a one-way communication and don't take into consideration journalists' needs or what actually makes up their jobs. Pang suggests that we need to

- Learn to write like a journalist to truly understand their needs;
- Show journalists we truly DO understand what makes something newsworthy to them;
- Know and respect their deadlines—journalists would like their stories to be balanced and to include as many viewpoints as possible in a story, but can't if we don't respond in a timely manner;
- Use our knowledge of various journalists' deadlines to time announcements and events to fit the needs of their outlets;
- Systematically monitor the media to target journalists who might be interested in our organizations or stories, as well as those journalists' news values;
- Build relationships with the journalists we target because their beats include our organizations, or because they write about topics similar to those we care about for our organization;
- Become a source of information journalists can trust to supply accurate and useful information within the legal and ethical constraints you are bound by.[29]

Although a useful model in terms of its tactics for media relations, the journalist-centric media relations model does not address planning; it focuses more on being systematic than being strategic. As Pang notes, "this model is instructive for new practitioners to view media relations as a holistic process involving a set of interacting influences rather than merely an information subsidy function."[30]

Professional Commentary

Tina McCorkindale, PhD, APR
President and CEO
Institute for Public Relations

In the 2016 Global Body of Knowledge (GBOK) project led by the Global Alliance for Public Relations and Communication Management, the group noted that knowledge of communication models and theories, as well as the skills and abilities to apply them, were necessary to practice and excel in public relations. Even though applying theory to guide decision-making is not top of mind in the day-to-day activities of public relations professionals, the use of theories is absolutely critical in an industry focused on building relationships. Compared to other industries where the impact of "X" results in a change to "Y," public relations can be challenging because of our interactions with stakeholders. Because humans are unpredictable, public relations professionals need guidelines and strategies for how to encourage adoption of messages, attitudes, and behaviors. Theory helps professionals better understand how people think and how they behave, which is helpful in building and maintaining relationships with journalists.

Journalists on social media platforms sometimes share examples of bad pitches they receive from public relations professionals. Typically, these pitches demonstrate how some public relations professionals do not understand that the key to media relations is in the term "relations" and the building of long-term, mutually beneficial relationships. Many public relations practitioners also operate from a strictly tactical perspective by casting a wide net when pitching to see if they land any hits rather than paying attention to the types of articles the reporter has written in the past. Pitching should focus on quality rather than quantity. Media relations must be regarded as a strategic function.

In media relations, the public relations professional acts as a two-way conduit between the journalist and the organization. Understanding how people think and behave by using theory as a guide better equips a public relations professional to develop a media relations strategy. For example, by applying diffusion of innovation theory by Everett Rogers, we can better understand where people fall on the spectrum of speed of adoption of a new product or idea, from the first person to adopt it to someone who

(Continued)

only accepts the new innovation after everyone else they know has already done so. The theory also emphasizes that the media build awareness and knowledge of an innovation (anything deemed to be new in society), while interpersonal networks influence adoption.

With that knowledge, a public relations professional can understand the importance of how the media can influence dissemination, followed by subsequent adoption of information, products, and services. Knowing how to best serve the ultimate audience benefits both the organization that wants its story told and the journalist who wants stories that are timely and relevant to his or her readers. The relationship becomes a mutually beneficial relationship, the heart of public relations and a win-win for both parties. Behavioral science theories can also give insight into how people think and behave. Borrowing theories from other disciplines, such as psychology, sociology, or even neuroscience, can help organizations determine how to influence attitudes and behavior.

I would be remiss if I did not address the important role of ethics in theory and public relations. Knowledge is power, and theory can be used for harm. While behavioral science and other communication-related theories can help us better understand people, the importance of being ethical in engagement should not be understated. Adopting an ethic of care philosophy that focuses on mutuality and reciprocity should be at the forefront of building relationships, and that includes the relationship between public relations professionals and journalists. As journalists are critical to the success of what public relations people do, engaging theory to have positive outcomes for both parties, is a win-win for both organizations (vis-à-vis public relations professionals) and journalists.

Tina McCorkindale Biography

Tina McCorkindale, PhD, APR, is the president and CEO of the Institute for Public Relations, a global industry nonprofit association devoted to research in the profession. Previously, she was a professor for 15 years with more than 10 years of prior experience working in corporate communication and analytics. McCorkindale serves on the boards of several industry associations and has received awards for her contributions to the profession. She has more than 150 presentations and publications in books and journals with a research focus in digital and behavior. She lives in Seattle, Washington.

Development of Expectations Management Theory

To solve the problem of having no true theory that has been developed specifically for use in the strategic practice of media relations, your authors have started on the road toward development of what we are calling the expectations management theory. As is discussed in Chapter 5 of this book, media relations is built on relationships between information suppliers—the media relations communicator—and the representative from the media outlet—the journalist or producer or blogger.

As defined in Chapter 1, media relations is the *systematic, planned, purposeful and mutually beneficial relationship between journalists in the mass media and public relations practitioners*. If you think about what is involved in successful, or mutually beneficial media relations, there are four expectations that need to be satisfied within the context of expectation management. Those expectations are (1) the *product*, or information subsidy; (2) the *process* of relaying the information; (3) the *roles* of the journalist and the practitioner; and, perhaps most important, (4) the *relationship* between the two.

Providing definitions is an essential step in developing theory that involves relationships.[31] Therefore, the first step in developing a theory of expectation management based on our definition of media relations was to define the relationship between the media relations practitioner and the journalist. The second step in establishing this new theory was to develop the background to that mutually beneficial relationship.

To do that we conducted several research studies and learned that there is important demographic background information that related to a positive relationship between those in media relations and those who work in the media. This, of course, is in addition to whether the person answering the questions was a media relations practitioner or a journalist, which was the first question we asked in the survey. The important demographics are the *years of experience* that the professional has, whether the professional was a *female or a male*, whether the professional holds a *managerial role*, and the *geographic location* of the professional. Each of these factors was shown by the research to have some impact on how the journalists and media relations professionals who were studied reacted to the very idea of media relations being a two-way and beneficial relationship.

The final step in developing the new expectations management theory was to define the outcome of the relationship. For some media relations practitioners, success is defined as placing an information subsidy in the mass media. However, for the purpose of a theory of media relations that is based at least partly on relationships, success should not be defined as solely the **placement** of an information subsidy, but rather as the initial **acceptance** of the message. What this means is that your information might not be placed immediately, or without changes, but it could be considered for inclusion in another story or used by the journalist to spark other story ideas.

What we always have to remember is that successful media relations is a two-stage process. In practical terms, as long as a journalist doesn't immediately disregard public relations information subsidies, and views that subsidy as holding value, then the subsidy can be viewed as successful, even though it might not be published as submitted for a variety of reasons. This is the acceptance stage.

The second stage in effective media relations messaging is adoption, during the process of which the message is accepted and used by the journalist in formulating a news item. While success in many settings may not be realized until the message is actually adopted or used in the medium, message acceptance is an important part of building media relations relationships. Public relations practitioners should attempt first to get their messaging accepted, which will help to build the relationship, ultimately leading to greater message adoption.

There are constraints to the media relations process, specifically, time and frequency of interaction, which make it different from other long-term-oriented relationships within public relations, such as those of employee or investor. Media relations is often accomplished through a series of short duration, intermittent interactions. Therefore, the dimensions of the relationship must be explored in those terms, not in terms of other types of continuing relationships.

Based on Broom, Casey, and Ritchey's scholarship about theory development, we began to develop the theory of expectations management. Figure 3.2 represents the concepts of the new theory and the proposed linkages. The three panels explain (1) the important background information that relates to a positive relationship, (2) the areas of expectations, and (3) the outcome—proposed here in two levels. Based on the constructs of the theory proposed here, the short definition of the media relations expectations management theory (EMT) is

> Whether a message will be accepted or adopted is dependent on the degree
> to which the public relations practitioner has met the expectations of the
> journalist.

To some of our readers, there may be nothing here that is new or unexpected. However, the proposed antecedents of message acceptance or adoption make this unique, as does the explanation—or concept—of the relationship with regard to *the product, process, roles,* and *relationships.* If both public relations practitioners and journalists are aware of these antecedents, and both also know about the expectations for the **product**—the information subsidy, **process**—the content and

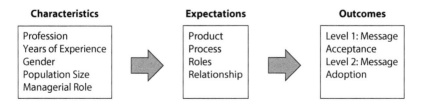

Characteristics		Expectations		Outcomes
Profession Years of Experience Gender Population Size Managerial Role		Product Process Roles Relationship		Level 1: Message Acceptance Level 2: Message Adoption

FIGURE 3.2 Expectations Management

means of communication, **roles**—range and limits of control of information, and **relationship**—frequency, expertise and nature of communication, then the likelihood of message acceptance or adoption will increase.

The second theoretical assumption is

The greater the level of message acceptance over time, the more likely it is to lead to a greater level of message adoption.

This assumption shows the two-step nature of media relations, as explained above, and highlights the need for increased awareness of whether or not a message is accepted by journalists. While the final goal—and organizational perception of success—may be for message adoption, media relations practitioners must be conscious of message acceptance, and its role in establishing expectations, thereby leading to a better relationship with the journalist.

"If You Want to Truly Understand Something, Try to Change It"

We hope you remember that quote by Kurt Lewin from the first paragraph of this chapter, and that we would be returning to it. We have now circled back, and you have, we hope, more knowledge about how to successfully undertake a strategic view of media relations. Lewin, a famous social psychologist, developed what has become known as field theory. He saw the social environment—remember, he was a psychologist—as a dynamic field that interacted with human consciousness. This means that your behavior is related both to your personal characteristics and to the environment, or social situation you find yourself in. You and that environment interact through your behavior, and change takes place in both you *and* the environment in which you live or work. So what does this have to do with the practice of media relations?

At the beginning of this chapter we wrote that in trying to change the practice for the better we have come to understand it more. That is indeed the case for your authors. The research we conducted over the past 15 years gave us insights about:

- What journalists, as well as media relations practitioners believe makes something newsworthy;
- How past studies have discussed the relationship between journalists and media relations practitioners;
- The changes that are taking place in how journalists collect and report the news because of social media, media online sites, and a reduction in staffing within media outlets; and
- The fact that media relations professionals are working hard to learn new skills to deal with this changing media environment

And, while conducting that research about the pieces that make up our current understanding of media relations, we came to a realization. Yes, understanding the past and seeing the changes that have occurred in the environment surrounding media relations are important. But having media relations continue to be considered a tactical process would never allow professionals in the field to contribute as much to an organization as their skills make possible. Only by accepting that a healthy program of media relations involves a strategic process can we truly understand its possibilities and capabilities.

Each of the theories discussed in this chapter shows you a way you can change how you practice—or plan to practice—media relations. You may already be using some of the theories, perhaps without even realizing it. But taking more of them into account could allow you to change the way you do things, and in so doing change the environment in which you work. By better understanding audiences, or how to frame your issue when writing news releases, or proving yourself to be a trustworthy spokesperson, or taking into account the constraints under which journalists work, you can change your behavior and affect the environment in which you work.

Even small changes, based on the theories presented here, can help you to better understand how to achieve successful and strategic media relations.

Key Concepts

In this chapter we discussed what *theory* is and how to evaluate whether a theory is *good or useful* for use in media relations. We defined a theory as *an abstract understanding of a process,* and, because our focus in this book is media relations, the process of importance for us is the process of strategic media relations. A theory attempts to provide an abstract understanding because the goal is not to describe just a single event or process, but rather all events and processes that are similar. A useful theory will help us to organize and summarize knowledge, focus observations on particular items, predict, clarify, and help us to control events.

Theories and models that can help us do our jobs better through understanding their concepts are the *two-step flow theory;* **agenda setting** *and* **agenda building; framing**, and within framing, **information subsidies** and **source credibility**; *cumulative effects theory*; and the *model of relationship management.*

There are only three theories or models that focus directly and specifically on media relations. They are the *model of media relations,* the *journalist-centric media relations model,* and expectations management theory.

REFERENCES

1. Miller, K. (2002). *Communication theories: Perspectives, processes and contexts*. New York, NY: McGraw Hill.
2. Littlejohn, S. W. (1996). *Theories of human communication* (5th ed.), pp. 31–32. Belmont, CA: Wadsworth.
3. Lowery, S. A., & DeFleur, M. L. (1988). *Milestones in mass communication research*. (2nd ed.), pp. 163–186. New York, NY: Longman.
4. McCombs, M. E., & Shaw, D. L. (1972). The agenda setting function of mass media. *Public Opinion Quarterly, 36*, 176–187.
5. Scheufele, D. A., & Tewksbury, D. (2007). Framing, agenda setting, and priming: The evolution of three media effects models. *Journal of Communication, 57*(1), 9–20; Weaver, D. H. (2007). Thoughts on agenda setting, framing, and priming. *Journal of Communication, 57*(1), 142–147.
6. Weaver, D. H., & Elliott, S. (1985). Who sets the agenda for the media? A study of local agenda-building. *Journalism Quarterly, 62*(1), 87.
7. Oliveira, M., & Murphy, P. (2009). The leader as the face of a crisis: Philip Morris' CEO's speeches during the 1990s. *Journal of Public Relations Research, 21*(4), 361–380.
8. Scheufele, D. A., & Tewksbury, D. (2007). Framing, agenda setting, and priming: The evolution of three media effects models. *Journal of Communication, 57*(1), 11.
9. Hallahan, K. (1999). Seven models of framing: Implications for public relations. *Journal of Public Relations Research, 11*(3), 221.
10. Entman, R. M. (1993). Framing: Toward a clarification of a fractured paradigm. *Journal of Communication, 43*, 54.
11. Zoch, L. M., & Molleda, J.-C. (2006). Building a theoretical model of media relations using framing, information subsidies, and agenda-building. In C. H. Botan & V. Hazleton (Eds.), *Public relations theory II*, pp. 279–309, Mahwah, NJ: Lawrence Erlbaum Associates.
12. Gamson, W. A., & Modigliani, A. (1987). The changing culture of affirmative action. In R. G. Braungart & M. M. Braungart (Eds.), *Research in political sociology* (Vol. 3, pp. 137–177). Greenwich, CT: JAI Press.
13. Petty, R., & Cacioppo, J. (1986). The elaboration likelihood model of persuasion. *Advances in Experimental Social Psychology, 19*, 123–205.
14. Berlo, D. K., Lemert, J. B., & Mertz, R. J. (1969). Dimensions for evaluating the acceptability of message sources. *Public Opinion Quarterly, 33*(4), 563–576; Mccroskey, J. C. (1966). Scales for the measurement of ethos. *Speech Monographs, 33*(1), 65; Meyer, P. (1988). Defining and measuring credibility of newspapers: Developing an index. *Journalism Quarterly, 65*(3), 567–588.
15. Turk, J. V. (1986). Information subsidies and media content: A study of public relations influence on the news. *Journalism Monographs, 100*, 3.

16. Lawler, E. J., & Thye, S. R. (1999). Bringing emotions into social exchange theory. *Annual Review of Sociology, 25,* 217–244; Lawler, E. J. (2001). An affect theory of social exchange. *American Journal of Sociology, 107*(2), 321–352.

17. Chibucos, T. R., & Leite, R. W. (2005). *Readings in family theory,* p. 137. Thousand Oaks, CA: SAGE.

18. Chibucos and Leite, 137.

19. Broom, G. M., Casey, S., & Ritchey, J. (1997). Toward a concept and theory of organization–public relationships. *Journal of Public Relations Research, 9*(2), 86.

20. Broom, Casey, & Ritchey, 95.

21. Toth, E. L. (2000). From personal influence to interpersonal influence: A model for relationship management. In J. A. Ledingham & S. D. Bruning (Eds.), *Public relations as relationship management,* pp. 205–219. Mahwah, NJ: Lawrence Erlbaum Associates.

22. Simon, R. (1980). *Public relations: Concepts and practices* (2nd ed.), p. 273. Columbus, OH: Grid Publishing.

23. Simon (1980) quoted in Toth (2000), p. 206.

24. Toth, p. 217.

25. Shoemaker, P., & Reese, S. D. (1996). *Mediating the message.* New York, NY: Longman.

26. Zoch and Molleda, p. 280.

27. Zoch and Molleda, p. 296.

28. Pang, A. (2010). Mediating the media: A journalistic-centric media relations model. *Corporate Communications: An International Journal, 15*(2), 193.

29. Pang, pp. 196–199.

30. Pang, p. 201.

31. Broom, Casey, & Ritchey, 1997.

4 UNDERSTANDING AUDIENCES

Although primarily concerned with journalists as an audience, media relations practitioners must also think strategically about other audiences in a variety of ways to effectively execute a media relations program. Thinking of journalists and other information disseminators as a targeted audience—and not just as a step on the way to reaching your ultimate audience—is something new for many people. That's because media relations is usually seen as a tactic to reach our ultimate audience of constituents and stakeholders. That ultimate audience might be comprised of consumers, shareholders, donors, volunteers, community members, activists, politicians, voters, a combination of all those constituents, or entirely different groups altogether. Our intended purpose for the outreach will define the audience.

For those of us in media relations, however, *journalists, or other mass communicators, are our most important audience, our primary audience*, for without them we would not have broad access to the other groups and individual constituents that matter to our organization or to our agency's clients.

This chapter will introduce you to—or perhaps remind you about—the variety of ways to categorize audiences; how people who are not our final target can help us to inform or persuade our ultimate target or targets; why transparency is important when dealing with all our audiences, but particularly with our primary audience of journalists; how to determine and speak to our audiences' objectives related to our communication; and how those who work in various media differ from other audiences.

Understanding the Makeup of an Audience

There are four terms that we use throughout this book to describe the individuals and groups important to an organization. The concepts behind these terms must be differentiated so that you can fully understand how the communication practiced by a public relations professional communicating directly with constituents differs from how we communicate when we act as a media relations practitioner. The terms are "public," "stakeholder," "constituent," and "audience." The media, and therefore media relations practitioners, generally communicate solely with the broadest and least defined of the groupings: the audience.

How Is a Public Different From a Stakeholder?

Public relations is one of those fields in which its practitioners and academics use many terms that *appear* to mean the same thing but often do not. Unfortunately, students of public relations often become so confused about the different words that are used for the various types of groups of people that they tend to refer to every group as either a stakeholder or a public without attempting to differentiate between them. You may find yourself using the two terms interchangeably because one or more of your instructors or colleagues does. However, the term "public" has a specific meaning in public relations that is far removed from the idea of a "general public," which is what most people think of when using the word "public." It is also different from "stakeholder," a word that comes originally from the business literature.

Stakeholders are any individual or group that can affect or be directly affected by the actions, decisions, policies, practices, or goals of an organization. Examples of stakeholders would be employees, or in a nonprofit, volunteers; customers or clients of the organization; suppliers to the organization; the local community; employees or elected officials at various levels of government; and even, to some extent, the media. Stakeholders can actively influence an organization's reputation. For example, their communication with others may affect whether an organization is considered legitimate by its customers and clients. Stakeholders can even alter an organization's income if they aren't satisfied with its products, social responsibilities, or other activities. Organizations must recognize the importance of their stakeholders and make an effort to communication directly with them. To know your stakeholders' expectations is the first step to fulfilling them.

Stakeholders are an important group to public relations professionals because they can—if they are not treated fairly or legally, if their expectations are not met, or if they are not communicated with on a regular basis—take the next step and start forming into a public.

A **public** forms when stakeholders recognize that a problem exists between them and an organization and they then *organize to do something about it*. You may be familiar with the authors James Grunig and Todd Hunt from other courses in public relations.[1] These two public relations scholars in 1984 wrote the first book about managing the public relations function within an organization. They also added the word "public," which originated in sociology, to the vocabulary of public relations.

The connection between these two concepts is that if an organization does not communicate with and react to its stakeholders' concerns quickly—and that is done using two-way communication rather than the media—stakeholders can easily come together to form a public. As Grunig and Hunt wrote, "members of a public function as a single system because they input and process the same information and output similar behaviors. Thus, we can define a public as a loosely structured system whose members detect the same problem or issue, interact either face to face or through mediated channels and behave as though they are one body."[2] Publics may receive their initial information about the problem or issue through traditional media, but organizations generally prefer more-direct ways to communicate with such groups once they form. Social media is one of the ways that is most commonly used.

What Is a Constituency?

A "constituency" is a relatively new term that has developed as public relations scholars came to believe the field was too focused on corporations and their interactions, and that the language we used was ignoring a large group of organizations in activist and nonprofit areas. According to Coombs and Holladay, "**constituencies** can be defined as groups of people in a similar situation. By this definition, stakeholders are constituencies and organizations are constituencies."[3] The point of reframing who public relations professionals communicate with— constituents, stakeholders or publics—is to remind us that relationships are interdependent, and that those we communicate with wear as many hats as we do. In other words, individuals are constituents of many organizations and take on many roles in society. They can be internal or external audiences, members of a public, or stakeholders in a corporation, depending on your point of view and the reason you communicate with them.

Media Relations Focuses on Audiences

Audiences, in general, are people who *receive* our communications, our information, our messages. "Receive" is the important word when discussing audiences, because audiences are seldom discussed in terms of two-way communication. We expect constituents or stakeholders to react in some way to us, our organization or our client—not always in words, but sometimes through the decisions they make or behaviors they undertake—and therefore we communicate with them with that expectation in mind. These groups are not considered an audience because they are targeted, and the relationship is two-way. Chapter 2 introduced you to the use of owned and shared media vehicles with which to communicate. Owned and shared media are excellent methods to reach out and connect with both external and internal constituents and stakeholders in a way that can start and continue conversations.

As described in Chapter 2, earned media reaches an audience through a media vehicle outside the organization and out of our control. Media relations often relies on this type of media to access a more general audience. As stated in earlier chapters, this book is proposing that using media relations should be a strategic decision made by an organization, and to be considered strategic it must in some way fulfill the overall goals of the organization.

> Why would an organization set a goal to reach a broad audience, which usually doesn't respond to communications from the organization, in a medium over which the communicator has no control?

First, it is important to realize that every audience is composed of individuals, whether they are listening to a symphony, attending a speech, watching television news, reading a newspaper online, checking a content aggregator, or even checking a Twitter or Instagram feed. The people who make up the audience, if you pick your media outlets wisely, may well be stakeholders—consumers of your company's products, for example. Alternately, they could be constituents of your organization, perhaps those who donate to your nonprofit organization; or members of a group that you seek to add as a constituent, such as new college graduates just starting their first jobs.

Second, it is equally important to remember that no matter how the mass media have been maligned in recent years, research indicates that most people would rather hear news from that primary source than from a secondary source, such as an aggregator or social media. People may access news digitally on their smartphones or computers, but by a large margin their sources remain traditional news media, like television or newspapers.[4]

And third, the job of media relations professionals is to build relationships with journalists and other information disseminators in those outlets that their constituents or desired constituents read, view, or listen to. As we mentioned above, and will discuss below, *those reporters, editors, producers, influencers, or bloggers are our primary audience.*

Defining Our Audiences

There are three general audiences that public relations professionals communicate with, and each type of audience potentially includes stakeholders and constituents, as well as members of an active public. These categories are internal audiences, general external audiences, and targeted external audiences. Depending on the topic, each of these audiences can be reached using media relations, although there are usually better methods to reach internal audiences. Perhaps surprisingly, determining what types of constituents make up each category can sometimes be more difficult than it would appear, because there is overlap depending on the topic you want to communicate about.

We have found that sometimes the best way to identify and explain the differences among these audiences is to use an example. Because it references an organization with which we're all familiar, for this illustration we'll use a college or university to briefly think through how to determine and identify our three audiences.

Internal Audiences

In our example, the internal audience, of course, would include students, faculty, administrators or managers, and staff members working at the university. That's the easy part. But what about alumni, parents of current students, donors to the university, or family members of faculty? Are they part of the internal audience? When would they be categorized as internal and when might they be considered an external audience? About what kinds of topics would each group be considered as internal constituents to the organization? What might topics be for which we would consider them outside constituents of the organization?

These are the sorts of questions you will find yourself asking with every media relations campaign you undertake. Audiences are made up of individuals, all of whom slot into more than one of the types of groups discussed above that we communicate with in public relations. Knowing which ones are which can help us determine whether media relations is the best way to communicate with them, or if more targeted and personal communication is needed.

External Audiences

External audiences can be just as confusing to differentiate, particularly because we must distinguish between two types of external audience. A targeted external audience might be composed of community members; it might be donors of any kind, including alumni—unless you have already decided that donors and alumni are both internal audiences for a particular situation. The audience might be the local city or town government; it might be potential students; it might be companies that provide the university with necessary supplies such as food, copy paper, technology, textbooks, and all the other articles that keep the organization functioning. For each target there can be overlap with other targeted audiences. There could be alumni in any of the other groups. There could even be faculty or students, therefore overlapping with the internal audience. And, of course, all these targets are part of a larger general audience, which the university must remain aware of and keep informed to fulfill its educational mission and uphold its reputation.

For those of us whose job it is to reach external media, another targeted audience is that of journalists and other information disseminators. And *our particular targets are those journalists, producers, editors, bloggers, and influencers with whom we work to build relationships* to best help our organizations reach the groups they want to target.

A *general external audience* is the type of audience for which most people would use media relations. If you think about this audience as a collection of individuals about whom you know little, but that each member might have some interest in whatever it is you want to communicate, then using traditional mass media would make sense. Even given your lack of information about them, that general audience can be targeted in some ways so that it remains broad, yet you know enough about them to be able to direct your efforts. Geography and demographics can help you whittle down how broad your reach needs to be as well as on which media vehicles you should put your focus.

Let's Set Up a Short Scenario: Audience Outreach

The university in question is a medium-sized public university in a state that, like most states, has budgeted less and less public money annually toward its colleges and universities. Because of that, the state legislature expects those colleges and universities to make up the difference in ways that don't include constantly raising tuition. In an effort to increase income and promote itself as relevant in today's world, the university has initiated an online degree program in cybersecurity. It is a popular area of research and a good employment opportunity for graduates.

Throughout the process of developing the degree, the university has kept students, faculty, staff, alumni, donors, and other friends of the university informed through announcements and articles in its emailed weekly newsletter, as well as featuring stories in its twice-a-year mailed magazine. There was also a short article in the closest city's newspaper when the state approved the new program, but that was published before the university had fully developed the curriculum, hired faculty and staff, or built additional infrastructure. Now it's time to let other important constituents know about the new program.

The internal audiences are already aware of the new initiative. Is our outreach with that group finished? Probably not, but as this book is about media relations, any further outreach we discuss will be in terms of outreach to external audiences. Because that's the case, our earlier conundrum about whether alumni, donors, and parents can be considered internal audiences is no longer relevant. Each of those constituent groups can also be reached through a variety of traditional and online media, and we need to start thinking about what their interest would be in this story—and how we can frame it for all of our potential audiences.

It is important to remember that, no matter what type of organization you work in or with, media relations is a collaborative venture. Our work is not the only way that our constituents receive information from our organization. In this scenario, if one of the university's goals is to recruit students into the cybersecurity program, depending on the level of the program, the undergraduate admissions office or the graduate affairs office will be involved. Although knowing that other communication efforts are being taken is important, that in no way precludes our efforts in media outreach.

Because you are working for a public university, at a minimum you would plan to reach out to traditional media vehicles across your state, if not beyond, to achieve several strategic organizational goals. You will want to introduce the new program; to emphasize its need and importance to the business community within the state; and to point out that, thanks to your university, these cybersecurity graduates will be highly trained and employable both within and outside your state. Employability of graduates is increasingly a goal within all universities. How many stories you will have to write to communicate all these points will depend on many variables. These considerations could include the geographic areas your incoming students primarily come from, other colleges with similar programs, whether there are cities or towns where corporations have a greater need for cybersecurity experts, and potential areas across the state where recognition of your university could be improved.

Whether this outreach is considered broad or targeted depends on the geographic areas you decide to cover. Do you want to cover the entire state or just those areas with the most prospective students or the most high-tech or computer-dependent industries?

The media outlets you choose to use within each area will depend on what you have found out from the demographic research you've conducted for this or earlier communication for the university. You never want to waste your time targeting media outlets that don't match the demographics that are most important to your client or organization. It will also be essential to your targeting to identify the journalists within each media outlet who will be interested in your specific topics. We discuss below how you can determine the solutions to both of these problems.

Types of Audiences to Consider

So far, we have discussed how to think about and separate the groups and individuals that make up our audiences and how to categorize the audiences with which we want to communicate. Now it's time to consider the idea that, in the sphere of media relations, while not all members of an audience may be our ultimate target, they are all important in terms of outreach. At first glance that may seem counterintuitive after discussing how we need to narrow our target audience geographically and demographically so as not to make outreach impossible, or a waste of our efforts. But as we'll explain, even audiences that are not our specific target can be useful to us as we map out how to reach the ultimate target.

Simply put, your *ultimate target audience* is the collection of individuals and groups you are, in the end, trying to reach to accomplish the goals set by your organization or client. Using the scenario we set up earlier, our ultimate target audience would be prospective students and prospective employers in whatever geographic areas we have determined. It could also include individuals in parts of the state that are underrepresented in the university's student body or even employers that currently don't have a need for cybersecurity employees but may later determine they do.

A second type of audience that all media relations professionals need to think about in terms of importance is what is known as a *moderating audience*. This audience is composed of individuals or groups that can influence your ultimate audience—usually family members or opinion leaders. In our scenario, this moderating audience would consist of parents, friends or classmates, teachers or guidance counselors, and perhaps others who are influential to potential cybersecurity students. For potential employers of those students, that moderating audience could be cybersecurity experts who are currently unaware of your program, or industry publications that emphasize the need for this type of security.

Often it is that moderating audience that first alerts your ultimate target about the information you want them to have. Parents are frequently as involved in their child's college searches as the student is. High school teachers may know the interests or strengths of their students and, perhaps more importantly, they are more likely than the students are to pay attention to news in both traditional and online formats. These interpersonal relationships are the important aspect of moderating audiences. The individuals who make up this type of audience are the opinion leaders referred to in the two-step flow theory. Understanding how awareness, knowledge, and decision-making works is also why sometimes knowing about theories can help you professionally.

The third type of audience is the most important one for media relations. It is called an *intervening audience*, meaning it is an audience that comes between those of us who represent and communicate for our organization, and the organization's targeted final audience. But for us, *it is our primary audience of concern*. This intervening audience is made up of the gatekeepers who either accept or reject our communication—in other words, the journalists and other information disseminators with whom we work to build positive relationships.

For those of us in media relations, these reporters, editors, producers, and digital workers are truly our primary audience. They are our targets so that we can reach the ultimate audience, those constituents and stakeholders that our organization has identified as important to its success.

Finding the Right Mix of Media Through Research

Earlier in this chapter we identified the audiences of concern for the scenario we have used throughout this discussion of audiences. These audiences we need to communicate with include both the ultimate audience, in this case potential students, and moderating audiences, in this case each student's opinion leaders. When viewing media relations as a strategic function, communication research is essential to every move we make. Only if media relations is viewed as a tactic do we, at our peril, ignore what we can learn through focused research.

In the cybersecurity degree scenario we brought up two important decisions that must be made prior to conducting the media relations efforts. Both of those decisions require knowledge that initially can only be gathered through research. Eventually you may have enough experience with your organization that you no longer need to conduct research every time you reach out to the media. But whenever there is a major change to your topic or audience, updating your research will be in order.

The two problems you need to solve before moving forward are

1. Which media outlets do I choose to contact with my story or stories?
2. Which journalists within those outlets do I target directly?

Remember, we are not talking here about using your owned and shared media. It is a given that you will put the information and all the stories about the new degree on your website and your social media accounts. Current students and potential students who are currently considering your university will see the information and may pass it on to others they know. In addition, you will be working in cooperation with others at your university to disseminate the information through interpersonal, two-way channels, such as outreach to high schools.

The media outlets you will use are those major newspaper, television, and radio outlets in the geographic areas you are targeting. Remember, you are targeting a broad, general audience. Your research in this case, first, should be to identify

1. The demographics of your current students, so you know at least in which geographic areas to start your outreach. Students will continue to come from those areas because you have already developed a positive reputation there.
2. The areas of your state, large cities in or close to your state, or nearby states, where technology, banking, manufacturing, military, or governmental organizations in need of cybersecurity experts are based. As this is an online program, potential students may be able to obtain the degree while still working full-time.
3. New, potential, geographic areas from which to draw students. For instance, areas that have two-year community or technical colleges or schools might be targeted.

From the results of that research, you can then determine the major media outlets in those areas. In addition, as you are targeting potential employers for your cybersecurity graduates, doing some research about the trade and industry publications and websites relevant to various business sectors is always a good idea.

Determining the journalists to target takes some reading and investigation on your part. The only way to know which journalists cover the topics you are reaching out to them with is to read what they write or view what they report. In our scenario, you would be targeting print reporters who generally cover the topics of education, business, and technology. The only way to know who that might be, is to read the print or online versions of the vehicle for which they write and look for bylines within the relevant areas. When targeting broadcast reporters—or more likely, producers as they assign the stories—and depending on the various markets across the areas you want to cover, you will likely find less specialization about news topics. Contacting the newsroom directly and asking who you should talk with is a good place to start.

As you begin to narrow in on who you will be contacting, you may discover that journalists often cite information disseminators from blogs or other social media platforms dedicated to education or cybersecurity. In doing this research, you may want to read what these nontraditional journalists have written and decide if you want to add these disseminators as potential targets for outreach with your stories as well.

Once you conduct the original outreach it will become easier to find the correct contact. If your organization conducts an active media relations program, you may find you already have some of this information. It is only when you enter new areas that you must update your contacts. Remember, there is a lot of job change-over in media outlets, particularly television, as reporters seek upward mobility to larger markets. Always check to see if a reporter is still working at a station before contacting them, especially if it's been a while since you have communicated with them.

Audience Objectives

Later in the book we will be writing about setting measurable goals and objectives for our communication efforts. Something people often forget, however, is that members of an audience have objectives too. Journalists need to deal with the idea of audience objectives all the time as they attempt to report stories about which their audience will be interested. Is it local? Is it relevant? Is there the potential for this story to affect those who are reading, viewing, or listening to it? Why would someone pay attention to this story?

In public relations in general, or specifically in the case of media relations, it's a very important concept for us to be aware of. Audience objectives involve thinking carefully about how our message can be tailored to our audience's self-interest. Most of us tend to be extremely selfish when it comes to our time. None of us wants to waste our time paying attention to things that aren't going to be interesting, entertaining, or helpful to us in some way. Audience objectives, therefore, tend toward the "what's in it for me?" view of the world.

Thinking about our audience's objectives is important whether we are concerned with our ultimate organization-determined goals or about our media relations' media-targeted objectives. For both audiences we need to think about

1. What we want the audience to know, to think, or to do—knowledge, attitude, or behavior changes, and
2. What they want to know from us—the reason/objective the audience has for paying attention to our information.

Ultimate audience objectives, in the scenario we have used throughout this chapter, are the objectives that a prospective student or employer would have in deciding to pay attention to the information they are receiving about the new program in cybersecurity. That means when you pitch or ultimately write a media release about the program, you need to think about bringing in information that would resonate with the audiences' self-interests—in this case, that information might be the potential to get a good job upon graduation or the possibility of having a larger pool of trained employees to hire from.

Additionally, although journalists are considered an intervening audience, because they are also media relations practitioners' most important target audience, we must consider the self-interests of journalists and others working for media outlets as well. The media's objectives, therefore, are what journalists want from us in order to be willing to accept and ultimately publish, in whatever medium or media they work, our information. The most important objective journalists have is to provide their readers, listeners, or viewers a story that is relevant or interesting, that will help their audience in their daily lives, or inform them about something new or useful to them. This is also the information we discuss in Chapter 7, and it involves us knowing what makes a story newsworthy, understanding the routines of journalists and the pressures on them, as well as external forces that affect journalists.

Satisfying media needs also involves our ability to give the reporter, editor, or producer what they need to fulfill the requirements of the medium in which they work. Do we have good visuals, either still photos or video? Can we have someone available from our organization, in this scenario, a university, to answer questions about the program? Are there students who have already committed to enrolling in the program who can talk about why they made that decision? What about potential employers? Could we provide someone who already hires cybersecurity employees who can talk with the media? Do we have statistics about employment rates in the field?

The more we can provide, in a manner and time frame needed by a media outlet, the more we are meeting the reporters' unspoken question of what's in it for them.

Perhaps of most importance, prior to reaching out to a journalist, is ensuring that the particular reporter we are contacting covers our topic or topics. For the scenario of a new program at a university, do the journalists and other information disseminators you are contacting cover education, economic development, or employment topics? If not, you are facing a negative response and time wasted.

Professional Commentary

Matt Kelly
Senior Vice President, Chicago Digital Lead
BCW Global

Most PR practitioners work with the information they have, based on what's happened before—not necessarily what's going to happen next. What if you could know what stories are going to drive the most engagement online using new digital tools, and use that knowledge to shape your media relations strategy?

I present a hypothetical situation:

It's 7:00 a.m. A negative story came out about your organization late last night. Now, you're receiving emails and texts from your team who are saying this story is massive news. In fact, they're saying they want to postpone a media event you'd slated for later today. The C-suite is holding an all-hands meeting at 8:30 a.m. You'll be expected to understand the story, who's shared it, what the reporter has covered before and other details about the situation to help your leadership team contextualize the story and act quickly. You're on the hook to report back regularly, starting this morning. You're expected to know the best way to respond to protect your organization's reputation.

Typically, you would start to build a response strategy: reaching out to the journalist, a press release, a statement from your CEO. . . . Whatever you do will be dictated by the perceived severity of the situation and how likely it is for the story to "go viral." For your 8:30 a.m. meeting, you'll need to bring options and defend them to people who need to know you have a handle on this, and that you're not wasting their time. What if you could go into that meeting with data, instead of your subjective POV?

In recent years, new technologies have started to allow us to see which news stories will drive social media interactions . . . before they happen. These tools work based on frequency of computer interactions, and they can reliably predict how much social media engagement a story will receive based on the engagement it has received during its life cycle since it was posted. The most sophisticated brands are using tools like this not only for predicting if a brand mention is worth a response in a potential crisis situation but to fundamentally guide their earned media outreach approaches and campaign strategies. Essentially, these are tools that marry your traditional earned approach with your social media strategy.

Two examples: Reebok uses a tool that does this, Newswhip, to monitor the general online conversation to see which stories are predicted to drive the most social interactions. When Starbucks unveiled its Unicorn Frappuccino a few years ago, they were able to see how earned media was starting to drive social interactions, and the company was quick to frame it in a way that was relevant to their audience of fitness enthusiasts. Starbucks released an intense workout to help their fans burn the calories they'd consume from the drink. This not only drove social engagement but the release was picked up by many media outlets that were also trying to capitalize on the Unicorn Frappuccino story. Social media data drove their earned media hits.

When you walk into your 8:30 a.m. meeting, don't bring guesswork based on what has worked in the past. Bring a thoughtful, earned media strategy rooted in predictive analytics and social media. You'll save yourself and your team from unnecessary reports delivered at contrived cadences. Most importantly, you'll understand what matters to your audiences so you can drive an integrated communication approach that resonates.

Matt Kelly Biography

Matt Kelly is senior vice president, Chicago Market Digital Lead at BCW Global. He has spent more than a decade in digital communications, working with top brands State Farm, McDonald's, Discover Card, BP, Dow Chemical, Walgreens, Nestlé Waters, S. C. Johnson, Conagra Brands, and others to protect and improve their online reputation and advance business objectives. He has been selected to present at the International Public Relations Research Conference multiple times, and has spoken at events such Social Media Week, International Association of Business Communicators (IABC), Word of Mouth Marketing Association (WOMMA), Meltwater Social Summit, and PRSA.

Transparency in Media Relations

Over the past 10 to 15 years, transparency has become a management catchword. Some articles in professional journals and websites even give the impression that being transparent can solve any organizational problem. Although that may seem an extreme claim to make, and we certainly don't believe it can solve all problems in an organization, we do believe transparency can go a long way toward building trust with constituents, including the media.

But what, exactly, is "transparency"? That's an interesting and complicated question, as the term is used in so many ways with regard to organizations. When working in media relations, though, transparency is all about communication. It means being as straightforward and honest as you can be with your media contacts; providing or making available all the information necessary to clarify a situation; responding to media requests in as timely a manner as is humanly possible; clarifying what information you are able to make available and why additional information can't be discussed; having a free and open dialogue about what you can and cannot discuss, and why—usually for legal reasons.

Perhaps David Grinberg, a strategic communication consultant, explained most simply, and in keeping with the goals of this book, why we need to be transparent with our media contacts when he wrote, "fostering transparency involves being honest, open and forthcoming with the media. This builds respect and goodwill in the short term, as well as a strong bond of trust over the long run."[5]

We frequently don't consider the need for transparency in our day-to-day dealing with the media. We communicate with our media contacts when we have a story, or information we would like them to cover. They contact us for comments on stories about our business or industry, even when our organization is not involved. It is when something negative happens in our organization, or it is facing a crisis, that transparency becomes essential.

We forget at our peril that our ultimate audience is our organization's stakeholders and other constituents. By not sharing the information we have quickly and honestly with our media contacts, we are allowing these intervening but primary audience members to jump to their own conclusions about what is happening. It is also allowing them time to go to other information sources that won't have the correct information to answer their questions. They will then pass on to our constituents this secondary information they have collected, and our organization's viewpoint will not be represented.

Transparency during a negative organizational situation is essential to our ultimate constituents as well as to the media. Transparency supports an organization's long-term reputation as well as its daily image and can go a long way toward repairing a bruised reputation and lost trust among your constituents. Although this is discussed to some extent in Chapter 6, which focuses on ethics, there are a few actions media relations professionals need to take regarding transparency that bear repeating:

- Always put your stakeholders and constituents—both external and internal—first when it comes to communicating what is happening within your organization. You will reach them through the media, while other members of your team reach them in other ways.
- The media are an important constituent. They will help you reach out to others, so ignoring them or refusing to comment on the situation is not a viable option.

- Be honest about what you know is going on, but be aware of legal, proprietary, and policy considerations that might stop you from communicating information you can't share with them to external audiences.
- If you can't tell a reporter something—see previous bullet—be sure to tell them *why* you can't. At least they'll have something to write about, even if it's to explain why they didn't get their question answered, and you won't ever have to use that terrible phrase—I'm unable to comment about that.
- If you don't know what's happening with whatever the situation might be, don't speculate. Be sure to let your media contacts know you'll do your best to find out and will get back with them.
- Get back with them.
- Be accessible to the media 24/7 and communicate frequently.

If your organization is involved in a full-blown crisis, there are other steps you'll need to take in communicating with the media to reach all your important audiences, including following your organization's crisis plan. At the end of this chapter we have included a short list of references to resources about crisis communication that you may find useful.

Key Concepts

There are three types of audience public relations professionals communicate with—*internal, targeted external*, and *general external audiences*. For media relations practitioners, internal audiences are not a common target of communication, however, important audiences are composed of individuals who are also members of groups vital to an organization, and that includes internal audiences.

We conceptualize and define the three groups that make up our audiences as *publics, stakeholders,* or *constituents* of the organization. There are also three types of audiences that communicators must think about. Not only is the *ultimate target* of importance, but also *moderating audiences*—comprised of family, friends, and opinion leaders—and *intervening audiences*—gatekeepers in the media.

The most important, or primary audiences, for media relations are the intervening audiences, as they are composed of people who work in a variety of traditional and digital media—reporters, editors, producers, bloggers, and influencers—that the targeted audience engages with.

Audience objectives, the "what's in it for me?" of why audience members might choose to pay attention to our messages, is an important aspect of outreach and persuasion that is often overlooked by media relations professionals. Thinking about the needs and wants of the audience can make crafting the message easier for the communicator.

The final point we've discussed is the importance of being as *transparent* as possible with all groups and audiences that are important to our organization.

Challenge Case

Earlier in the chapter we set up a scenario involving a university that had developed a new cybersecurity program to grow its enrollment and to improve the economic health of the state by providing a trained workforce in a needed area.

Put your college or university into this scenario in place of our generic midsized public university. Thinking about your state, other universities in the state, your current and potential student population, and important corporations and industries, how would you target your media relations communication? What types of media vehicles would you use and why would you use them? Think both traditional and digital. Would you limit your outreach geographically, target your whole state, or even reach outside your state boundaries? For each answer, try to explain *why* you made the decisions you made.

Resources for Communicating During a Crisis

Coombs, T. (2019). *Ongoing crisis communication: Planning, managing, and responding* (5th ed.). Thousand Oaks, CA: SAGE.

Fearn-Banks, K. (2016). *Crisis communications: A casebook approach* (5th edition). New York, NY: Routledge.

Fink, S. (2013). *Crisis communications: The definitive guide to managing the message*. New York, NY: McGraw-Hill Education.

Ulmer, R. R., Sellnow, T. L., and Seeger, M. W. (2017). *Effective crisis communication: Moving from crisis to opportunity* (4th edition). Thousand Oaks, CA: SAGE.

REFERENCES

1. Grunig, J. E., & Hunt, T. (1984). *Managing public relations*. Boston: Cengage.
2. Grunig & Hunt, p. 144.
3. Coombs, W. T., & Holladay, S. J. (2010). *PR strategy and application: Managing influence*, p. 4. West Sussex, U.K: Wiley-Blackwell.
4. Pew Center. (2019, March 26). For local news, Americans embrace digital but still want strong community connection. Downloaded March 30, 2019. https://www.journalism.org/2019/03/26/for-local-news-americans-embrace-digital-but-still-want-strong-community-connection/.
5. Grinberg, David B. (2018, April 2). Media relations 101: Why transparency always triumphs. Downloaded April 28, 2019. https://medium.com/@DBGrinberg/media-relations-101-why-transparency-triumphs-2e9f720d2bfd.

5 THE RELATIONSHIP BETWEEN MEDIA RELATIONS PRACTITIONERS AND JOURNALISTS

The relationship between journalists and the media relations practitioners who provide them with news has a long and fraught history. The following snapshot of the time period when media relations was starting to look and act as it does today will help separate two very different attitudes toward the purpose of this field.

A 2014 article about how the developing profession of public relations was viewed by journalists during the pivotal early years of the 1900s stated that,

> in the earliest days of the 20th century when public relations was emerging as a separate, recognized field of professional practice, journalists and [the public] alike were either unable or unwilling to accept the distinctions between those who sought publicity just for the sake of publicity, and those who sought to link the publicity needs of clients with the news needs of journalists by supplying accurate, truthful information.[1]

That link between clients and journalists is the key to media relations as we practice it today. Of course, the relationship goes back much further than that, and *the emphasis on publicity transitioning into an emphasis on news* is what made the early 20th century so important to what was to become the field of media relations.

A Quick History of the Relationship Over the Last Century

In a well-known historical article about the relationship between journalists and media relations practitioners, two communication scholars, Denise DeLorme and Fred Fedler, indicated that the well-accepted hostility between the two disciplines began somewhere between 1900 and the end of World War I in 1918. They wrote, "journalists feared that publicists' efforts to obtain free publicity would reduce newspapers' advertising revenue."[2] Another study found that "journalists and PR practitioners seemed to perceive the worst in each other, but that some differences were based on fact" not just perceptions.[3] Other researchers, publishing in *Communication Yearbook*, conducted a long-term study of public relations practitioners as the source of news. They determined that journalists have continued to be reluctant to work with media relations professionals for a number of reasons, including this perceived adversarial relationship.[4] Even today, the questions continue. Is this history of dislike and distrust still a real problem, or has the perception of antagonism between journalists and their primary sources of news—us—become a problem of the past?

Factors Affecting the Relationship

The historical analysis done by DeLorme and Fedler identified a number of related areas they believed over time contributed to what they determined as real hostility by journalists toward public relations professionals today. They found the negative attitude had continued from the beginning of the modern use of media relations until the time of their research, which was conducted in 2002. The five causes they uncovered were[5]

1. **Hunger for publicity.** They found that historically—and we don't see much change in this today—Americans want attention for their personal as well as professional lives. What that meant for the media, primarily newspaper as it has been around the longest, was that the work in the newsroom was constantly being disrupted by unwelcome advertisers, lobbyists, and those conducting stunts to get attention.
2. **Situational context of publicity's origins.** As discussed in the first chapter of this book, media relations started out as publicity, and publicity, at least in the beginning, was not conducted professionally. That created more work for journalists who had to turn amateur writing into usable prose, edit heavily, or simply throw away a great number of stories with no news value.
3. **Methods of early PR practitioners.** People conducting early media relations sometimes depended on bribes, gifts, and stunts to get their information published. Even though these methods have long since become unacceptable in the United States, and relevant ethical codes are now in place, many journalists still hold the belief that media relations practitioners are unethical or deceitful.

4. **Early criticisms of PR practitioners.** Journalists have always accused PR practitioners of being inaccurate and unqualified. We have listed journalists' four main complaints about those conducting media relations, along with our comments.

   a. *Public relations practitioners wanted free advertisements.* We find it interesting that public relations has always had the problem of being confused with advertising, even though advertising is paid communication, while public relations is earned communication.

   b. *The use of stunts and fake stories weakened public confidence in every story.* We certainly can't argue with that one.

   c. *They made it difficult for journalists to report legitimate stories.* This concern is still relevant today, as some media relations practitioners do indeed conceal facts and don't make important sources available to the media.

   d. *They violated the basic rules of newswriting.* This is another valid point, and the main reason PR writing or newswriting are required courses in every public relations program—or should be. Over time, journalists developed a concise, facts-first style of writing that has not always been duplicated by media relations practitioners.

5. **Journalists had their own problems.** In addition to pointing out several times in their article that many journalists make midcareer moves into public relations, DeLorme and Fedler synopsized these problems when they wrote:

   > Given journalists' own problems and reputations, some of their criticisms of PR practitioners seem puzzling, even hypocritical. Problems within the newspaper industry contributed to journalists' shift from newsrooms to related fields, including public relations. Whenever journalists gathered the talk moved "to the lack of reward, the hopelessness as to the future, and the general worthlessness of newspaper work as a career." [6]

More recently, in his book *Journalism and PR: Unpacking "Spin," Stereotypes, and Media Myths*, Jim Macnamara wrote that by the time of his 2014 publication, it was likely that more than 200 research studies had looked at the public relations–journalist relationship.[7] Macnamara also conducted a review of quantitative studies that analyzed how much media content either comes directly from media relations activities or is influenced in some way by PR. Over the past 100 years, researchers have found the percentage of content to range from 30–80%, with 50–80% being a common estimate.[8]

These findings are important because they tell us that no matter how troubled the relationship between journalists and public relations professionals, they have in the past, and still do, depend on each other to do their jobs successfully.

The Relationship Today

There are currently three different views of the relationship between journalists and their communication counterparts in media relations, according to a 2019 article by D. E. Clementson. The first viewpoint is that, along with all the new media now at both fields' disposal, the difficult relationship that continued for more than 100 years has also entered the 21st century. The second view is that the groups—journalists and those who practice media relations—are in competition, but each group attempts to keep its own untrustworthy members under control, so they won't hurt the relationship with the other group. The third view of the relationship is that a mutual dependency on the other group has kept them sharing a professional link, even if a shaky one.[9] So what is the truth? Has there been a change of attitude? A truce? Clementson reported in his article that many studies found "the two professions are both hostile and cooperative at the same time."[10]

In a series of in-depth interviews with both journalists and public relations practitioners specializing in information technology, Macnamara also discovered what he called the paradox of PR–journalist relations. He wanted to answer the question, "How do journalists and editors explain and justify regularly using PR material and relying on PR contacts, while holding negative perceptions and being publicly critical of PR?"[11] What he found was rather surprising in such a long-term relationship as journalism and PR—ignorance and hypocrisy on both sides.

Journalists in his study tended to classify only information presented using standard tools and tactics—such as media releases, news conferences, or other written materials—as being media relations. Information on organizational websites, briefings, social media, research studies and reports, and exclusive interviews, for example, were not seen by those he interviewed as public or media relations. When asked about the media relations professionals they work with regularly, the journalists *recategorized them* as "specialists," "experts" in their industry or field, "authorities," or "trusted sources." It appeared from his interviews that the journalists excluded the practitioners they knew the best and communicated with the most from the field of public relations.[12] To lower the conflict they felt in working with PR sources, they denied to themselves that this was what they were doing, and didn't think of their sources as practicing media relations.

Public relations or media relations practitioners are not blameless in creating, or continuing, the antagonism with journalists. If you work in the field, you know that journalists think you will deceive or *spin* them at every opportunity.

"Spin," a concept that originated in politics and remains an active practice there today, is a word many public relations practitioners dislike. It means deflecting a journalists' questions or not answering questions, and then immediately coming back to the point you wanted to make. Acting in this way encourages journalists to think you will mislead them, as well as the public, at every opportunity.

Hope Moving Forward

And so continues the relationship—in a careful and easily unbalanced manner. Each side needs to be educated about the other—their needs, how they work, the stresses inherent in the job.

Yet nine of ten public relations professionals, and eight of ten business people interviewed in a recent study believe earned or independent media are more credible than controlled media.[13] At the same time, journalists not only continue to work with media relations professionals who contact them but also have adopted media catching—which will be discussed later in this chapter—by the tens of thousands.[14]

A final note, this one from a study conducted in Europe. The authors wrote that "in spite of the conventional wisdom that there is a love-hate relationship between the two professions, this study shows that maybe it is time to reevaluate this assumption. . . . It seems public relations specialists underestimate journalists' opinion of the communication profession. They seem to perceive the relationship as more adversarial than it really is."[15]

Professional Commentary

Janet Morrissey
Business Reporter

Media relations people—good ones—can be really important sources for a journalist. I always welcome emails and tips from them when looking for story ideas to pitch to my editors, and I also contact them when seeking sources, customers, and investors for stories I've already been assigned.

As a business writer, I've worked as both a full-time staff reporter—for Dow Jones Newswires/*Wall Street Journal*—and as a freelance reporter—for such publications as the *New York Times*, *Fortune*, and *Time* magazine. I rely far more heavily on PR people as a freelancer than I ever did as a full-time staffer. And here's why: When I was full-time, I covered one particular beat, and a big part of my job was knowing the companies inside out so that I could break news on a regular basis. I spent considerable time getting to

(Continued)

know CEOs, CFOs, COOs, big investors, auditors, fund managers, attorneys, investment bankers and others—anyone who could provide insight into those companies. With all of these inside sources keeping me on top of the latest news in my beat, I had little need for outside PR people. But as a freelancer, I write features, profiles, and trend stories across many different beats, and I'm constantly looking for innovative angles, new trends, and companies that haven't been covered by a regular staff reporter. So, I welcome ideas from PR people. Also, I will work hard to get a particular story approved and published because I only get paid when a story is published. (A staff reporter is paid whether the story runs or not).

Here are some tips that, for me, define a good PR person from my perspective as a business journalist.

1. The PR person knows the client—and the client's business— extremely well. And if they don't know the answer to a question, they're close enough to the CEO, CFO, or founder that they can pick up the phone—or send a text—that will get the answer quickly. This is particularly important when I'm preparing a story pitch to my editor. If I have to wait many hours—or even days—to get answers to basic questions, I usually see this as a "red flag"—where it raises concerns about this PR person's ability to set up the interviews with the CEO and investors in a timely manner once the story is approved by my editor.

2. It's important that a PR rep be able to get accurate numbers—sales data—from a client that will back up a CEO's claims about the company's growth. This is particularly true when writing a profile on a startup company: We need data that shows a company has seen significant year-over-year revenue growth as proof-of-concept—so that we don't wind up writing about a company that goes belly-up a month after the story is published. We can't just take a CEO's word that demand for a product/service is soaring without numbers to back it up.

3. The best PR people know all about a client's investors, customers, and competitors. If I'm writing a profile on a company, I need to speak with the CEO/founder—but also with customers, investors, and competitors. A great PR person knows who these people are and can arrange interviews quickly with customers and investors.

4. If a PR person pitches a particular angle for a story, it's important the client knows about this pitch. I've had situations where a creative-thinking PR person promoted a particular edgy angle—but the CEO had no clue about it and was unable to verify the PR person's statements when I interviewed him.

5. If the PR person is pitching a particular story, that professional makes sure the CEO/founder will be available if the story is approved. I recall one PR person who pitched me a great story idea. At the time, I was tied up on two other stories, and told her I would

pitch her story to my editor when I finished the other stories. She was very persistent—dogged me for weeks—emailing me every couple of days for updates. She insisted she had the founder, customers, and investors lined up to speak with me. But when my editor approved the story and I reached out to the PR person—through emails and phone calls—to set up the interviews—there was "radio silence." She had disappeared. Poof. It was truly bizarre. When she finally responded a day or two later, she told me she was "working on it"—and "might" be able to set up an interview the following Monday or Tuesday—which was five days after the story had been approved. I wasn't impressed.

6. Sometimes a PR person will come up with a great idea for a particular column—like the *NYT* media/advertising column that I sometimes write. This can be really helpful when I'm looking for new innovative ideas.

7. A good PR person is always honest and encourages a client to be honest when speaking to a reporter. Never lie. Most reputable reporters do their homework and fact-check every statement and claim that a source tells them. If the source or PR person is caught in a lie, it makes us question everything the person has said. I remember attending a conference in LA many years ago, and the CEO of a large company told an auditorium filled with investors and others about a deal he had just signed and what it would mean to the company. The PR person went berserk—and ran over to me, lied—and told me that I wasn't allowed to legally report about this deal for at least another day. I pointed out that the CEO had just announced this deal to a room filled with 300 people, and so, of course, I was going to file a report about it immediately. It turns out the PR person had promised the deal story as an exclusive to a reporter who wasn't attending the conference and was now in panic mode because I was breaking the story first.

8. There's a difference between in-house and outside PR people. I'll be honest—I try to avoid dealing with in-house PR teams whenever possible. I will call CEOs and CFOs directly, ask an investor to get a CEO to call me—just basically do anything to avoid dealing with those dreaded in-house PR people. The reason? In many cases, I've found they are slow to respond, often don't know answers to questions, and seem extremely hesitant to call a CEO or CFO to get answers to questions as if they're afraid to bother them. Delay, defer, and block—that seems to be their MO. It's really annoying. Of course, not all of them do this—but I've run into a significant number who do.

So, if you're an in-house PR person, please have a good working relationship with senior executives, who you can contact for answers and get on the phone for interviews in a timely manner.

9. The relationship between a journalist and PR person needs to be a two-way street. I'll give you an example of what I mean. Back when I worked

(Continued)

at Dow Jones, I was approached by a PR person, who asked if I would write a profile story on her client—a real-estate company that was based overseas. I'm not going to mention the company's name, but it was offering a "WeWork" kind of service—except this was long before WeWork was around. Its concept was a little ahead of its time, and it was having trouble getting its story out and attracting U.S. investors/analysts. I thought the concept was an interesting one and so I agreed to do the story.

My story touted the company as a diamond in the rough with incredible potential upside ahead of it. After the story was published, U.S. investors and analysts suddenly became interested in the firm and it took off. I continued to follow the company and wrote small updates as it grew.

About year or so later, the company made a huge game-changing merger deal that would expand its business into the United States and trade publicly in the United States. But, instead of giving me the blockbuster news in advance so that I could break the story—the company gave it to a competitor who had never written a single story about this company ever.

Here's the kicker: The company made a series of business missteps over the year or two following the merger—and took such a hit that it was struggling to survive financially. Remarkably the PR person contacted me to ask if I would write another story on the company to lay out its comeback plans to help restore investor confidence in the firm. Needless to say, I politely declined.

10. Sometimes, a PR person will invite me to a client's company cocktail party following a conference. When this happens, I really appreciate it when the person takes me over to the company's senior executives and introduces me to them—rather than have me wander around the room alone looking at name tags to identify people.

In general, when I find a PR person who's knowledgeable and reliable; offers great story ideas, responds quickly, can get answers to questions fast; and arranges interviews with clients, investors, and others in a timely manner, I'll contact them again and again for stories. They can become important core sources for me, and sources like that are golden.

Janet Morrissey Biography

Morrissey is a freelance writer for the *New York Times* and other publications, including *Fortune* and *Time*. She covers all areas of Wall Street and business news—start-ups, entrepreneurs, bitcoin/cryptocurrencies, branding/advertising, corporate profiles, M&A deals, industry trends, personal finance, venture capitalists, real estate, private equity, hedge funds, ETFs, and geopolitical events that affect the markets. She formerly worked for *Crain's Investment News* and Dow Jones Newswires as a senior staff reporter.

Importance of Source Credibility

In our field, it is always important to remember that for a journalist the media relations practitioner is a source, often nothing more and—we can hope—nothing less. Therefore, when we talk about building a relationship with a journalist the concept of source credibility becomes important. Source credibility was discussed briefly in Chapter 3 when we paired it with information subsidies as two essential building blocks in media relations.

Source Credibility Defined

Source credibility has been defined as "judgments made by a perceiver concerning the believability of a communicator."[16] From a psychological viewpoint it is a "weight" that can increase the value of information in a message.[17] A definition of source credibility from a journalistic perspective can be developed from Yoon's 2005 study of medical and science reporters in which she wrote that credibility is "an organization's believability as a source of information. It is the degree to which information from an organization is accurate, fair, unbiased and trustworthy."[18] In that study, when Yoon wrote about the credibility of the organization, she was really referring to the accuracy, fairness, lack of bias, and trustworthiness of the news sources from an organization. For us, that means the communicator or media relations practitioner. This definition was also used by Reich in a study about source credibility and journalism.[19]

Both Reich and Yoon also noted that the way journalists determine credibility is not always objective. Yoon wrote "it is based on the perceivers' subjective evaluation rather than objective facts. In other words, credibility in this study is in the eye of the beholder."[20] Other researchers found that no reporter believes his or her sources can be totally relied upon, and therefore the information they provide must be verified as much as possible.[21] "Those they talk with frequently can be evaluated over time," and therefore are more trusted.[22] This statement is one of the best arguments to be made for developing continuing relationships with journalists and other information disseminators.

Do Journalists See Us as Credible Sources Today?

Several years ago your authors conducted a research study in which we administered a questionnaire to journalists in all 50 states to measure how credible they thought the media relations practitioners with whom they worked were.[23] The journalists included members of the American Society of Journalists and Authors (ASJA), some members of the Society of Professional Journalists (SPJ), as well as a national sample from a media list supply organization. Five hundred thirty-five (535) journalists responded. They were employed by daily newspapers, weekly or

Competence	Goodwill	Trustworthiness
Intelligent	Cares about me	Honest
Trained	Has my interests	Trustworthy
Expert	at heart	Honorable
Informed	Not Self-centered	Moral
Competent	Concerned	Ethical
Bright	Sensitive	Genuine
	Understanding	

FIGURE 5.1 **Scale Items by Credibility Factor** McCroskey, J. C., & Teven, J. J. (2013). *Source:* Credibility Measures. Measurement Instrument Database for the Social Science. Retrieved from www.midss.ie

biweekly newspapers, broadcast radio, satellite radio, broadcast television, cable television, print magazines, online magazines, online-only news sites, blogs, and the catch-all "other." We discovered from their open-ended answers that many of those checking "other" were freelancers who worked for a variety of media types.

We used a well-tested scale that specifically evaluated how people viewed the credibility of sources with whom they interacted. We changed the question wording slightly to refer to the media outlet of the journalist answering the questions, as well as their personal experience. Each item making up source credibility was presented with a positive and a negative—for example, expert and inexpert, informed and uninformed, or cares about me/my media outlet and doesn't care about me/my media outlet—and a 7-point scale. The higher the number chosen, the more positive. This scale had 18 items that, when analyzed to see which items grouped together, had been found over time to divide into three aspects of source credibility: competence, goodwill, and trustworthiness.[24] "Goodwill" was viewed as the intent of the PR practitioners toward the journalist[25] and perceived caring.[26] "Competence" was defined as expertise and intelligence, while "trustworthiness" refers to qualities such as honesty and character. Figure 5.1 shows the breakdown of the 18 scale items.

What we found in this study astounded us. Our expectations had been very low after reading all the history about the negative relationships between PR and journalists. And the more recent literature, indicating the relationship between journalists and practitioners was both hostile and cooperative at the same time, hadn't presented us with much hope either.

We know that most studies involving a questionnaire are just a snapshot in time. They are the thoughts from one group of people—those who cared enough to answer—on a particular day. In this case, as in most surveys, the 535 people who responded can't really be generalized to all journalists working in the United States. So yes, we know that more and larger research studies need to be conducted to verify what we found is true. But what we found does give us cause for optimism.

Table 5.1 shows all 18 items we used in the scale along with the mean, or average, of where those responding put each item on the continuous scale of 1 to 7. The higher the number, the more positive the response. No mean response was

Table 5.1 Mean Scores of Each Item of Source Credibility
Higher means are an indication of more-credible qualities.
(i.e., Intelligent = 7, Unintelligent = 1)

Scale Item	Credibility of PR Source/ Practitioner
	Mean
Intelligent; Unintelligent	5.46
Trained; Untrained	5.39
Expert; Inexpert	5.19
Informed; Uninformed	5.32
Bright; Stupid	5.22
Cares about me/my media outlet; Doesn't care about me/my media outlet	4.73
Has the interests of me/my outlet at heart; Doesn't have the interests of me/my outlet at heart	4.44
Self-centered; Not self-centered	4.42
Concerned with me; Not concerned with me	4.45
Sensitive; Insensitive	4.82
Understanding; Not understanding	4.98
Honest; Dishonest	5.14
Trustworthy; Untrustworthy	5.14
Honorable; Dishonorable	4.97
Moral; Immoral	4.97
Competent; Incompetent	5.31
Ethical; Unethical	5.08
Genuine; Phony	4.85

*In the survey, some items were reverse coded and questions were mixed to reduce agreement bias.

Table 5.2 Means of Source Credibility Scales and Reliability

	Competence	Goodwill	Trust
Mean	5.32	5.02	4.64
Reliability (α)	0.93	0.90	0.95

lower than 4.42, which is slightly more positive than 3.5, which is halfway between the highest and lowest numbers on the scale. What was even more positive to us was that the three groupings that make up credibility—competence, goodwill, and trustworthiness—were also well above the midrange. This information can be seen in Table 5.2.

What the Research Means for Media Relations

These findings are good news for how journalists perceive the credibility of media relations sources. Your authors' research supports other studies that show journalists and other information disseminators trust those with whom they work the most. It means that in answering the questions on the questionnaire, those who responded thought about the practitioners with whom they most often communicated. It means that although the journalists who responded have a healthy skepticism about media relations practitioners as sources, they find that those they contact the most are competent, trustworthy, and are generally trying to help them do their jobs. In other words, those PR people with whom they work the most have goodwill toward them.

Here are a few quotes from journalists talking about good media relations practitioners they've worked with. The interviews were conducted as a follow-up after the questionnaire was completed. These journalists' comments further supported the idea that PR practitioners have credibility as sources.

- *I love when PR professionals are permitted to comment for stories,* on behalf of the individual or entity they're working for—and can provide me with good quotes—because that makes my job so much easier. I currently know a handful of PR people *who I can rely on* for quick, good quotes. Also, PR people have to always be reliable and available—reporters often have to get information very fast—so PR individuals need to be ready, and they have to be able to reply or get a response from someone else very, very quickly.
- The guy I am working with now . . . is *getting me everything I need and keeping me so informed it is almost too much, but I love it*—he has lined up all the interviews I need, gotten me all the research, even some I should have gotten myself! So be available, be helpful, get the reporter what they need in a timely manner, always know a reporter's deadline and work within it! Don't demand that your product be in the story in a certain way . . . give us the benefit of the doubt that we will mention your organization the best we can.
- As the outlet for their stories, they should *work on developing relationships with us* and telling us not just how something is interesting, but *why* it's interesting to us.
- Most of the public relations practitioners I have worked with *are passionate promoters of causes that they truly believe in, or they are hard-working employees* trying to do their best for their institutions. I enjoy working with them. Spammers, screamers, schemers and incompetents are another story.
- The relationship between a public relations practitioner and journalists is mutually beneficial. In order to maintain a successful relationship both parties must work together and *trust one another*.

- Each of us has a job to do. I hope most PR people recognize that. I can't say how they perceive us for certain though, because I simply don't know. All I know is that here, I *have been able to develop great relationships with local PR practitioners founded on mutual respect and honest communications.*

From the perspective of source credibility, journalists prefer to work with media relations professionals with whom they have a history. It is very similar to any relationship; the longer you know someone, the better you understand each other's needs. If you find that isn't happening after a while, and you know you need to continue the relationship, it's time to have an honest talk and figure out how you can work better together. Or, it's time to move on to someone else, or another medium you *can* work with.

Building Relationships for Media Relations

There are several important pieces involved in building good working relationships with journalists and other information disseminators. One of those aspects, which we call assessing news, we discuss at length in Chapter 7. In that discussion we examine what makes something newsworthy enough to attract media coverage, similarities and differences across the various media, how organizations and journalists view news differently, thinking strategically about how to achieve media coverage, and a variety of other issues involved in achieving coverage in the media.

For now we are going to consider the interpersonal elements of building good relationships with those in the media.

Cultivating Journalists and Others in the Media

Many working professionals, researchers, academics, and websites populated by all three, advise similar approaches to connect with and build relationships with those who write for the media. In this section we provide a compilation of the best and most successful ideas we have found, or learned ourselves, to develop and cultivate media relationships. At this point you may be wondering what cultivating a journalist or a relationship means.

Cultivation is truly what builds a relationship in any situation. It is a notion that comes from the field of fundraising, or development as it is often called, and is a word that is based—of all things!—in farming. Outside of farming, it means to nurture, to promote, to encourage. Cultivation is one of the nine cardinal principles of fundraising.[27] As one professional wrote when discussing the steps in raising money, "You cannot expect to receive donations from people until they know about your organization; you should not ask people for money until they

Professional Commentary

Melissa Brown, Senior VP
Weber Shandwick

There are two factors that separate exceptional media relations professionals from everyone else—storytelling and relationships—with the latter, relationships, being the most critical to success. Being seen by journalists as a resource to help them do their jobs is incredibly valuable and can ultimately lead to better outcomes for your clients. Media relations professionals' careers are built or broken by their relationships with journalists and begin by focusing on the human element of the job. At the same time, if you don't have a compelling story, only so many favors can be called in and it's part of my responsibility to generate ideas on my client's behalf or help them understand when a story arc is flat. Both factors are strategic and artful and take years to cultivate and finesse.

The way I see it, my job has two main functions:

1. Understand the ins and outs of my client and their industry
2. Understand the media landscape.

Understanding the ins and outs of my client and their industry—I have to become a subject-matter expert and keep my finger on the pulse of every issue or opportunity relevant to my client and their competitors. Eighty percent of the time, I found out about competitors' moves from a journalist asking me if I know anything about it. From there, I can strategize with my clients if the issue affects them and still be a resource for the media.

Understanding the media landscape—and it has changed, a lot. No more than a decade ago newsrooms were flourishing. Journalists had strong job stability and stayed with the same outlet for many years—oftentimes for a print publication with an online viewership. The pervasiveness of social media, shifting ad budgets, and an ever-fragmenting media landscape have left skeleton crews in newsrooms and layoff announcements on Twitter are a daily occurrence. To illustrate the competition for attention, there are approximately six media relations professionals for every one journalist! People also consume news differently and seek out podcasts, newsletters, or peruse Twitter and Instagram for bite-sized nuggets of news.

Clearly, the media landscape is multifaceted and to navigate it effectively you have to know your people. Journalist–PR relationships must be a two-way street built on trust, fluidity, and honesty.

Knowing that I, the media relations person, and the journalist both need and want something can prove to be challenging to any relationship—even tumultuous, at times. I want the journalist to include my client favorably, but I can't always provide the journalist with a spokesperson to talk about the matter. For example, there's one journalist at a conservative major news organization that I deal with often. He's a lovely human—his kids are amazing, his wife is hilarious, but we argue at least once a week. He calls at ungodly hours because he must fill a 24/7 news cycle and wants to be the first to break a story. We sometimes argue about him calling me at 1:00 a.m. but we usually argue about me not being able to get him access to an executive to speak about the breaking news in question–at 1:00 a.m. He screams at me for not giving him the CEO and I scream at him for screaming at me. At the end of the day, it's my job to protect my people as well as provide journalists with information. There are few breaking news instances that warrant a 3:00 a.m. interview with the CEO. That doesn't mean there aren't applicable scenarios, and he knows I'll give him what he needs if that were to happen, but it's not at 1:00 a.m. at the break of a new product offering or slight stock price drop.

When breaking news happens or a journalist is under fire to produce, I want to be one of their first calls because they know I'll give them the truth. It'll be entirely self-serving on behalf of my client, but I'll never lie to them and it's crucial that the journalist knows that. During difficult situations, organizations can feel like the journalist is the enemy. They simply have a responsibility to their readers to present the truth in an unbiased and fair way—but I have an equal responsibility to my client to ensure their remarks are not tinted with cynicism, falsities, or inferences not based in truth or reality.

But you can guarantee, the moment you don't communicate with your journalists is the moment the relationship takes a turn for the worst. I have a personal rule that I answer every journalist phone call or text, no matter if I'm in a meeting, at dinner with friends, or in bed. Every email from a journalist must be answered within 20 minutes or else they'll move on. These are my rules and they've worked for me. I am, at the center of my function, a conduit to a resource the journalist needs. If the journalist can't reach me, they'll make their own assumptions, print something inaccurate, or find another source. None of these scenarios is favorable for bolstering relationships.

Melissa Brown Biography

Melissa Brown is a Roanoke, Virginia, native currently living and working in New York as a senior vice president at Weber Shandwick, one of the world's largest public relations organizations. She is a communication strategist and storyteller with over a decade of experience building brand equity for clients with cross-industry knowledge in enterprise technology, consumer packaged goods, e-commerce, and retail. Melissa brings strategic partnerships, savvy media relations, and thoughtful crisis communication approaches for *Fortune* 500 companies, billion-dollar unicorns, and emerging brands across the globe.

Melissa received her Bachelor of Science and Master of Science in Communication from Radford University.

are ready. Getting them ready is called cultivation."[28] It also means to support or to help, words that connect better to cultivation in media relations.

A Starting Point in Building the Relationship

Of course, different people suggest different first steps for reaching out to those in the media with whom we want to build relationships. There is no "only," or perfect answer for what to do, or how to handle it. The one thing that every source we read does agree on is that *building the relationship is in the hands of the media relations practitioner.* You cannot count on journalists reaching out to you, even if you are a believer in using the online services where journalists post requests for sources. They may reach out, but you have to respond and work to build that first outreach into a relationship.

Know What They Write

An article on the website for 5W Public Relations has a suggestion about how to start the process that we agree with totally:

> The easiest thing that you can do is for you to become an ardent fan of a relevant journalist first. You should also note that print journalists may write long or short form on social networks because they also have a tendency of having personal blogs and digital responsibilities. You should find multiple sources in order to read the work of a journalist. You can then use other means to get alerts or subscribe to the sources via newsletter and RSS feed as soon as you find them.[29]

Other similar suggestions come from journalists we interviewed for the credibility study discussed earlier in this chapter. The point they made again and again was that PR professionals need to know what individual reporters write about, and how. What are they interested in? Are there certain topics that they specialize in? This could be crime, a particular community, the local or regional arts scene, sports, or any other focus. One journalist from New England wrote, "Anything that doesn't relate to my beat—what I usually cover—I immediately delete. Don't send a breaking science news release to a politics reporter; don't send a release about something going on in Hingham if they're covering Natick."

A host of a television morning program told us, "To be honest, as a host I rarely read press releases, instead, my producer tells me which story I need to cover. However, hypothetically speaking, I would be reluctant to read a press release that isn't relevant to the stories I cover. If a PR practitioner received my contact information, then they should know that I am a lifestyle reporter."

Another journalist told us, "I could write a book about what PR folks do wrong. I read most press releases that come through my inbox. Most of them are inane.

I mean, I write about books and culture and the occasional hard news story and the very occasional food story, and yet I get countless press releases about pointless—to me!—new products, which I never, ever write about. I don't take this personally—I know PR folks are just trying to do their jobs—but I do disregard about 98% of press releases that cross my desk because they're completely irrelevant to anything I would ever consider writing about."

If a media representative is ignoring your press releases because they aren't relevant, they are also ignoring you. There goes the chance to start building a relationship.

Start Interacting Slowly

Much of the research we reviewed on cultivating journalists emphasized that you should strive to grow an established relationship prior to really needing a journalist's help with a story. You do not want to wait until you have a really important pitch or are in the middle of a situation that has the potential to grow into a crisis.

Jim Dougherty, a writer for the Cision blog, recommends you start interacting with journalists on social media. He writes, "The level of accessibility that social media offers is unprecedented. The fact that Twitter and other social media platforms are used so widely by journalists is important for the PR profession. . . . Social offers a means to stay up-to-date on journalist interests and to share low-key social interactions."[30]

A practitioner we interviewed during our research told us, "This takes time. The best way to go about building a relationship is to engage them. Like any relationship, it starts with communication. *Call them on the phone*, introduce yourself. Show respect for what they do and let them know how you can support them. Always remember that their job is not to promote your client, products, or services. Their role is to bring viewers/readers useful information that they could use to improve their lives. Another aspect of building relationships is to identify their needs. This requires doing some research. Learn their reporting patterns, their focus areas, whether they publish their stories through [social media] platforms as well as the news websites, etc. The more you know about the reporter, the better source you can become."

We hope you noticed that this media relations professional made what might be considered a very old-fashioned suggestion: that you call the journalist or other information disseminator on the phone to introduce yourself. Of course, know their deadlines before taking too much of their time. Telling them about you and your organization, what your expertise is, what you have done before, can be very helpful to you in the future. But it can also be helpful to journalists when they have a need for a source with your background to add to a story they're writing.

Perhaps even more old fashioned is the advice to *interact in person* with those who work in the media if at all possible. Suggestions by Cision's Dougherty in one of his blog posts are to set up a time to talk over coffee, drinks, dinner, or at industry events you both are attending. He notes that some journalists don't form long-lasting relationships on social media or email because they do better with people in person.[31] And that makes sense. By definition, journalists' work requires they conduct many interviews, so being comfortable talking with people, either in person or on the phone, is part of the job description.

Work to Be Helpful

In a recent article about how the role of a journalist has changed over time, Mike Schneider of Muck Rack writes about how media writers, whether full-time or freelancer, are responsible for building their own brands—that means finding additional places to share their work and build their own audiences. A recent Muck Rack survey indicated "more than 41% of journalists consider the potential "shareability" of a story when deciding what to write about and 68% of journalists worldwide track how many times their stories are shared on social media."[32]

What that means for us is that journalists are always looking for stories that will appeal to their audience. We can be helpful by contacting those who write for the media—whether they are journalists at a national newspaper, local television reporters, or online bloggers, when we have information or an idea or a source that can be helpful or useful to them. One of the most effective relationship-building strategies we can use is to help our media contacts do their jobs better by sending them information relevant to their journalistic focus.

An interview with a sportswriter provided us with other ways to be helpful, but also made clear this journalist recognizes the limits to what a media relations person can accomplish. To this reporter we say thanks. We appreciate you recognizing our needs and limits too.

> Access is the most important aspect of reporting for a columnist or feature writer, and access is harder and harder to get. If a PR person is willing to help me find someone in a crowded room or get someone out of a locker room that is closed to me, I appreciate that a great deal. A PR person who gets someone on the phone for you—that usually requires the PR person to dial the number while standing next to the athlete and hand him the phone, can't be paid enough. I also appreciate a PR person who will explain to coaches, players, athletic directors, owners, whoever, that reporters have a job to do and hiding from them or otherwise hindering them when they are doing that job benefits no one. That takes a PR person who is willing to speak truth to power, if you will, which is increasingly harder to find.
>
> I also appreciate PR professionals who recognize when one or two people will be in great demand and make everyone's life easier by putting that person or persons on a podium to take questions rather than forcing

every reporter to fight for an opening to first get close enough to a player, then to get in a question. Every reporter wants one on one. Sometimes that isn't practical and the PR person who understands that and makes it possible for everyone to do the job is greatly appreciated.

Be Aware of Contact Preferences

Journalists also have individual expectations about aspects of our and their roles in the developing working relationship. Being aware of their needs and preferences is important for us in developing good relationships. The way they want to be contacted about story ideas, pitches, or media relations, although a personal choice, do tend in one direction or the other. Surprisingly, most journalists chose one medium as their choice.

Although social media have had an impact on journalists' newsgathering process, they have not been as significant as was expected at their inception. Three recent industry surveys of journalists, two by the TekGroup, an online newsroom software provider, in 2018 and 2019; and one slightly older report in 2016 by Business Wire, a major distributor of media releases in 2016, all support the contention that traditional methods of media relations are not dead. The 2019 TekGroup survey, although primarily focused on online newsrooms, found that 100% of journalists responding *preferred to receive information from an organization via email*, rather than through phone calls, text messages, or Twitter.[33] One year earlier they also found 94% of journalists prefer to receive story ideas or pitches via email.[34]

Business Wire had similar findings, with 66.5% of respondents preferring an email alert with a link to a full press release from a company and 73.5% preferred a pitch to be sent via email. Even though the survey was conducted by a newswire, only 20.9% of respondents chose a newswire press release. In this case, for pitches, the percentage of those who chose using social media postings was at 0.9%, text messages at 0.5%, and blog posts at 0%.[35]

And So Many More

As we noted in the opening for this section, our list is just a starting point in building a relationship with media representatives and other disseminators of information who are important to us and our organization. This isn't the end of the discussion by any means, and as you work your way through this text, the subject of the journalist–media relations practitioner relationship will come up many times. If this is a topic that concerns or interests you, pay particular attention to Chapters 7, 9, 10, 12, and 13.

Will You Be Working With Digital Influencers?

Although we know the reach of influencers has been growing rapidly, we have decided to address them differently and separately from other journalists and writers with whom we may find ourselves working. Why? Because attention by most influencers is not strictly earned media coverage.

It is most likely we will work with influencers if our media relations job is, to some degree, product based. That is because, by their very nature, influencers are individuals who have "the power to affect purchase decisions of others because of his/her authority, knowledge, position or relationship with his/her audience."[36] Influencers generally have a specific niche and attract others who are also interested or involved in that niche.

For those of us in media relations, our interest is in those influencers who are active in social or shared media because through their posts they can create trends. Trends usually involve products or activities, and influencers have power over their followers' purchasing or involvement decisions. As Mike Schneider wrote in Muckrack.com, "Unlike their traditional celebrity counterparts, these digital influencers have earned their fame (and their money) directly through the endorsement of products and services to their online audiences, rather than first catapulting into the spotlight through some other medium. This shift has made it much more difficult to truly identify the right influencer for a particular campaign, because who holds influence is different for everyone."[37]

Some influencers, even "microinfluencers" who have smaller but very engaged audiences, are able to support themselves and grow their audiences through their relationships with specific brands. Hold that thought! What this means for media relations is that influencers cannot be considered in the same way that journalists and other more unbiased information disseminators are. Why? Because they are biased toward the brand or organization that pays them. They endorse products, services, or activities, for which they are paid. If your organization works with an influencer, it will be a *marketing* relationship. Because of the breadth of our jobs, however, we will talk more in Chapter 13 about how working with influencers could still be related to media relations.

Media Catching as a Relationship-Building Strategy

Media catching is a fairly recent means of building relationships with journalists. What makes it different from other methods is that, unlike in traditional media outreach, media relations practitioners are—at least for the first contact—responding to journalists' requests for information. In an article that studies the use of this outreach method in Russia, the authors write that "media catching is the reversal of the traditional public relations process of pitching story ideas to journalists using press releases, feature pitch letters, and other techniques. In media catching, journalists working on specific stories reach out to large numbers of public relations practitioners using a variety of technologically aided services with queries for specific information."[38]

Media catching, in effect, turns traditional media relations on its head *at the beginning of the relationship*. It allows a journalist to reach out to hundreds of potential sources and receive many responses from people who can serve as sources—or who have access to others in their organization who can serve as sources—for the article. Practitioners who respond to these specific requests are indicating they have expertise in the area the reporter or blogger is working in. They are also expressing that they are willing to participate in the process of putting together an accurate and well-researched story. When the outcome results in a story the reporter is pleased with, both of these factors can help to develop a longer-term relationship between the journalist and the media relations practitioner.

How Media Catching Sites Work

The act of "media catching," a term coined to describe the process for media relations professionals, originated in the early 1990s with ProfNet, which is a service of *PR Newswire* that allows journalists and bloggers to post requests for sources and information on topics they are covering. Those requests are sent out several times a day to registered "experts," generally public relations practitioners who, unlike reporters and bloggers, must pay for the service.[39]

Although ProfNet may be the oldest of these services, HARO—Help a Reporter Out—claims to be the largest and most frequently used by both journalists and media relations practitioners. The website indicates it distributes "more than 50,000 journalist queries from highly respected media outlets each year," as well as reaching 800,000 sources and 55,000 journalists and bloggers.[40] Similar to ProfNet, the service sends reporter requests out to potential sources three times a day. There are three levels of paid subscriptions plus a free basic subscription for sources. Journalist and blogger requests for sources are free. If interested, the source, generally a media relations professional, is then expected to send an email pitch to a concealed email address listed in the source request. The site also indicates that "if the journalist is interested, they'll reach out."[41]

Related services are provided by Muck Rack, SourceBottle, Pitchbox, and others. Each one has its fans and detractors. One complaint about all the sites, especially among potential sources, is that they are supporting the sites with their monthly subscriptions, while reporters have free access. Yet, for the most part, media relations professionals see the benefit of getting their organizations, or themselves, exposure. But frequently the requester is in a geographic area or is a writer for a specialty publication, or a blogger, who won't help the practitioner communicate with his or her target audience. Additionally, most of these services hide the media outlet identification until the requesting journalist or other media representative responds back to the practitioner answering the request.

Some sources don't use the services to build relationships with media outlets but rather to improve their organization's website search engine optimization—SEO—efforts. Many blogs, online news sites, and online sites for traditional media include links to their source's organization, which help to boost their search engine results. But the best outcome for most communicators who have acted as a source, is when they develop a continuing relationship with a publication that includes members of their organization's target audience.[42]

Usefulness of Media Catching

To date, only one article has been published about the most successful methods public relations professionals use in media catching in the United States, and it focused solely on HARO. We believe, however, that no matter which service you use for media catching, if you respond to reporters or others making requests in a way and with the information that is best for them, it will give you the *possibility* to start building a relationship.

In 2012 researchers Tallapragada, Misaras, Burke, and Waters conducted a small survey of media relations practitioners who use HARO.[43] Their study produced a number of suggestions for how to successfully respond to media requests and, we hope, start to build relationships. We base the following list on that survey's findings, rather than relying on the various sites' suggestions or information found online, because the responses come directly from practitioners who are using the site. We have added our comments and explanations:

1. Know the rules of the service you're using and how to use it. This will help you reply appropriately and in the way the reporter wants you to.
2. Read every listserv message that comes out, usually several times a day, so you don't miss anything that might be relevant to you or your organization.
3. Don't rely on Twitter notifications without checking back to the listserv because they don't contain all the information you'll need to respond.
4. Taking the time to create a well-thought-out pitch, as long as you meet the reporters' deadlines, is more successful than rushing to be first.
5. Also take the time to be sure you are fulfilling the specific needs of the journalist with the request.
6. Be certain that all your contact information is correct so the reporter can get back to you. If it's wrong, and if they can't reach you quickly, they will probably just go on to another person who responded.
7. You should not only include the correct information (email, phone, social media information) but also *be available* to respond to journalists if they get back to you.

8. If you can't provide the information the reporters need but can steer them to someone who can—do it. Journalists will appreciate it and will generally get back in touch with you.
9. Sometimes a request comes out that you can answer because of your expertise, even though doing that won't directly help your organization. Answer that one too.

As we emphasize throughout this book, media relations is all about building relationships with journalists. "Media catching" sites don't necessarily make that easier, but simply provide additional venues through which to introduce yourself to journalists. Numbers eight and nine on this list relate directly to building relationships, even if the actions won't help your organization right at that time. As the authors of the study wrote, "these actions demonstrate a commitment to the journalist–public relations practitioner relationship. The practitioner genuinely is helping the journalist rather than trying to secure a placement for an organization or client. This assistance proved to be worthwhile in media catching as it turned the practitioner into a more trusted source for future information requests."[44]

Key Concepts

The antagonistic relationship between journalists and media relations practitioners has been a problem for both groups of professionals since the early 1900s. Today, that relationship seems to be changing to one of more-grudging cooperation.

We discuss the importance of being, and being seen as, a *credible source,* and what that means in our relationship with those working in the media. Research studies have been conducted about what makes up the concept of being credible, particularly in the media relations–journalist relationship. Three aspects of credibility are *goodwill, trustworthiness,* and *competence.*

Building good working relationships with journalists is important to your success in media relations. We discuss some ways to *cultivate* those working for the various media we need to do our jobs.

Media catching is a potentially useful relationship-building strategy that should be considered as a beginning point. The new term is defined and suggestions for how to use it effectively are discussed.

REFERENCES

1. Zoch, L. M., Supa, D. W., & VanTuyll, D. (2014). The portrayal of public relations in the era of Ivy Lee through the lens of the *New York Times. Public Relations Review, 40*(4), 723.

2. DeLorme, D. E., & Fedler, F. (2003). Journalists' hostility toward public relations: An historical analysis. *Public Relations Review*, *29*(1), 100.

3. DeLorme & Fedler, p. 10, citing Sallot, L. M., Steinfatt, T. M., & Salwen, M. B. (1998). Journalists' and public relations practitioners' news values: Perceptions and cross-perceptions. *Journalism & Mass Communication Quarterly*, *75*(2), 73.

4. Cameron, G. T., Sallot, L. M., & Curtin, P. A. (1997). Public relations and the production of news: A critical review and theoretical framework. In Brant R. Burleson (Ed.), *Communication yearbook* (Vol. 20, 111–155). Thousand Oaks, CA: SAGE.

5. DeLorme & Fedler.

6. DeLorme & Fedler, p. 108.

7. Macnamara, J. (2014). *Journalism & PR: Unpacking "spin," stereotypes, & media myths*. New York, NY: Peter Lang.

8. Macnamara, p. 127.

9. Clementson, D. E. (2019). Do public relations practitioners perceptually share in-group affiliation with journalists? *Public Relations Review*, *45*(1), 49–63.

10. Clementson, p. 51.

11. Macnamara, J. (2016). The continuing convergence of journalism and PR: New insights for ethical practice from a three-country study of senior practitioners. *Journalism & Mass Communication Quarterly*, *93*(1), 130.

12. Macnamara, p. 131.

13. Howes, P. A., & Sallot, L. M. (2014). Does media coverage matter? Perspectives of public relations practitioners and business professionals on the value of news coverage. *Public Relations Journal*, *8*(4). www.prsa.org/prjournal

14. Cision HARO about us (2017). Retrieved from https://www.helpareporter.com/about/?nav_location=footer

15. Verčič, A. T., & Colić, V. (2016). Journalists and public relations specialists: A coorientational analysis. *Public Relations Review*, *42*, 528.

16. O'Keefe, D. J. (1990). *Persuasion: Theory and research*, pp. 130–131. Newbury Park, CA: SAGE.

17. Anderson, N. (1971). Integration theory and attitude change. *Psychological Review*, *78*, 171–206.

18. Yoon, Y. (2005). Examining journalists' perceptions and news coverage of stem cell and cloning organizations. *Journalism and Mass Communication Quarterly*, *82*(2, Summer), 283.

19. Reich, Z. (2011). Source credibility and journalism: Between visceral and discretional judgment. *Journalism Practice*, *5*(1), 51–67.

20. Yoon, pp. 283.

21. Gans, H. J. (1979). *Deciding what's news*. New York, NY: Pantheon; Manning, P. (2001). *News and news sources: A critical introduction*. London: SAGE; Tuchman, G. (1978). *Making news*. New York, NY: Free Press.

22. Gans, pp. 129–130.

23. Supa, D. W., & Zoch, L. M. (2014, August). *Does social media use affect journalists' perceptions of source credibility?* Paper presented at the Association for Education in Journalism and Mass Communication conference, Montreal, Canada.

24. McCroskey, J. C., & Teven, J. J. (1999). Goodwill: A reexamination of the construct and its measurement. *Communication Monographs, 66,* 90–103.

25. McCroskey, J. C., & Young, J. Y. (1981). Ethos and credibility: The construct and its measurement after three decades. *Central States Speech Journal, 32*(1), 24–34.

26. Teven, J. J., & McCroskey, J. C. (1997). The relationship of perceived student caring with student learning and teacher evaluation. *Communication Education, 46*(1), 1–9.

27. Broce, T. E. (1986). *Fund raising: The guide to raising money from private sources.* Norman: University of Oklahoma Press.

28. Howe, F. (1991). *The board member's guide to fund raising: What every trustee needs to know about raising money.* San Francisco, CA: Jossey-Bass.

29. 5W Public relations. How to grow, foster and maintain a relationship with a journalist in public relations. https://www.5wpr.com/new/building-relationships-journalists/

30. Dougherty, J. (2015 February). 7 ways to build better relationships with journalists. In Comms best practices blog. https://www.cision.com/us/2015/02/7-ways-to-build-better-relationships-with-journalists/

31. Dougherty

32. Muck Rack and Zeno Group (2018). Shareability, credibility & objectivity: The state of journalism today. https://info.muckrack.com/journalistsurvey

33. TekGroup (2018). The online newsroom survey report. Marketing.tekgroup.com/2018-online-newsroom-survey-report

34. TekGroup (2019). The online newsroom survey report. https://www.tekgroup.com/marketing/online-newsroom-survey-report/

35. Business Wire (2016). Business Wire's media blueprint: 2016 media survey results. https://education.businesswire.com/hubfs/2018%20US%20White%20Papers%20/Business_Wire_Media_Blueprint.pdf?submissionGuid=3f07c488-7ee7-46fe-928f-66a87207a063

36. What is an influencer? (2019) https://influencermarketinghub.com/what-is-an-influencer/

37. Schneider, M. (2018). What's the difference between a journalist and an influencer? [Blog]. Retrieved from https://muckrack.com/blog/2018/10/18/whats-the-difference-between-a-journalist-and-an-influencer

38. Erzikova, E., Waters, R., & Bocharsky, K. (2018). Media catching: A conceptual framework for understanding strategic mediatization in public relations? *International Journal of Strategic Communication, 12*(2), 145–159.

39. What is ProfNet (2019). Retrieved from https://profnet.prnewswire.com/ProfNetHome/What-is-Profnet.aspx

40. Cision HARO about us (2017). Retrieved from https://www.helpareporter.com/about/?nav_location=footer

41. Cision HARO sources: How it works (2017). Retrieved from https://www.helpareporter.com/sources/?nav_location=main_menu

42. Fried, N. (2018). The truth about using HARO! HARO sources tell us their honest experiences. Retrieved from https://fupping.com/natty/2018/04/28/the-truth-about-using-haro-haro-users-tell-us-their-experiences/

43. Tallapragada, M., Misaras, I. C., Burke, K., & Waters, R. D. (2012). Identifying the best practices of media catching: A national survey of media relations practitioners. *Public Relations Review*, *38*, 926–931.

44. Tallapragada et al., 930.

6   ETHICS

Think about the relationships you have with people you admire. What is it you admire about them? Common responses might include that you admire those people who are trustworthy, reliable, straightforward, truthful, and hardworking. Those same characteristics also apply to the relationship between media relations practitioners and journalists. Within the pages of this book, we are increasing our understanding of media relations by examining the constructs of the relationship between practitioners and journalists. Two of the pieces that fit into that relationship are how to effectively work in partnership to achieve both the needs of journalistic audiences *and* organizational messaging, and how to strategically think about media relations in light of our organizations' goals. This chapter takes a step back to look at one of the fundamental aspects of the relationship between practitioners and journalists—how to behave ethically in that relationship.

People have remarked that ethics cannot be taught, that they are intrinsic to who we are as humans, and that the ethics that guide us are some combination of genetic inheritance and conditioning from the time of our birth. And while this chapter—or this book—is not the place to debate whether ethics are innate or not, we will examine two types of ethics: personal and professional. It is important to note that a third type of ethics, organizational ethics, may also impact your media relations experience. Organizational ethics are the ethics that specifically exist within a particular workplace, or within a certain industry. Obviously, as you enter a workplace or a particular subfield, you will want to learn the ethics associated with those groups. However, organizational ethics are difficult to generalize, and we will therefore address the ethical components common to many areas of media relations practice.

Personal Ethics

The decisions you make every day and the beliefs that you hold about what is right or wrong are reflective of your personal ethics. Your personal ethics often come into play when you interact with others. For example, if your best friend wears an outfit that you feel is outlandish, do you say something negative, offer a compliment, or say nothing at all? During a crowded commute, will you get up from your seat on the bus to allow someone else to sit? In a job search, will you accept multiple offers knowing that you will have to go back on all but one of them? These are each examples of where you will need to make a decision based on what you feel is the right thing to do.

In practicing media relations, it is likely that at some point you will need to make a decision based on what you feel is right or wrong. This might come in the form of taking on a new client, in creating a media relations campaign, or in working with a journalist. While there may be societal and field-specific ethics to guide you, ultimately the decision will be yours to make.

For example, let's suppose you are working at a public relations agency that has just signed on a new client company with holdings in tobacco. The agency is giving you the choice of whether you want to work with this client or not. Your role would be to work with journalists who cover healthcare and also those who cover the farming industry. You would communicate information about the tobacco company, provide information about the smoking-cessation programs it is sponsoring, and write about new products. What will you choose to do? Your decision will likely be based off your personal ethics, the experiences you have had, and ultimately whether you are comfortable working on behalf of the client.

In the example above, it should be noted that your agency is likely acting ethically in giving you the choice about whether to work with the client. What if your agency assigned you the client without asking—and told you that if you couldn't work with the client, that you would be fired?

With personal ethics, there is no right or wrong response. However, if you want to work in the media relations field, there is one personal ethic that you should adopt: *Don't lie to a journalist.* You may get away with it once, but if that lie is discovered, you have very likely ended any hope of a successful relationship with that journalist, and you will soon establish a reputation that will make it very difficult for you to be successful in media relations.

Professional Ethics

Each profession has had an evolution of ethics throughout its history. Public relations practitioners started out primarily as press agents who would seek publicity through any means possible. Journalists have gone through various phases of sensationalism in their production of "news." We will discuss this history more in the next section, but it is sufficient at this point to say that modern day public relations and journalism have both become significantly more ethical than they were at their inception.

In part, this march toward professionalism—and the ethics associated with that—has come as a result of professional organizations that have sought to create an atmosphere of better practices. The two standard bearers of each profession's standards, the Public Relations Society of America (PRSA) and the Society of Professional Journalists (SPJ), each have a code of ethics that are not only meant for their members but are intended for the professions as a whole. These codes represent the standard for ethical practice in each field, though neither organization can hold them as legally binding documents. In Box 6.1 are the preamble and tenets of each organization's code, and a brief explanation of those principles.

In thinking about each of these values, we can see there are clear connections between ethics and practicing media relations. **Honesty**, of course, is integral to building effective relationships with many audiences, but especially to journalists. You might get away with being dishonest with a journalist once, but it's likely you won't get a second opportunity to be dishonest—since the journalist will probably never deal with you again.

BOX 6.1
Public Relations Society of America Code of Ethics[1]

Preamble: This Code applies to PRSA members. The Code is designed to be a useful guide for PRSA members as they carry out their ethical responsibilities. This document is designed to anticipate and accommodate, by precedent, ethical challenges that may arise. The scenarios outlined in the Code provision are actual examples of misconduct. More will be added as experience with the Code occurs.

The Public Relations Society of America (PRSA) is committed to ethical practices. The level of public trust PRSA members seek, as we serve the public good, means we have taken on a special obligation to operate ethically.

The value of member reputation depends upon the ethical conduct of everyone affiliated with the Public Relations Society of America. Each of us sets an example for each other—as well as other professionals—by our pursuit of excellence with powerful standards of performance, professionalism, and ethical conduct.

Emphasis on enforcement of the Code has been eliminated. But, the PRSA Board of Directors retains the right to bar from membership or expel from the Society any individual who has been or is sanctioned by a government agency or convicted in a court of law of an action that fails to comply with the Code.

(Continued)

Ethical practice is the most important obligation of a PRSA member. We view the Member Code of Ethics as a model for other professions, organizations, and professionals.

PRSA Member Statement of Professional Values: This statement presents the core values of PRSA members and, more broadly, of the public relations profession. These values provide the foundation for the Member Code of Ethics and set the industry standard for the professional practice of public relations. These values are the fundamental beliefs that guide our behaviors and decision-making process. We believe our professional values are vital to the integrity of the profession as a whole.

ADVOCACY: We serve the public interest by acting as responsible advocates for those we represent. We provide a voice in the marketplace of ideas, facts, and viewpoints to aid informed public debate.

HONESTY: We adhere to the highest standards of accuracy and truth in advancing the interests of those we represent and in communicating with the public.

EXPERTISE: We acquire and responsibly use specialized knowledge and experience. We advance the profession through continued professional development, research, and education. We build mutual understanding, credibility, and relationships among a wide array of institutions and audiences.

INDEPENDENCE: We provide objective counsel to those we represent. We are accountable for our actions.

LOYALTY: We are faithful to those we represent, while honoring our obligation to serve the public interest.

FAIRNESS: We deal fairly with clients, employers, competitors, peers, vendors, the media, and the general public. We respect all opinions and support the right of free expression.

Loyalty is also an important element. When we work with organizations we are often given information that, if shared with the public, could be detrimental to the organization. Media relations practitioners need to be loyal to their relationships with journalists, but of course not at the cost of being disloyal to the organizations with which we work.

Advocacy and **fairness** can work in concert. Our role is to provide information to audiences, in our case journalists, on behalf of our organizations. In doing so, we must embrace fairness by providing information in a timely way that is useful to journalists. We must also embrace the idea that when we send a journalist information, they can use it or not use it as they desire. Understanding and respecting the job journalists must do is a major component of fairness.

The PRSA Code of Ethics also contains provisions of conduct (see Box 6.2). In addition to the professional values, the provisions of conduct are meant to act

BOX 6.2
PRSA Code Provisions of Conduct

FREE FLOW OF INFORMATION

Core Principle
Protecting and advancing the free flow of accurate and truthful information is essential to serving the public interest and contributing to informed decision making in a democratic society.

Intent
To maintain the integrity of relationships with the media, government officials, and the public.
  To aid informed decision-making.

Guidelines
A member shall:

- Preserve the integrity of the process of communication.
- Be honest and accurate in all communications.
- Act promptly to correct erroneous communications for which the practitioner is responsible.
- Preserve the free flow of unprejudiced information when giving or receiving gifts by ensuring that gifts are nominal, legal, and infrequent.

COMPETITION

Core Principle
Promoting healthy and fair competition among professionals preserves an ethical climate while fostering a robust business environment.

Intent: To promote respect and fair competition among public relations professionals; To serve the public interest by providing the widest choice of practitioner options.

Guidelines
A member shall:

- Follow ethical hiring practices designed to respect free and open competition without deliberately undermining a competitor.
- Preserve intellectual property rights in the marketplace.

DISCLOSURE OF INFORMATION

Core Principle
Open communication fosters informed decision making in a democratic society.

(Continued)

Intent
To build trust with the public by revealing all information needed for responsible decision making.

Guidelines
A member shall:

- Be honest and accurate in all communications.
- Act promptly to correct erroneous communications for which the member is responsible.
- Investigate the truthfulness and accuracy of information released on behalf of those represented.
- Reveal the sponsors for causes and interests represented.
- Disclose financial interest (such as stock ownership) in a client's organization.
- Avoid deceptive practices.

SAFEGUARDING CONFIDENCES

Core Principle
Client trust requires appropriate protection of confidential and private information.

Intent
To protect the privacy rights of clients, organizations, and individuals by safeguarding confidential information.

Guidelines
A member shall:

- Safeguard the confidences and privacy rights of present, former, and prospective clients and employees.
- Protect privileged, confidential, or insider information gained from a client or organization.
- Immediately advise an appropriate authority if a member discovers that confidential information is being divulged by an employee of a client company or organization.

CONFLICTS OF INTEREST

Core Principle
Avoiding real, potential or perceived conflicts of interest builds the trust of clients, employers, and the publics.

Intent
To earn trust and mutual respect with clients or employers; To build trust with the public by avoiding or ending situations that put one's personal or professional interests in conflict with society's interests.

Guidelines
A member shall:

- Act in the best interests of the client or employer, even subordinating the member's personal interests.
- Avoid actions and circumstances that may appear to compromise good business judgment or create a conflict between personal and professional interests.
- Disclose promptly any existing or potential conflict of interest to affected clients or organizations.
- Encourage clients and customers to determine if a conflict exists.

ENHANCING THE PROFESSION

Core Principle
Public relations professionals work constantly to strengthen the public's trust in the profession.

Intent
To build respect and credibility with the public for the profession of public relations; To improve, adapt and expand professional practices.

Guidelines
A member shall:

- Acknowledge that there is an obligation to protect and enhance the profession.
- Keep informed and educated about practices in the profession to ensure ethical conduct.
- Actively pursue personal professional development.
- Decline representation of clients or organizations that urge or require actions contrary to this Code.
- Accurately define what public relations activities can accomplish.
- Counsel subordinates in proper ethical decision making.
- Require that subordinates adhere to the ethical requirements of the Code.
- Report practices that fail to comply with the Code, whether committed by PRSA members or not, to the appropriate authority.

as *core principles* for the Code of Ethics and provide more-specific guidelines for working in public relations. Those provisions are presented here.

While the provisions of conduct provide a glimpse into how to apply the ethical dimensions advocated by PRSA, some are particularly important for media relations. The free flow of information, as a provision of conduct, lies at the heart of media relations practice. One of the main goals of media relations is to ensure that audiences have access to information about an organization. This means—or should mean—both the good and the bad information. As a media relations practitioner, you should not expect journalists to cover your story about how employees are volunteering to help the community, but then expect them to not cover the story when those same employees get laid off.

Of course, the free flow of information must be balanced with disclosure of information and safeguarding confidences. In media relations, we hope for an exchange of information that is mutually beneficial and also free-flowing, but both journalists and practitioners must also understand there will be times when information cannot be shared. As we will discuss later, there are ways of working through these situations that can maintain our ethical obligations and our relationships.

Documents such as codes of ethics are meant to be *normative*—in that they seek to provide guidance for every situation. For PRSA, their Provisions of Conduct are intended to provide more concrete guidance on how to follow the code of ethics. Similarly, the Society of Professional Journalists Code of Ethics contains similar guidance and is also meant to be normative. Like the PRSA Code of Ethics, it is intended for adoption by its members, but is written to address the field of journalism, members and nonmembers alike. As a general principle, most journalists hold the SPJ Code of Ethics to be the industry standard. As you examine the SPJ code in Box 6.3, see if you notice any similarities between the ethical standards presented for each of the professions.

BOX 6.3
SPJ Code of Ethics[2]

Preamble: Members of the Society of Professional Journalists believe that public enlightenment is the forerunner of justice and the foundation of democracy. Ethical journalism strives to ensure the free exchange of information that is accurate, fair and thorough. An ethical journalist acts with integrity.

The Society declares these four principles as the foundation of ethical journalism and encourages their use in its practice by all people in all media.

SEEK THE TRUTH AND REPORT IT

Ethical journalism should be accurate and fair. Journalists should be honest and courageous in gathering, reporting and interpreting information.
Journalists should:

- Take responsibility for the accuracy of their work. Verify information before releasing it. Use original sources whenever possible.
- Remember that neither speed nor format excuses inaccuracy.
- Provide context. Take special care not to misrepresent or oversimplify in promoting, previewing or summarizing a story.

- Gather, update and correct information throughout the life of a news story.
- Be cautious when making promises, but keep the promises they make.
- Identify sources clearly. The public is entitled to as much information as possible to judge the reliability and motivations of sources.
- Consider sources' motives before promising anonymity. Reserve anonymity for sources who may face danger, retribution or other harm, and have information that cannot be obtained elsewhere. Explain why anonymity was granted.
- Diligently seek subjects of news coverage to allow them to respond to criticism or allegations of wrongdoing.
- Avoid undercover or other surreptitious methods of gathering information unless traditional, open methods will not yield information vital to the public.
- Be vigilant and courageous about holding those with power accountable. Give voice to the voiceless.
- Support the open and civil exchange of views, even views they find repugnant.
- Recognize a special obligation to serve as watchdogs over public affairs and government. Seek to ensure that the public's business is conducted in the open, and that public records are open to all.
- Provide access to source material when it is relevant and appropriate.
- Boldly tell the story of the diversity and magnitude of the human experience. Seek sources whose voices we seldom hear.
- Avoid stereotyping. Journalists should examine the ways their values and experiences may shape their reporting.
- Label advocacy and commentary.
- Never deliberately distort facts or context, including visual information. Clearly label illustrations and re-enactments.
- Never plagiarize. Always attribute.

MINIMIZE HARM

Ethical journalism treats sources, subjects, colleagues and members of the public as human beings deserving of respect.

Journalists should:

- Balance the public's need for information against potential harm or discomfort. Pursuit of the news is not a license for arrogance or undue intrusiveness.
- Show compassion for those who may be affected by news coverage. Use heightened sensitivity when dealing with juveniles, victims of sex crimes, and sources or subjects who are inexperienced or unable to give consent. Consider cultural differences in approach and treatment.

(Continued)

- Recognize that legal access to information differs from an ethical justification to publish or broadcast.
- Realize that private people have a greater right to control information about themselves than public figures and others who seek power, influence or attention. Weigh the consequences of publishing or broadcasting personal information.
- Avoid pandering to lurid curiosity, even if others do.
- Balance a suspect's right to a fair trial with the public's right to know. Consider the implications of identifying criminal suspects before they face legal charges.
- Consider the long-term implications of the extended reach and permanence of publication. Provide updated and more complete information as appropriate.

ACT INDEPENDENTLY

The highest and primary obligation of ethical journalism is to serve the public.

Journalists should:

- Avoid conflicts of interest, real or perceived. Disclose unavoidable conflicts.
- Refuse gifts, favors, fees, free travel and special treatment, and avoid political and other outside activities that may compromise integrity or impartiality, or may damage credibility.
- Be wary of sources offering information for favors or money; do not pay for access to news. Identify content provided by outside sources, whether paid or not.
- Deny favored treatment to advertisers, donors or any other special interests, and resist internal and external pressure to influence coverage.
- Distinguish news from advertising and shun hybrids that blur the lines between the two. Prominently label sponsored content.

BE ACCOUNTABLE AND TRANSPARENT

Ethical journalism means taking responsibility for one's work and explaining one's decisions to the public.

Journalists should:

- Explain ethical choices and processes to audiences. Encourage a civil dialogue with the public about journalistic practices, coverage and news content.
- Respond quickly to questions about accuracy, clarity and fairness.
- Acknowledge mistakes and correct them promptly and prominently. Explain corrections and clarifications carefully and clearly.
- Expose unethical conduct in journalism, including within their organizations.
- Abide by the same high standards they expect of others.

In looking at each of the codes, were you able to recognize the number of similarities? Both call for building the public trust, truth in communication, and independence—including accountability—in action. It stands to reason that media relations practitioners and journalists truly should complement each other, so long as all participants adhere to the principles set forth by leading organizations. Unfortunately, this is not always the case, as the expectations for the public relations–journalist relationship are not always followed.

Knowledge of how journalists seek to disseminate information ethically is vitally important to media relations practitioners. In the end, it comes down to respect. If you, as a media relations practitioner, can respect the ethical obligations of journalists and can show that respect by acting in an ethical manner with an eye toward understanding their job, then it is likely that same respect will be afforded to you. Ethical media relations may not always result in the successful sharing of information, nor end necessarily with the journalist disseminating your information, but as long as integrity and ethical conduct are maintained, there will likely be another opportunity in the future.

Field Ethics

When we refer to field ethics, we are referring to a more hands-on subset of professional ethics. Field ethics are *descriptive*, that is, they reveal how things may sometime happen in practice, as opposed to normative ethics, which tell us how we *ought* to act.

It is how media relations is actually practiced that often defines the ethics of the field. Unfortunately, past practices have had an impact on the perceptions of today. Earlier in this chapter we alluded to the questionable ethical practices of historical media relations. While we would likely not refer to early attempts to gain the attention of the media as media relations, many of the tactics—or antics—used by people like P. T. Barnum have continued to affect the perception of media relations practitioners.

"Barnum knew the media, and knew how to garner attention for his 'amusements.' Whether it was parading through Europe with Tom Thumb, promoting Jenny Lind across the United States, or plowing a field with an elephant in North Carolina, he attracted attention like few others. He was the father of modern publicity, and has served as the inspiration for many people, and tactics, in public relations."[3]

Prior to Ivy Lee's Declaration of Principles for public relations in 1906—and unfortunately sometimes after it, as well—those who wanted to gain the attention of the media would often "create" news events that were sensational, with the hope that journalists would cover them, and subsequently, their organizations. Unfortunately, this ultimately had the effect of labeling these "press agents" as charlatans, though some of these *pseudo-news events* have worked their way into our cultural memory as having been, and now continue to be, legitimate events. Awards shows, parades, and groundbreaking ceremonies are all examples of early events that were designed by communication professionals to drum up media coverage and have now become recognized events.

Other tactics were decried by some journalists at the time—and they would surely be illegal now—as news fakes, and an article in *Editor & Publisher* from 1920[4] called for a national law to prevent press agents from engaging in these tactics. As part of its call, an intrepid reporter named Margaret Elmore was able to interview Harry Reichenbach, referring to him as the "king" of press agents. She asked about his tactics to promote the latest *Tarzan* movie. He responded:

> Well, that was also very simple and this is how I handled it. I knew the manager of the Belleclaire Hotel in which this story was "planted" and I asked his permission to "pull" the stunt. He granted my request, and went on a vacation, leaving the assistant manager in charge. The next day Mr. T. R. Zann registered at the Belleclaire and asked the clerk in charge if he might have a piano moved that afternoon into his room, and if he would have the window taken out so it could be put in. Late in the afternoon the piano box, and it was a real piano box, was raised outside the window, but in it was not a piano but something which under ordinary circumstances could make quite as much noise.
>
> Nothing more or less was it than a large lion which I had procured from a park in Yonkers. We strewed animal books quite carelessly around the room to give the impression that Mr. Zann was a lover of the jungle and I stayed there with him most of the night, arranging for the work of the next day. When the waiter came to take his order for breakfast, he also ordered 25 pounds of raw beef, and when the waiter exclaimed in amazement asking whom it was for, Mr. Zann drew aside the curtain and showed the lion, resting peacefully in his lair.
>
> Excitement reigned supreme and the manager rushed up and ordered both the lion and master remove themselves immediately if not sooner. Mr. Zann coolly suggested that the manager put him out. Trooping in a few minutes later came the police, who were not especially eager to approach Mr. Zann and his pet. Then officials of the Gerry Society put in their appearance, but had no warrant for an arrest, so for a little while their activities ceased. The news reached the papers, which carried long stories that afternoon and the following morning, and the aftermath of the stunt was the picture shown a few days later, advertising "Mr. T. R. Zann" or "Tarzan" who stayed with his lion at the Belleclaire Hotel. (p. 8)

In the same article, Reichenbach referred to a New York law that would take effect that September, making it a misdemeanor to supply false news to newspapers, stating he was "not worrying at all. New Jersey is entirely too close to New York for that to give me any concern." However, he also later pointed out that to appease the journalists who were duped by his "events" he would offer payment in the form of cash or expensive gifts, which he indicated were readily accepted.

Fortunately, the ethics of media relations have evolved significantly over time—as have animal protection ordinances. Today it is not realistic for a modern media relations practitioner to use a lion in a hotel room to garner media coverage. Nor would a journalist accept a cash payment in lieu of their journalistic integrity, at least in the United States. We will explore various international practices, which are very different from those followed in the United States, in Chapter 13. Nevertheless, there are still many circumstances within the United States that media relations people are involved with today that raise some ethical questions, and where the "right" thing to do is less clear. Let's look at a few of these ambiguous areas.

The Embargo

In Chapter 3 we introduced the idea of information subsidies—the information that is provided by media relations practitioners to journalists. In Chapter 9, we will take a closer look at what those subsidies look like. Up until recently, a common inclusion with all written communication tools used by media relations practitioners was the *embargo date.* This was the date the journalists were free to use the information they were given. It was a common practice when information was mailed out in hard copy because there was often no way to judge when the information would reach the journalist. It was better to send the news early rather than have it come after the deadline. Today, the embargo date raises an ethical dilemma.

Suppose you are a media relations practitioner who knows about a major corporate announcement that is going to happen next week. Because you have worked to establish effective relationships with journalists and want to reinforce that relationship, you let several journalists with whom you work regularly know what is going to happen, but ask them to not disseminate the information until the announcement is made.

This raises an ethical question for the journalists who, although having the information and a duty to report news to the public, is being asked not to publish the information until the next day. Journalists also have a duty to their outlets, and being the first to publish the information could result in increased web traffic, increased prominence, and ultimately, in increased revenue for the outlet. Assuming the information does not have an embargo for legal reasons—perhaps national security or information with financial implications—the journalist must decide whether to honor the embargo requested by the media relations practitioner.

If the value of the relationship with the media relations person is stronger than the value of releasing the information early, then it is likely the journalists will honor the embargo. However, if the relationship is not valuable—or perhaps nonexistent—then it is unlikely the embargo will be honored.

As a rule, media relations practitioners should not send information to journalists unless they are willing to have the information immediately disseminated. If it is necessary that a news embargo be used, then it must be very clear as to its purpose, and there should be some agreement ahead of time with a journalist before the information is shared. In other words, you should only rely on an embargo if there is a significant amount of trust with the journalist, and even then you need to realize that an embargo is putting the journalist in a potential conflict of interest.

Exclusives

An *exclusive* is information, or access, that the media relations practitioner is only going to give to a single journalist, or a single media outlet. While the exclusive itself is ethical, and an excellent way to build a relationship with a journalist or outlet, the process through which the exclusive comes about, and the ramifications of it, can be fraught with ethical challenges.

Usually an exclusive that is initiated by the media relations practitioner is a significant news event or represents access to a person or event that would normally be off limits to a journalist. A one-on-one interview with a major corporate CEO, a new product launch, or the bankruptcy of a major organization are all examples of news items that might be considered for an exclusive with a journalist. However, as journalist Paul Gillin wrote in a blog post, "exclusives make one friend at the expense of making a lot of enemies."[5]

Media relations practitioners may decide an exclusive is the best approach for a particular organizational announcement, but its use should be limited to times when it will be, as Gillin points out, "a win-win proposition." Whenever this is not possible, the media relations practitioner needs to weigh the benefits for the organization of a single outlet covering an event versus the possibility of affecting the relationships with other journalists who cover the organization and with whom you have built relationships.

No Comment

There are times when, as a media relations practitioner, you will not be able to disclose information to journalists, even if you know it is in your organization's best interest to do so. This presents an ethical challenge to the relationship between you and the journalists and often represents an example of what happens when the legal wing of the organization gets involved with organizational communication. However, there will be times when, as a communications professional, you really shouldn't share information with the media, but as any textbook on public relations will tell you, usually the worst thing you can say is "no comment."

Variations on "no comment" include statements such as "our organization does not comment on issues of pending litigation" or "while we have no comment at this time, our organization is committed to its customers and will be making a statement soon." Do you see a theme? Most of the time, organizations "don't comment" when something is going wrong. Choosing to not make a statement to journalists is usually the safe thing to do, legally speaking, but will often result in negative coverage.

Unless the legal department is clearly warning you to say absolutely nothing, you can, however, choose to make a statement that will clearly indicate to the journalists with whom you have built relationships that you cannot legally or ethically answer their questions right now. You may be able to comment in the future, however. Telling a journalist that something is a personnel matter, or the situation is under review, or it is too early for you to have all the facts is sometimes necessary. Also telling them that you will get back to them as soon as you can—and then doing it—will go a long way toward building your credibility and enhancing your honesty quotient, even if it initially leads to a negative story.

As a media relations practitioner, you are sometimes at a crossroad. You must decide whether to try to get your organization to offer some form of statement to preserve the relationships you have established with journalists, or to follow the advice of the legal department and not make a statement to journalists. Ultimately, your organizational leadership will make the decision, but as the person who has worked to build those journalist relationships, you will likely feel conflicted.

Stealing Thunder

The concept of stealing thunder is borrowed from crisis communication and refers to getting ahead of a news story by revealing information from the organizational perspective directly to your targeted audience before a journalist can disseminate the information. The goal behind doing this is to ensure the organization's voice is the first to be heard. One example of this tactic is moving up a product launch if you find out a journalist has already seen the product and plans to announce it—think of a tech executive using a new phone and accidentally leaving it somewhere.

Stealing thunder, as a tactic, is easier to accomplish in this age of social media when an organization can communicate in its own voice directly to its audiences. In fact, it need not necessarily be a crisis situation, but any information that an organization wishes to disseminate. Circumventing journalists and announcing information directly via a social platform is a great way for those of us who work with marketing to ensure the message being sent and received is exactly the message that was planned. However, stealing thunder can have negative ramifications for media relations.

Engaging in this tactic may alienate journalists who regularly cover your organization because they could feel as though you are hiding information that they could have used. It may also have the unintended consequence of reaching fewer people, as journalists may not cover information that has already been released. Finally, by disseminating the information on your own, you are eliminating the third-party credibility that comes with earned media placement.

As with all decisions in media relations, you will need to learn to strike a balance—in this case, between releasing the information directly to your ultimate audience or working with journalists to disseminate the information. If you are consistently releasing your own information, then it will likely have a negative impact on your relationship with journalists, but you will retain control of your message. It is your duty as the media relations practitioner to understand the consequences, and to advise your organizations on the best course of action.

Pay for Play

Journalists should never ask you to pay for a story to be published. You should never offer to pay a journalist to publish a story. In the United States, that should be the end of the story. (We will address how media systems in other countries work in Chapter 13.) Nearly every journalist and media outlet forbids the practice of paying for placement of editorial information. This is one of the clear differentiators between earned and paid media—and the difference between a professional journalist and an influencer—though, today there are even standards for influencers that social media platforms have instituted to indicate paid content. In other words, paying for placement of editorial content is nearly nonexistent in the modern American media environment.

Nearly.

Working with major media, national broadcasters, newspapers, online outlets, and major blogs and magazines means that you will likely never be asked to pay for the placement of a story. But what if these major outlets are not the best way to reach your ultimate audience? Perhaps your organization would be better served by working with independent media outlets or small, niche outlets that reach a targeted audience. And, in the course of working with a journalist, or an editor, or a website owner, they offer you the opportunity to purchase an advertisement that would run alongside a story that the outlet is planning about your organization. Smaller outlets, after all, may have limited staff—and the person responsible for writing the story may serve double-duty as the advertising sales manager. While clearly against the SPJ Code of Ethics, you have a decision to make: Is the price of the advertisement worth it in comparison to the potential reach of the story?

It should be noted that this is unlikely to happen to you, as transparency has become increasingly important for media outlets. But it should also be noted that many of the examples used in the text of this book are not hypothetical, so you will need to be prepared for anything.

Off the Record/Anonymous Sources

Journalists don't like using anonymous sources. In an era where journalistic integrity is often called into question, an anonymous source could be perceived in any number of ways, including that the journalist is making up the source to cover their own speculations about something. And while anonymous sources are still used, there is usually a substantial vetting process that involves multiple people. Also keep in mind that while there are legal protections in place for industry or organizational whistleblowers, laws protecting the journalist's right to not reveal sources vary from state to state. In other words, if you ask to speak with a journalist as an anonymous source, you may be asking them to put both their integrity, and potentially their freedom, on the line.

Similarly, asking that a journalist keep something off the record can be problematic. As a rule of thumb, don't tell a journalist something that you don't want to see tweeted out a few minutes later. However, there may be times when it's necessary to go off the record to preserve the relationship you have built with a journalist. For example, imagine that you have worked with a journalist to set up an interview with your organization's CEO, and the CEO cancels at the last minute. You will likely want to let the journalist know, off the record, that the interview was cancelled due to a family emergency involving the CEO. If the emergency doesn't impact your organization, an ethical journalist will likely respect the request to keep it off the record. Of course, if you tell the journalist that it was a family emergency, then that had better be the truth. Overall, you should be leery of speaking with journalists off the record; it puts both you and the journalist in an awkward situation of not being able to execute the basic functions of the media relations relationship.

Blacklists

Relationships are fickle, and media relations relationships are no different. While certainly not something that is often talked about, certain organizations and journalists, or media outlets, don't work well together. Or in the case of a media blacklist, don't work together at all. This can be the result of a journalist disseminating information that an organization's CEO found to be offensive or unflattering, or an organization refusing to work with politically charged media, or any number of reasons.

As a media relations professional, your job is to avoid a situation where your organization would not work with a journalist or a media outlet, but we can't always be successful. If your organization has decided to not share information with a certain journalist or outlet, it puts you in the difficult situation of, perhaps, deciding how you will handle requests from that journalist. Whenever possible, you should attempt to repair any dysfunctional relationships between a journalist, or an outlet, and your organization. If that is not possible, you will need to determine how you will handle your organization's desire to not work with specific outlets.

A Few Notes on Laws Relating to Media Relations

Ethics and law are decidedly different areas. It is important to note that there are very few areas where law intercedes in media relations, and effective relationships with journalists are heavily dependent on ethics. In other words, there are very few "rules" when it comes to how to conduct media relations. However, depending on your area of media relations practice, there may be some regulations that you will want to keep in mind.

The financial industry is one area where there is some regulation regarding information dissemination. Release of corporate earnings statements, financial outlooks, mergers and acquisitions, and nearly any information that could have financial implications for stockholders or investors are closely monitored and regulated by multiple government agencies, but most often by the Securities and Exchange Commission (SEC). If you are working, or plan to work, in media relations involving financial information, you will need to familiarize yourself with the laws surrounding that dissemination.

Another area of media relations that is often subject to legal regulation is working within the government. Much information that the government holds is meant to be for open records, in that a journalist can request information and the government is compelled to share. This is often through a Freedom of Information Act (FOIA) request. However, some information is exempt from FOIA requests, such as information that has been deemed classified, would be an invasion of privacy, or would reveal commercial secrets, such as patent applications. Additionally, individual states also have different restrictions on what information can be shared, or not shared, with media. It is imperative that if you are working in media relations for a government agency at any level that you study, understand, and implement applicable laws regarding information dissemination.

Generally, the First Amendment of the Constitution allowing for freedom of the press, the right to petition the government, and the freedom of speech has been the predominant legal standard for media relations. Journalists are independent and are allowed to engage with information, and media relations practitioners are free to speak on behalf of their organizations. Absent a specific law that is narrowly focused, the First Amendment is generally the fallback, thus the necessity for ethics to serve as the guiding principles for the media relations–journalist relationship.

At the end of this chapter we have provided information on the one law book that specifically focuses on laws affecting public relations and advertising. Of course, there are also good texts that cover the broader area of media law.

Key Concepts

Because there are few laws regarding the interaction between the fields of journalism and public relations, effective media relations practitioners must attempt to follow personal, societal, and field ethical standards in their interactions with journalists.

The discipline of ethics often means there is no correct answer, and organizations and practitioners should develop a common set of standards they will use to react to any potential ethical dilemma.

It is incumbent on the media relations practitioner to balance the needs of the organization with the needs of maintaining effective relationships with journalists.

Challenge Case

Using the example in this chapter of Harry Reichenbach's promotion of *Tarzan*, imagine you have been hired as a media relations practitioner by the movie studio to re-establish the damaged relationships with the affected audiences, including journalists. Your image restoration campaign will be primarily done through media relations efforts. How would you go about establishing new relationships with journalists, given what Mr. Reichenbach has just done? What message would you try to convey? And how would you seek to establish transparent and trustworthy relationships with journalists so that future films might continue to be featured in the media?

Resource for Public Relations Law

Maye, C., Moore, R. L., & Collins, E. L. (2019). *Advertising and public relations law*. (3rd ed.). Abingdon, UK: Routledge.

REFERENCES

1. Public Relations Society of America. (2018). Code of ethics. Retrieved from https://www.prsa.org/ethics/code-of-ethics/
2. Society of Professional Journalism. (2014). SPJ code of ethics. Retrieved from https://www.spj.org/ethicscode.asp
3. Zoch, L. M., Supa, D. W., & VanTuyll, D. R. (2014). The portrayal of public relations in the era of Ivy Lee through the lens of the *New York Times*. *Public Relations Review*, *40*(4), 723–732.
4. Elmore, M. (21 August 1920). National law against news fakes needed to protect public. *Editor & Publisher*, *53*(12), p. 8, 19.
5. Gillin, P. (14 October 2010). Are exclusives a good idea? In a word: No. http://gillin.com/blog/2010/10/are-exclusives-a-good-idea-in-a-word-no/

7

ASSESSING NEWS

To best understand why one story or media release is accepted by the media and another is not, media relations practitioners must be aware of how members of the various media we target determine a story to be "newsworthy." This chapter will investigate the phenomena of news from both the public relations and journalistic perspectives and discuss the differences in perception between media relations practitioners and the journalists we are targeting. We will also look at how the targeted medium affects newsworthiness and consider why our timing in releasing information is important. Finally, we will discuss what it means to be strategic in our media relations.

What Is Newsworthiness?

The discussion of what makes something newsworthy has been a debate of long standing, not only from the media relations perspective, but from the journalistic side as well. The adage that *news is what an editor says it is* may no longer be applicable in our changing media environment. Decisions on what is or is not news still lie, to some extent, with editors, but also with journalists, photographers, bloggers, freelancers, publishers and, in some media, the members of the public themselves. While the editor may be the final decision-maker in print news, he or she may not always be our target.

Media relations practitioners must take into account the differences in how individual media vehicles disseminate news, and also need to understand that each vehicle may in fact have individual needs or individual values about what constitutes news. This is a truism in the field of media relations and is a recurring theme in articles written by both academics and practitioners:

Media relations practitioners must know the media they are targeting, both in style and in newsworthiness values.[1]

Although we will talk about this later in the chapter, for now, think about the *different requirements for a story* that is to be disseminated across print vehicles, online news sites, television, radio, social media, and to online bloggers.

If you were to do an online search using the questions: *What is newsworthiness? What makes a story newsworthy?* or *What are the "characteristics" of newsworthiness?*, you would find dozens of answers. Those answers would include many lists of varying lengths that include the factors within stories that one source or another considers to be newsworthy. For this chapter, we compiled our list of the factors included in stories that can be considered newsworthy a bit differently. We conducted research and discovered dozens of academic studies that were written between 1950 and the present that all attempted to determine what comprised a newsworthy story. Then we narrowed the list to factors that multiple authors had listed as important across the more than 65-year period of our study.[2]

General Factors of Newsworthiness

- **Localness** or **proximity** indicates the news is happening in the local area or that it relates to local issues, trends, or events. News consumers pay much more attention to company openings or closures, and job gains or losses in their own or nearby communities than they do such changes in other states, for example.
- **Timeliness** means the news is current and generally involves hard news. Hard news is commonly considered front-page news. Hard news most often deals with international, business, political, crime, economic, or national news. Timeliness might also be a different angle on events that have previously been covered but the update is new information. An update on a hard news crime story indicating the suspected perpetrators have turned themselves in, for example, is still very timely. Feature, or soft, news can also be considered timely, if it is used within a reasonable time frame. Coverage of a new trend, or an article about seasonal fruits and vegetable, would be timely feature news as long as the season hadn't already passed!
- **Immediacy** is frequently called breaking news. It might be preceded by the words "announced today" or "this just in." Immediacy is most often used by real-time media such as television, radio, or online outlets. It is news being reported while it happens or shortly thereafter. Photo 7.1 is an example of how immediate news could be handled by television.
- **Prominence** concerns famous or well-known people, institutions, or events. Stories are often published or broadcast because they have already

PHOTO 7.1

received attention from other media. This factor is not often used by media relations practitioners working for organizations, although those working in the entertainment industry will have a different experience.

- **Significance** or **importance** is information people should know because it has general importance or is useful to the consumer of the news. The winner of the election for a state's governor is information we should know about, whether or not we care about the outcome. A new supermarket coming to our community is useful for us to know about.
- **Unexpected** is exactly what the word tells us. It is surprising, astonishing, or unanticipated. A story about a family getting up in the morning and finding a bear in their swimming pool is unexpected. So was a story widely distributed in summer 2017 of a human chain of 80 people rescuing a family swept away from shore by a riptide.
- **Human interest** is unusual or entertaining information. It is about people in a personal rather than a business sense. It sometimes stirs the news consumer's emotions or causes people to talk about it. To be told the CEO of a large corporation that has just made a considerable donation to the regional Ronald McDonald House is the parent of a teenager who survived cancer at a young age, gives us an insight into why that cause was chosen. It also tells us something about the person who initiated the donation.
- **Cultural proximity** is the final factor we identified and is also perhaps the most difficult to understand. It involves making a nonlocal story relevant or interesting to local readers by relating to local interests, culture, or geography. People pay attention to others like themselves. For example, during the summer of 2016 pregnant women in the south demanded tests for the Zika virus before it had even reached the United States. Why?

PHOTO 7.2 Maria Fernanda Ramirez Bolivar talks to reporters as she carries her baby Micaela Milagros Mendoza Ramirez, during a news conference, Friday, August 26, 2016, in Miami. Ramirez Bolivar contracted the Zika virus when she traveled to her native Venezuela; at the time she was three months pregnant. She tested positive for the virus in April 2016 after experiencing symptoms, including rash and body aches. Ramirez Bolivar delivered 8 lb 1 oz Micaela Milagros on June 28, 2016. The baby remained at Holtz Children's Hospital's neonatal intensive care unit for more than 2 weeks, where she underwent a series of tests to measure the impact of the virus.

Because the tragic consequences to babies of pregnant women in South America who contracted the disease made them concerned for their own unborn children. This was an extremely relevant story for them. Photo 7.2 shows why Zika was relevant in the Miami, Florida, area of the United States during the outbreak in South America.

It is also important to note that a story, or in the case of a media relations practitioner, a media release or other information subsidy, may, and probably should, include more than one of the factors discussed above. The more newsworthy factors you include in a pitch or a story, the more likely your subsidy will be accepted, or your story covered, by that medium.

Differences in Perception of News

The eight factors discussed above came from articles written by scholars, not by working journalists or public relations practitioners; to make this information useful to us in writing our own stories, we need to have the answers to three questions. First, *Do journalists and media relations practitioners agree with these factors of newsworthiness?* Second, *Are there any differences in how important media relations writers see each of the factors compared to journalists?* Third, *Which factors do those working in media relations use most often in their outreach to the media?*

A research study we published in 2014 in the Public Relations Society of America's *Public Relations Journal* attempted to answer these questions as well as several others.[3] The study was broken into two parts.

Survey of Opinions

The first part was a **survey** of journalists and media relations practitioners in three states—one each in the southeast, midwest, and northeast. We used a five-point scale, called a Likert scale, to measure how important each of the people who responded to the survey thought the eight newsworthiness factors are. For each of the factors, the respondents were asked to rate its importance from 1 = very important to 5 = not important at all. Table 7.1 shows a comparison of the mean or midpoint of the responses for each of the eight newsworthiness factors. The table is separated into the responses of journalists on the left and media relations practitioners on the right.

What we found from this survey answered the first two questions listed above: *Do journalists and media relations practitioners agree with these factors of newsworthiness?* and *Are there any differences in how important media relations writers see each of the factors compared to journalists?*

As we can immediately see, the average for each of the newsworthiness factors leans toward importance in the responses from those in both professions. Therefore, we can safely answer that representatives from the two professions agree that all of the eight factors of newsworthiness are important. Timely

Table 7.1 Comparison of Means of Newsworthy Factors

(1 = Very important, 5 = Not important at all)	Journalist	Media Relations
1. Immediacy	2.59	2.63
2. Timely news	1.60	1.47
3. Local news	1.68	2.14
4. Significant news	1.98	1.76
5. Prominent news	2.62	2.66
6. Human-interest elements	2.28	2.07
7. Cultural proximity	1.47	1.82
8. Unexpected information	2.66	2.86

news (timeliness) and cultural proximity are most important to journalists while timely news and significant news are most important to those in media relations.

What Does This Mean to Us?

Although there were slight differences in how respondents from each profession answered, there were no meaningful differences between groups, and most responses were very similar. Therefore, for the second question, we can determine that although there are slight differences between the two professions, no factor was considered extremely different in importance. For those of us in media relations, that's good news because we now know that the two professions generally agree on the types of information that *should* be in a media release and ultimately in a story in the media.

Actual Use in Media Releases

The third question couldn't be answered using a survey. Because surveys may represent what people *say* they do, and not what they *actually* do, a survey couldn't be accurate enough to determine which factors of newsworthiness media relations practitioners actually use in their media releases and the articles on their organizational websites. To answer the question, *Which factors do those working in media relations use most often in their outreach to the media?* we conducted a **content analysis** as the second part of our research.

For this we performed a systematic analysis of the contents of media releases found on the media websites of 50 large companies. Half of the companies were public, and half were private. Of course, we were particularly interested in measuring how frequently the eight factors of newsworthiness were used in news releases produced by corporations. After all, the characteristics were determined by journalism and public relations researchers over a period of 65 years to contribute to the newsworthiness, and therefore the acceptability, of the story by the media vehicle.

What we learned is that, even though media relations writers may *know* what should be included in a media release to make it newsworthy, they didn't always include those factors. Although we found seven of the eight factors of newsworthiness somewhere in the 200-plus releases we analyzed (we didn't find unexpectedness coming from the organizations we reviewed), the practitioners relied primarily on two of the factors—timeliness and immediacy. Forty-nine percent of the releases contained themes or information showing timeliness and 46.5% contained themes relating to immediacy. The two factors considered most important by journalists in the survey, localness and cultural proximity, were used in only 25% and 20.6% of releases respectively.[4]

What Does This Mean to Us?

Timeliness and immediacy are drilled into the heads of public relations students and practitioners alike. We are told repeatedly not to put anything out there that isn't "news" with "new" being the important part.[5] The phrase "For Immediate Release" has become the standard on media releases, and this timely but not vital type of announcement is "by far the most widely used type of release."[6] But stopping at timeliness is never a good idea. What is it about the timely information you are trying to get accepted that will be of interest to the audience you are trying to reach? Does it relate to the local community or region? Is it significant to a group of people you're trying to reach by choosing this particular medium? Perhaps you can find some human-interest hook the media vehicle would be interested in.

The most important point to remember is that you're not the only media relations practitioner reaching out to this or that media outlet. Your goal is to make your organization's release or pitch stand out among all the rest. There are several more important points we need to discuss to help you accomplish that.

Viewing Newsworthiness From an Organizational Perspective

Although most organizations employ communications or public relations staff, not all of them employ those with expertise in dealing with the media. That is because organizational managers view dealing with the media and the work of media relations in a variety of ways, not all of them positive. There are four major organizational paradigms when it comes to attracting media attention: (1) the media is one of our stakeholders and they should be communicated with regularly, whether the news is good or bad; (2) only get in touch with the media when something positive is going on; (3) only talk with media representatives when they contact you; (4) never deal with the media—keep your head down and pretend they don't exist. If you're reading this book you are most likely dealing with an organization that works within paradigm one or two. and therefore believes in reaching out to the media, or you have an instructor who understands the importance of reaching out to the media.

One of the biggest challenges facing us in media relations is getting others in our organization to understand when an announcement or activity or product or any number of other daily actions is or is not newsworthy. Ideally, you are the arbiter of newsworthiness within your organization but, as we all know, many bosses—from supervisors to CEOs—think they know best. Generally, in such circumstances the main problem is that your superior thinks *everything* the organization does is newsworthy. And each item may be newsworthy to some audience, such as employees, shareholders or a weekly business round-up of new hires and promotions in the local newspaper. But all items are not newsworthy to every audience, every time.

In such a situation, identifying "real" news within your organization then becomes your opportunity to take one or all of the following actions:

- Act like a reporter within your own organization and find news that will be of interest to one or more external media.
- Be proactive with the media, rather than only reacting to their requests for information, and pitch some ideas to a reporter whose work you know.
- Be as creative as you can be to find a positive connection within your organization to something happening in your environment—community, similar organizations, business subset, type of industry or service—that will interest an external audience.
- Put on your counselor suit and share your knowledge of the needs and expectations of various media outlets and vehicles with your superiors.

Of course, there are lots of other choices you can, and need, to make when working internally and preparing your information subsidies, or tools and tactics as we call them. We will discuss many of them in Chapters 9 and 10.

Viewing Newsworthiness From Journalists' Perspectives

As we wrote in Chapter 3, Augustine Pang developed a journalist-centric media relations model he called the mediating the media model.[7] He saw his model as being helpful to new media relations practitioners because he believes, as we do, that it is important to see media relations as a systematic process. Odd though it sounds, we all work within a system that seeks to be as logical and orderly as possible. An organization has certain expectations for how we all must do our jobs to achieve the goals of the organization, and journalists have the same situation. No matter how much we might want newsworthiness factors to be the only measure of whether a story is newsworthy, that simply isn't the case.

Reflecting the work about journalists conceptualized by Shoemaker and Reese,[8] Pang argues there are many additional forces that shape media relations besides the newsworthiness factors discussed earlier in this chapter. He breaks down these factors into five influences on the news which the journalist has to balance. Three of the factors are internal and two are external.

Internal Forces

These include the journalist mindset, journalist routines, and the media organization's routines. The *journalist mindset* is a similar view within each media organization that guides reporters' opinions about what must be included in a story to be considered news. And what it ultimately comes down to is that each journalist "faces the daily task of selecting and trimming large volumes of information to what is considered news."[9] *Journalist routines* are developed over time, based on the needs of the organization. Deadlines are part of every reporter's routine as we will discuss in the next section. Finally, the *routines of the media organization* itself can influence how a story is reported and shaped. Examples of this are when editorial decisions are influenced by advertising, either because the story is about a major advertiser, or because advertising must be given a portion of what is limited space or time because it pays the bills. Stories then may need to be cut.

External Forces

These forces come from outside the media organization and may include extramedia forces as well as media ideology. *Extramedia influences* are issues facing journalists like obtaining press credentials for important special events, or laws placed on journalists that restrict what they can include in a story. It also might be something positive for you, such as the need to obtain a credible source for a story, or background research about a new product from a government agency, both of which you can provide for the story. *Media ideology* refers to a newspaper, magazine, television, or radio newscast, or website or blog having a liberal or conservative bent. Knowing this tells you the type of reporting you'll find in that outlet, as well as the audience you will reach by contacting reporters from each media outlet. It also helps you to understand the types of stories you will find in various publications, and the viewpoint of the reporters writing those stories.

Commonalities of Newsworthiness Across Media

As noted above in looking at newsworthiness from an organizational perspective, we have to continually be aware, and unfortunately accept, that journalists, and especially bloggers aren't always interested in what an organization's representative, you, considers important news. Those that write for any media vehicle are interested in news that their audience will find interesting and important. But each audience is different, and all audiences are diverse, so what is the commonality?

Perhaps surprisingly, that commonality is one that public relations practitioners as well as journalists can get on board with: *The focus must be on the reader, listener, or viewer of the story.*

The American Press Institute (API), quoting from the book *The Elements of Journalism*, describes journalism as "storytelling with a purpose," and lists a number of traits that make a good news story, *one that audiences will consider to be newsworthy and worth paying attention to.*[10] Every media outlet, whether in print, on air, or online, seeks to attract attention and convince its audience that the best, most personally relevant news and information can be found by using that medium. No matter how different media outlets, or journalists, are from each other, each seeks to capture the largest possible audience. According to the API, some of the aspects of a news story that will do that include:

- Stories that are *important and interesting* to the targeted audience or audiences. This will vary across media, but all journalists, no matter the medium they work with, look for this connection to their audience.
- Stories that *prove their relevance* to the audience. People care most about things that affect them, that speak to their lives, that focus on something close to them in distance or in interest, and that causes an emotional response, either positive or negative.
- Stories that have *strong central characters*. Although this may sound more like fiction writing, a good news story brings out the humanity in the people who are being written about—politician, CEO, victim, or thief. The ability to use visuals as well as words to draw someone into a story has become a universal method to attract an audience.
- Stories that *connect to deeper themes* can draw in and hold an audience, no matter the topic of the news story. A visual that makes a connection to a larger story helps audience members see the relevance of a story to them. A story about increased security at a local courthouse or middle school, for example, connects easily to the increase in mass shootings across the country. Photo 7.3 of children going through metal detectors to enter their school building is an example of this.

PHOTO 7.3 Students at William Hackett Middle School pass through metal detectors on the first day of school on Tuesday, September 6, 2016, in Albany, New York. (AP Photo/Mike Groll)

- Stories that *provide context to a complicated issue* can help that issue stick in the heads of audience members. Even the most important stories out there aren't newsworthy if people can't understand them or if they can't see how a story has any connection to their lives. The best news stories about complex issues start with a reporter asking, "What does my audience need to know about this issue?" and then clearly following through by making connections to his or her audience's lives.[11]

Of course, researchers have discovered a variety of reasons that news stories are selected and, unfortunately for those of us in media relations, many of those reasons are based on newsworthiness values that it wouldn't be wise to include in our stories because of the type of organization we work for. Examples of those types of news values were reported in a 2016 article in *Journalism Studies*, and although some of the values match those identified by API, or your authors, others do not. The following list comes from the *Journalism Studies* article.[12] You will probably immediately note in the following list the news values it would not be wise to use relating to your organization!

1. **The power elite**. Stories concerning powerful individuals, organizations, or institutions.
2. **Celebrity**. Stories concerning people who are already famous.
3. **Entertainment**. Stories concerning sex, show business, human interest, animals, an unfolding drama, or offering opportunities for humorous treatment, entertaining photographs, or witty headlines.
4. **Surprise**. Stories that have an element of surprise and/or contrast.
5. **Bad news**. Stories with particularly negative overtones, such as conflict or tragedy.
6. **Good news**. Stories with particularly positive overtones, such as rescues and cures.
7. **Magnitude**. Stories that are perceived as sufficiently significant either in the numbers of people involved or in potential impact.
8. **Relevance**. Stories about issues, groups, and nations perceived to be relevant to the audience.
9. **Follow-up**. Stories about subjects already in the news.
10. **Newspaper agenda**. Stories that set or fit the news organization's own agenda.

Looking at the list it's easy to see overlaps with the previously discussed areas of newsworthiness and news values, but it's also clear that this list, developed by journalists, comes with a focus of "*all* news" not just "*your*—the media relations practitioners'—news." Most journalists today, whether print, broadcast, or online, are not heavily resourced. That translates into too much work for those available to do it, and not enough time or money to cover all worthwhile stories. *What that means to us* is that if a reporter has a sensational or high-profile story to cover, such as a murder, a massive recall of products that can kill, or a chief financial officer of a large corporation convicted of perjury, our stories come second. Even if our stories are timely and carry other aspects of newsworthiness, they will probably be set aside to be used only if there is time and space available.

Thinking Strategically: All News Media Need Content

Being put on the back burner can be discouraging, but sometimes we can make it work to our benefit. How? It's all about filling a need, and doing it very, very well. Although the very, very well part will be discussed in depth in later chapters, what you need to think about now is how a well-written and presented news subsidy, such as an expertly done media release with interesting visuals, can help journalists fill their news hole while they're working on that other high-profile story.

What will keep your release from being set aside for an undetermined amount of time to one being considered as a newsworthy story to be included in the time frame you had targeted is the *writing, presentation, and visuals* you make available. If you (1) have done your job and built a relationship with the journalist you have targeted with your news and (2) have something newsworthy to offer; (3) if you first pitched the story to the journalist in a helpful way and then (4) sent it to them in the way they wanted; (5) if you understand the needs of their particular medium or media—see discussion that follows—and (6) have learned to write and present your information in an acceptable journalistic style; (7) if you have visuals or graphics to go with the story or (8) you have interview subjects lined up *it's unlikely your story will be immediately deleted.*

That last statement may seem negative at first glance, because, of course, we always want our stories to be actively considered and, better yet, used by the media vehicle we're targeting. Knowing what is important to a particular journalist with whom you have built a relationship, meeting journalistic expectations in terms of writing and presentation, and making additional information available to the journalist will go a long way toward having your newsworthy release both considered and accepted, even in a time of competing news. But a final, equally important piece of information in your strategic process will add to your success. That is an understanding of the unique needs of the various media vehicles you are targeting.

Differences Across Media Vehicles

To get your news covered by your targeted media, it is important to be as strategic as possible with *every* pitch and release. That's because you never know what other news a day or week might bring. It is not always enough to pull out everything in your toolbox to make your story acceptable to journalists; it is equally important to appreciate that journalists, like us, want their hard work to be consumed by their audiences. Therefore, understanding the focus and standards of the medium for which your intended journalist reports and/or writes is important as well.

Earlier in this chapter we asked you to think about the different requirements for a story that is to be disseminated across print vehicles, online news sites, television, radio, and online bloggers. There are a variety of ways to talk about these differences, but one of the easiest is to think about the needs of the writers, reporters, editors, or producers working for the various media you may be reaching out to.

Deadlines

Yes, they still matter, even in our online, never-stop world. Knowing when each journalist you work with, in each media vehicle you're targeting, wants your information is an important part of a successful strategy to reach your ultimate audience. If your news is timely, you have already been in touch with the journalist several times in preparation for an article and know what they want from you. You probably have also put them in touch with people to interview or given them any additional materials they requested. But if you have not done so already, finding out the final deadline for the journalist is essential.

Each media vehicle with which we communicate has its own deadline, even if that deadline is set only by the writer of a popular blog we work with. As the oldest medium, the paper version of *newspapers* keep to the strictest deadlines. Journalists must submit their stories in time for that version to be sent to press, and, when dealing with print reporters you have to consider the entire timeline for the publication of a story. Because most newspapers today are published to come out in the morning, printing is done overnight so the papers can be delivered as early as possible. The larger the region the newspaper covers, the earlier the printing time, and therefore the earlier the deadline the journalist has to meet. If your news is timely, and not a soft news, or human-interest piece, make sure you know well in advance what the reporter's deadline is, and what the timing is for your submission *for this particular reporter*. If you've built multiple relationships within the same media vehicle, you already know that each journalist varies in their "need by" time frame.

Other *print* outlets such as popular or technical magazines and trade and industry publications have longer deadlines and are often weeks or months in production. This helps with deadline planning, but also limits the ability for media relations professionals to submit timely news to these outlets. Targeting trade and industry publications, however, has the benefit that we know very specifically who makes up the ultimate audience, and thus can direct our efforts only to those publications that have readers we wish to reach.

Television or radio journalists or producers will have multiple deadlines throughout the day based upon the number of newscasts or news breaks each station programs. Make sure you are familiar with the types of stories that are covered during each of these broadcast opportunities. Knowing who the audience is for each day part is also important in terms of getting your news accepted. Remember that journalists want their audiences to pay attention to what they cover, and to think the stories are newsworthy. As with newspaper journalists, get in touch with the producer in charge of the particular newscast or the journalist who usually covers the type of news you are communicating for your organization or client. That way you will know what information they need from you, and when.

Influential blogs targeting an audience that may be interested in our organization's products or services are also vehicles we need to be familiar with. The bloggers who write them generally operate on their own schedules and do not have set deadlines. Active and popular blogs, however, do publish a set number of times a week. Being familiar with the general publishing schedules, and how far in advance the bloggers plan, will help you as you strategize and schedule your outreach for news.

Almost all mass media, even the smallest outlets, have websites that carry breaking news; updates of stories that have already been reported; longer, more in-depth stories about topics that have already been published in print or broadcast on air; and stories that did not make the traditional media versions of the outlet for lack of space or time. Deadlines are of much less importance for the communicator who chooses to introduce their news online. Although there may be excellent reasons to take this route based on the final audience being targeted, it is wise, however, to think carefully and strategically about the ultimate impact of a story being introduced first on a media vehicle's website. This is of special importance if the news doesn't make the transition to the off-web medium you were originally targeting.

Fit

This is a simple idea, but one we may overlook when identifying media or reporters for our stories. How well does what we want to communicate fit the medium or the journalist we are targeting?

Both radio and television want news or ideas that can be communicated quickly and succinctly to an audience. These media are based on time, and most stories get very little of it. If what you want to publicize—and I use that word purposefully—can't be communicated in a minute or less, sometimes much less, then this isn't the medium to target. As some examples, we have found that upcoming special events, plant or business openings, expansions, or closings, or human interest stories that relate to a community work very well for these broadcast media.

Example 7.1 is a radio release for a summer day camp for children. As it timed out at 45 seconds, you might find the station needs to cut some of the details, as many radio spots are rewritten for the time available. News that involves longer explanations or background information is not a good fit. Of course, there are other concerns with these media, and we discuss those both above and below.

Print media, newspapers as well as magazines, trade, industry, and professional publications, can be pitched and ultimately provided with more detailed information for a story because of longer deadlines as well as a larger news hole—more space to fill with news. Print vehicles are often the medium of

---

Example 7.1 Format for Radio Release for a Special Event

Floyd County SPCA
17 Mercantile St.
Floyd, WV 25231

Bethanne Cicero
Director of Communications
304-890-1212
bcicero@floydspca.org   Time: :45
May 15, 2019

Floyd County SPCA gets requests every day from parents about opportunities for children who love pets. Animals Helpers 3-day camp may be the answer.

Do you have a child between 6 and 8 who can't get enough of animals?! Does he or she want to learn more about caring for animals? If so, this is the perfect camp! Children will learn how to properly interact with and care for cats and dogs as they work with the adorable rescued fur-babies that are available for adoption at the Floyd SPCA.

Campers will also be visited by guest speakers from law enforcement, canine working dogs, and service-dog handlers.

Animal Helpers is scheduled from June 17 to 19.

For information about costs and more details go to FloydSPCA.org and click the link for Animal Helpers.

Radio Release: A radio media release should include the time it will take, in seconds, for the newscaster to read it. Usually they are submitted double or triple spaced so they can be easily marked up, although few releases will actually be read as is. As noted in the text, they should be as succinct as possible yet still be memorable.

choice for stories about financial information or economic issues, new products or services, changes in top-level personnel, or any other story you might want covered in some depth. For the purpose of showing the difference between radio and print style, the same day camp is used in Example 7.2 of a print media release.

Bloggers, of course, should only be targeted if your product or service fits neatly and clearly into the area on which they blog. For example, a company developing a new sunscreen that will not damage coral reefs could target numerous bloggers across a variety of interests: environment, snorkeling, or healthy skin care, for example.

Fit is less of an issue with websites connected to an offline medium because the news hole is infinite and, with regular updating, time constraints don't come into play.

Format Variables

Whereas fit is a simple concept, format variables have become a very complicated one as most media vehicles have added websites to complement and enhance their offline media.

Outreach to television hasn't changed as much as other media vehicles because we are used to providing producers and reporters with short, succinct information; audiovisual materials; and, if we are called to provide an interview, with the well-known "soundbite." Of course, sound is the format of necessity for radio, and both bloggers and online websites want links to visuals and audiovisuals. The biggest transformations have occurred in newspapers and other print vehicles, and not necessarily only because they now also manage websites.

Although media relations professionals have not traditionally thought first about visuals beyond photos when targeting print media of any kind, that type of thinking needs to change. Over the last several years, journalism has been evolving to include more data in articles to support the points made or conclusions that are being drawn. Journalists are concerned with the increasing suspicion in which their work is being held. That concern includes information or stories we, as communicators, send them. A 2018 international study by Muck Rack and Zeno Group indicated 49% ($n = 520$) of journalists would be more likely to pay attention to a media release if it included *an infographic.*[13]

The importance of visuals to all journalism was also emphasized by several recent academic articles.[14] One of those articles, which looked at what properties determine whether a story is or is not considered newsworthy, found that *in both newspapers and broadcasting having good pictures available was an important aspect of any story being covered.*[15]

Example 7.2 **Format for Print or Online Release**

Floyd County SPCA
17 Mercantile St.
Floyd, WV 25231

FOR IMMEDIATE RELEASE

Kids and Pets Make for Happy Campers

FLOYD, WV, May 15, 2019—Animal Helpers Day Camp for 6- to 8-year-olds starts its second year on June 17. Children who love animals will learn how to properly interact with and extend care to cats and dogs as they spend time with the adorable rescued fur-babies that are available for adoption here at Floyd County SPCA. The day camp runs June 17–19 from 9:00 a.m.–4:00 p.m. each day, and costs $150 per child. Healthy snacks will be provided, but campers must provide their own lunches. Register at www.FloydSPCA.org and click the link for Animal Helpers.

Children will learn what it means to be a great pet owner through age-appropriate lessons, which will include topics about pet rescue, the different breeds of cats and dogs, and some training tips—along with fun arts and crafts projects. Campers will be visited by guest speakers from local organizations, such as law enforcement and canine working dogs, as well as service-dog handlers. We are excited to have new topics this year, so prior campers can experience something new with us!

Floyd County SPCA seeks to change the traditional definition of an animal shelter by offering services and programs to benefit the community, the people that live there, and the pets they love. The organization operates the largest private animal shelter in Floyd County, as well as a low-cost Community Pet Clinic and farm animal sanctuary. Our mission is to improve the lives of both people and their pets in Floyd County, with special emphasis on keeping animals in their homes, innovative placement programs, and eliminating companion-animal euthanasia in our communities.

Contact:
Bethanne Cicero
Director of Communications
304-890-1212
bcicero@floydspca.org

Media Release: This media release for the business section in print or online publications is set up to be sent over a business wire. It would be sent out on the HumanCare letterhead.

Audience Interest

Now is a good time to reiterate a point made elsewhere in this book—media relations professionals need to think about the interests of *all* audiences we are trying to reach. But, unlike with other types of public relations communication, the journalist, reporter, or producer is the *first audience* whose interest we need to arouse. Yes, we certainly want the media vehicle's ultimate audience to be interested, whether that is readers, listeners, or viewers of the medium, but if we don't first pique the interest of our *connection* to that audience—the journalist who is receiving the story from us—that story may never reach our primary audience. It will instead be ignored or simply deleted.

While presenting information we want to reach our *final* audience—consumers, investors, community members, industry opinion leaders, for example—our focus must always first be on what in other contexts are considered an "intervening" audience: the media gatekeepers. Of course, we all know these journalists serve not only as gatekeepers between our organizational information and the audience we are focused on, but also as an important audience on their own. It is essential that we provide newsworthy information that interests them too. As noted, journalists want a good news story, *one that audiences will consider to be newsworthy and worth paying attention to.* Both their jobs, and ours, rely on all of us understanding this very basic premise.

Key Concepts

This chapter emphasizes that the newsworthiness of your topic, although important, is only the first step in having your story accepted by the media vehicle or vehicles you are targeting. To be successful in media relations, you need to understand a host of issues that affect how journalists determine which stories, based on their organization or platform, are worth pursuing.

First, you need to remember that, although similar, journalists and communicators don't always perfectly agree about what makes a story newsworthy; and to make the situation even more complicated, our bosses often have totally different ideas of what is a newsworthy story.

As a media relations professional you act as a boundary spanner between your organization and the media you're reaching out to, so you need to understand both sides of the newsworthiness equation. As do you, journalists have particular mindsets and routines based on the medium for which they work. They also work on deadlines and are usually understaffed. They need content to do their jobs, but want content that will attract their readers, viewers, or listeners and that has some visual aspect to it, even if the medium is print based.

Finally, although media vehicles have many commonalities in how they operate and what they want from you in terms of news subsidies, they also have many differences, and it is up to you to be aware of those differences and cater to them.

Challenge Case

The following challenge is to get you thinking about how you might conduct outreach and provide information subsidies to journalists from a variety of media vehicles.

Although it's been fairly hush-hush up to now, your organization has been working with the economic development department of a city in a neighboring state about moving your operations there in return for a tax break and a land deal on which you can build a new facility. Your company is not big, employing only a little more than 100 people, but you're fairly sure not all your employees will want to move with the company, *and* the new building will provide room for growth, both of which will lead to additional jobs for residents in the new city. Of course, the move will also leave some existing employees in your current city without jobs, and will, at least minimally, hurt your current city's economy.

As things are looking good with the deal, your CEO has decided it's time to let your employees know what's going on and about the changes that will occur within the next year or so. As a communicator, you are well aware that once your employees know, the word will be out in both cities. You ask your boss for a day or two to prepare announcements to be issued concurrently in both cities.

Working either alone, or in a group to help you brainstorm, list the news stories that will need to be pitched in both cities—old and new—not forgetting you'll need to coordinate with human resources in your organization and the economic development people your CEO has been working with. Determine how each story will be presented as newsworthy—the values you'll be emphasizing—in the two cities. How will the two stories vary between cities? What sort of information subsidies do you need to prepare? What visuals will you use based on the medium—photos, illustrations, videos, infographics? How will you pitch the stories to various media vehicles based on their needs?

REFERENCES

1. Supa, D. W., & Zoch, L. M. (2012 August). *Seeking an updated understanding of the Public Relations-Journalist relationship in the age of social media.* Paper presented to the Public Relations Division, Association for Education in Journalism and Mass Communication (AEJMC), Chicago, IL.

2. Zoch, L. M., & Supa, D. W. (2014). Dictating the news: Understanding newsworthiness from the journalistic perspective. *Public Relations Journal, 8*(1). Retrieved from https://prjournal.instituteforpr.org/wp-content/uploads/2014ZochSupa.pdf
3. Zoch & Supa.
4. Zoch & Supa, p. 16.
5. Zoch & Supa, p. 18.
6. Bivins, T. H. (1999). *Public relations writing*. Lincolnwood, IL: NTC Business Books.
7. Pang, A. (2010). Mediating the media: A journalistic-centric media relations model. *Corporate Communications: An International Journal, 15*(2), 192–204.
8. Shoemaker, P., & Reese, S. D. (1996). *Mediating the message*. New York, NY: Longman.
9. Pang, p. 196.
10. American Press Institute (2018). Retrieved from https://www.americanpressinstitute.org/journalism-essentials/makes-good-story/
11. American Press Institute (2018).
12. Harcup, T., & O'Neill, D. (2016). What is news? *Journalism Studies, 18*(12), 1470–1488. doi:10.1080/1461670X.2016.1150193
13. Muck Rack & Zeno Group (2018). Shareability, credibility & objectivity: The state of journalism today. https://muckrack.com/blog/2018/05/22/2018-muck-rack-survey-results
14. Allern, S. (2002). Journalistic and commercial news values. *Nordcom Review, 23*(1–2), 137–52; Caple, H., & Bednarek, M. (2015). Delving into the discourse: Approaches to news values in journalism studies and beyond. University of Oxford: Reuters Institute for the Study of Journalism; Dick, M. (2014). Interactive infographics and news values. *Digital Journalism, 2*(4), 490–506.
15. Strömbäck, J., Karlsson, M., & Hopmann, D. N. (2012). Determinants of news content: Comparing journalists' perceptions of the normative and actual impact of different event properties when deciding what's news. *Journalism Studies, 5*(5–6), 718–728.

8

MANAGING GOALS, OBJECTIVES, AND EXPECTATIONS

To successfully use media relations as a strategy to help an organization achieve its goals and objectives, media relations practitioners must learn to (1) work within the organizational structure and (2) effectively manage the expectations of managers and organizational leadership. In this chapter we address the need for connecting media relations objectives to organizational goals and objectives. We also emphasize the need for establishing realistic media relations objectives, and the importance of establishing them early in the process. We discuss what a strategy is and what it means to think strategically through your media relations process. The chapter also goes through the media planning process, including a discussion about various types of media and why they may or may not be important to our organization in various situations. Finally, we discuss the importance of managing expectations for your client organization and for your management team.

Connecting to Organizational Goals Is Essential

When talking about media relations in the classroom, there are three points we find ourselves repeating throughout the semester. Those points foreshadow what we will be discussing in this chapter, and they are:

1. Our jobs as media relations professionals, under the umbrella of a public relations or communication department, are to *serve the organization we represent*. What that means is that no matter how creative or forward thinking our ideas for media outreach might be, we must always put the needs of the organization first. Is this story idea, this B roll, this pitch

to an online influencer going to help our organization reach its targeted and ultimate audiences? Will it reinforce our organization's reputation, support our marketing, espouse our core values, or promote our most recent fundraising effort? Am I being strategic in my choice of the media I intend to use; do those in our target audience pay attention to these media?

2. Media relations objectives must *work to support and fulfill organizational goals and objectives.* It is not our job or our role to develop a media relations objective because we know it is something media relations can achieve. The belief that doing something—anything!—is better than doing nothing is often a mistake made by new employees. Everything we do must connect back to the overall needs, mission, and goals of the organization. We won't have our job or our role very long if we don't work cooperatively with everyone else who is striving within their own departments or teams to achieve overall organizational success. That means linking everything we accomplish to the whole.

3. Our jobs *exist to support the organization's strategic plan.* Public relations, and media relations within it, are strategic functions. But what does it mean to be strategic? For us, it means we have to set our priorities toward obtaining media coverage for whatever it is our organization has determined is important to move its overall vision and mission forward. We have to focus our resources and our energy on achieving success and be willing to work with others who are focused on the same goal—helping the organization be successful.

Defining Goals, Objectives, and Strategies

The terms we're going to use in this chapter can be, like the "publics" and "stakeholders" we discussed in Chapter 5, confusing, because different people and different organizations define the terms in a variety of ways. Your authors developed our use of the terms "goals," "objectives," and "strategies" from the book *Public Relations Management by Objectives,* which was written by Norman Nager and T. Harrell Allen at about the same time as the first public relations management book by James Grunig and Todd Hunt was published.[1] As time has moved on, the management by objectives (MBO) philosophy morphed into management by results (MBR) and then lost favor in the field of management because it was seen as too controlling of employees by their managers. The concepts, however, have remained the same, and setting goals and objectives, and using strategies to achieve them, is a process that takes place in every organization.

Defining Goals and Objectives

The main confusion can occur between the words when using "goals" and "objectives" to mean the same thing. Although the terms work in concert, objectives *support* goals and are more short term.

An organization's *goals* are long term and point the organization and its staff in a general direction. Goals are also quite broad and general. They provide the framework to achieve determined outcomes or point the organization in the direction in which it wants to move in the long term. Most organizations set one-, three-, or five-year goals.

An organization's goal might be to

- Become the top medical service provider in the area;
- Demonstrate the coal industry's commitment to operating more cleanly;
- Increase public cooperation with the city's police force;
- Gain additional market share in the eastern region of the state;
- Grow shareholder value;
- Increase fundraising opportunities within the community.

Departments or divisions also set goals that are written to support the organization's goals. As a media relations professional you will most likely be working for either an agency in support of an organization (externally), or as part of an organization (internally). In the second case, depending on the organizational structure, you might find yourself working in a communication, public relations, marketing, or even advertising department or division.

Examples of departmental goals related to the organizational goals listed above might be to

- Provide better communication with our area clients;
- Establish a robust national media relations presence;
- Work more closely with neighborhood groups in the city;
- Develop a plan with the marketing department;
- Leverage earned and owned media to grow value;
- Develop relationships with other nonprofit organizations.

Objectives do more than point your organization in a general direction; they tell you specifically where it is going. They are, Nager and Allen tell us, our ends in view. Objectives are the way we can determine if we are "progressing satisfactorily in the direction of our goals;"[2] and objectives allow that because they can be measured and evaluated. When we write our first objective, we have headed in the direction our goals are sending us, but we've also started to develop a map to get there. We know we cannot get to the goal in one step or, continuing the metaphor of a map, in one day, so we have broken the journey into shorter trips that, when added together, help us reach the destination. Each objective we successfully complete gets us closer to the goal.

The acronym SMART is often used when discussing how to successfully write objectives, and covers the five criteria of being **specific, measurable, attainable/ achievable, relevant,** and **time-based**.[3] People who believe goals and objectives are the same thing will use these criteria in writing goals, but in this book and throughout this discussion goals and objectives are very different, and only objectives contain this degree of detail.

"Specific results operationally defined"[4] is the way Nager and Allen explained the first criterion for an objective. They added "operationally defined" because they believed there should be no room for ambiguity in what is being written, so that anyone reading it would instantly know what is required to fulfill this objective.

Measurable can mean several different things within an objective, but in general you have to make sure you answer the question of *how much*—how much change do you want to achieve? To do that you need to include words that indicate how much. Some of those measurements would include numbers, percentages, monetary costs, or even the time it takes to accomplish the objective; and you would strive for what you're measuring to go up, in most cases, or down, when we are talking about costs or human resources, from the past.

"Attainable" or "achievable," it's your choice which word to use, but it simply means making sure that you are being realistic in what you say you can accomplish within the objective. It is always better to underpromise and overachieve than to go in the opposite direction and promise more than you can accomplish in the time and with the resources you have.

Relevant is making sure your department or team objectives link directly to both the departmental and organizational goals. That's what will make your decisions strategic as you go forward. By planning the connections from what you're doing to the overall goals of the organization, you're making a direct contribution to success.

Time-based objectives mean you are setting a time frame within which you will accomplish the objective or assigning a deadline for when it will be completed.

Thinking Strategically

Once we know our organization's and department's goals, it's time for us to start thinking about how we can strategically use media relations to help move those goals forward. For some of us, though, the concept of what constitutes a strategy can be fuzzy at best or confusing at worst. That's because there are so many

Analyzing Objectives

Following are some examples of objectives for the media relations aspects of the public relations departments' goals listed on page 139. As you read each of them, think about what other objectives you could write to move toward the departmental goal. Why, in your mind, is each one a successful or unsuccessful objective? Are they all SMART? Do they each address the listed departmental goal? The organizational goal? How will a story about successful corporate social responsibility help grow shareholder value? What is missing in the objective for the nonprofit organization?

- By the end of the month, pitch a story to local television about a client our organization has helped, showing the versatility of what the organization can do.
- Within two months, work with one national media outlet to develop a story featuring our new clean initiatives.
- In coordination with our community relations outreach, pitch a story to the local media about the police department's commitment to community policing, as soon as meeting dates are set.
- Once a cooperative plan with the marketing department has been set in place, work with regional media contacts to achieve at least one story about our new product within the following two months.
- Within a year, achieve placement of at least one story covering our company's successful corporate social responsibility initiatives in a national media outlet.
- Reach out to reporters who cover community issues with a story idea about how joint fundraising events can help all types of nonprofit organizations.

different kinds of strategies we could use. So let's start with a couple of definitions and go from there.

A strategy is a plan of action that someone puts together when they know what they want to accomplish and how to achieve it. Strategic thinking, which is what we are really talking about here, is being able to look at the problem or opportunity that our organization is facing and come up with an effective plan to help resolve the situation or to achieve the organization's goal. For us, as media relations professionals, it also means accomplishing that within the framework of what we do best: using communication to reach out to a variety of media outlets to help disseminate information—and perhaps use it persuasively—relating to that goal.

Being a strategic thinker is a skill that can be learned. In fact, you're probably already on your way to understanding how to think strategically once you've learned the steps in putting together a public relations campaign or plan. You may have learned the process by using an acronym such as RACE, PIE, or ROSIE, but in each case it is a roadmap of the steps needed to achieve success and prove that success. It's a process, as is a strategy, connected to your organization's mission and goals.

Erika Anderson, a founder of Proteus, a firm that focuses on leadership training, has developed six steps that support strategic planning within an organizational setting,[5] and they merge well with the steps you've learned to develop a successful public relations plan.

1. Define the challenge you are facing or the problem you are trying to solve.
2. Figure out where your organization is now in terms of that challenge.
3. Imagine your ultimate goal—that is, the organizational goal you are linking to.
4. Identify the obstacles in your path.
5. Outline the path you will take—including your core strategies and the tactics for implementing them.
6. Re-evaluate your strategy and your tactics as conditions change.

Using this template as our starting point, to be successful from a media relations perspective you start developing your strategy by defining your organization's, and therefore your, challenge in achieving the goal it has set. You, or members of your team, conduct some research to make sure you understand where things stand now and what the obstacles in the path to success may be. You then set your own goal, strategy, and measurable objectives for media relations. You create your strategy or plan for using media relations to accomplish your goal and objectives. Finally, you plan to evaluate and re-evaluate your path to success as you move forward with the strategy.

Strategy Is the Step Between Goals and Objectives

As we discussed in Chapter 1 of this book, the two basic types of *purposeful* media relations programs, otherwise known as media relations plans or strategies, are proactive and reactive programs. Because media relations is generally considered a proactive strategy—our focus, after all, being to conduct outreach to journalists—we will primarily discuss those instead of reactive strategies. As a reminder: Reactive strategies can be useful depending on the organization's goals. As noted in Chapter 1, *organizations that seldom have new information to share, or whose news could be considered controversial, often use reactive media relations programs.* A reactive strategy doesn't mean that communicators for the organization are against working with the media, it just means they react to requests rather than conduct outreach to the media.

Simply presenting newsworthy information to the media—applying what we have talked about in this book about relationships, audiences, and newsworthiness—is a proactive strategy that many public relations or communication departments use.[6] More-specific strategies can be created by those of us within the role of working with the media. Thinking about the examples of organizational goals and related departmental goals already presented in this chapter, a strategy for the organization that wants to "become the top medical-service provider in the area" might be

- Reach out to all reporters, producers, freelancers, influencers, and bloggers within the company's area who focus on healthcare and technology.

That strategy would allow you to cover the media of importance in your company's area while doing outreach with the most important journalists and other information disseminators.

A strategy for the association that wanted to "demonstrate the coal industry's commitment to operating more cleanly," and where the public relations department's goal was to "establish a robust national media relations presence" could be

- Reach out through email or phone to all media outlets across the country we have had positive interaction with in the past to discuss our new clean initiatives.

Those are big, broad goals and, with the reality of climate change, your association is facing a difficult challenge to attract the attention it wants. This strategy can at least set you on the path to reaching media outlets that will listen to stories about change in the coal industry.

No matter the situation, getting the attention of appropriate media outlets is always a concern for media relations professionals. What strategies can you think of to address the other examples of organizational and departmental goals from earlier in this chapter?

Although some people use the idea of a strategy as a way to pull together all of the objectives they have set into something cohesive, that would be looking at strategies backwards. Objectives should not be set until you have first determined an overall plan, and that plan can't be developed until you have conducted research and analyzed the situation you're facing. What will be your guiding insights from the research? How will you move forward using what you have learned?

For a public relations department, using media relations to reach out to a determined audience could be the overall strategy. As the practitioner in charge of that strategy, however, you need to set your own plan, or strategy, for how to effectively reach that audience.

Successfully Connecting Media Relations to the Whole

As indicated at the beginning of the chapter, connecting to the organization's overall mission and goals is essential, and as we've just discussed, defining the situation currently facing the organization is the first step in thinking and acting strategically. Because media relations is only one of the several functions that make up public relations within an organization, we usually find ourselves working as part of a communication team. Each person, or specialized unit, is one segment of the whole, which can consist of a variety of segments, depending on the needs of the organizations. In fact, to take a step backward, public relations might even be considered a segment of a larger communication unit that is composed of, for instance, marketing, advertising, employee relations, and public relations.

An internal public relations department, or unit, can be structured in a variety of ways. One common method of structure is by function—media relations, employee communication, online communication, special events, and crisis management, for example. Another is to structure by stakeholders or constituent relations—such as community, public affairs/government, consumer, financial/investor, and media. Those who work in a public relations firm or agency might find themselves working with any of those areas and in any structural configuration. But since our focus is on media relations, we will limit the discussion to that functional area.

The point of this brief discussion about structure is to emphasize that, unless you are a one-person shop in a small company or nonprofit, you will always be part of a team that works together to provide various types of communication for the organization. Media relations practitioners are part of a team. Coordinating our work, part of which is to build relationships with professionals in external media and with others who work within the communication arena of an organization, can save everyone time and resources.

Defining the Problem or Challenge

Very few organizational challenges, or even opportunities, appear out of thin air. Sudden crises caused by forces outside the control of the organization are perhaps the only exceptions. What that means for us on a normal day is that defining the challenge our organization is facing isn't that difficult, although it might be time consuming, and we will have help in figuring it out because we work with others who are also involved.

Professional Commentary

Jonathan Withington
Chief, Plain Language Division
U.S. Citizenship and Immigration Services

While addressing cadets at West Point, former Secretary of Defense Robert Gates said, "The press is not the enemy, and to treat it as such is self-defeating." His affirmation was welcomed by the Pentagon press corps and military public affairs officers like myself. Armed with this openness, all of us working in military media shops still had to maneuver within the new media landscape and gain leadership buy-in.

A seismic shift has occurred in media relations in the decades since my first public affairs job decades ago. Intense competition for audience engagement has fractured the information ecosystem. One thing has not changed: Media strategy effectiveness hinges on preparation, setting expectations, and sound planning of goals and objectives.

Incorporating media relations as part of a communication strategy lets us share our story with audiences in a way that advances organizational goals.

Throughout my career, beginning in the army, with later stops in a national nonprofit association and federal government public affairs, I witnessed the evolution of new media forms gaining market share at the expense of traditional media, bringing radical change to how people get their news. Despite this, communicating deliberately, truthfully, and with a purpose can still cut through the clutter.

Preparation begins with cultivating press relationships. While the communication strategy includes all important channels, like congressional or stakeholder notification, and paid and owned media, it must also include earned media. Media relations cannot be an afterthought or a mere tactic. Key media relationships require an investment of time and energy beforehand to build mutual trust and understanding. Introducing yourself to reporters on the eve of a rollout or during a crisis will not produce good results.

Media engagement is vital. Start by asking, "What is my ROI (return on investment)?" Earned media, or press exposure generated by your own editorial influence, can lend credibility to your organization if journalists provide third-party endorsements or accurately acknowledge your position. It can also increase brand or issue awareness, especially in the private

(Continued)

sector. In government public affairs, the ROI is public trust, confidence, and accountability.

Successful media relations strategy requires a long-term view. While in business or politics the ROI may appear more quickly via increased sales or hits in the polls, in government public affairs it takes longer to inform public opinion. Also, unflattering news should not lead organizations to stop engaging. The more you engage, the more opportunities you have to tell your story, and more balanced stories will come.

Leadership buy-in is essential to an effective media strategy. Understandably, pushback is commonplace because some senior leadership may not appreciate the value of working with the media. Demonstrating value will help you overcome any reservations. The strategy should let leadership know what to expect. It should explain

- What are the opportunities for engaging and the risks of not engaging?
- How will our media strategy shape the narrative?
- What is the attribution?
- Can we expect accuracy and balance?
- What are competitors or opposing voices saying?

Identifying media strategy goals and specific objectives synchronizes team efforts and defines success. Your communication goal must link directly to your operational goals. Ask yourself a couple key questions. How does our media strategy advance the organizational goals and objectives? Why are we doing this, and what do we want to achieve? Establish your goals and specific objectives to provide direction and focus. Otherwise you cannot evaluate success or demonstrate value.

In Iraq, we wanted to increase American trust and confidence in the army's ability to conduct operations. We embedded media with units so journalists could learn more about the soldiers and better understand our operations. We also reassured families by using a satellite uplink system to establish live feeds and regularly communicate with news outlets near our home station. Bypassing the news organizations on the ground in Iraq enabled us to provide human-interest angles that would not have been covered by the Baghdad-based national and international media.

When I served in Korea, we prepared strategies for many scenarios, from provocations to political crises in North Korea. Our media strategy always complemented the operational goals of reassuring our South Korean allies, deterring further provocation, and showing resolve, all while working closely with our South Korean allies.

After one instance of military provocation, we flew South Korean media and CNN out to a Navy aircraft carrier participating in exercises off the Korean coast to watch joint air operations training. We sought to shape the narrative by facilitating independent coverage of professional U.S. and South Korean military operations. In the following days, the combined operations saturated the Asian press. Meanwhile, CNN broadcast imagery of our air operations worldwide—visibly portraying our resolve to millions of viewers.

In another example, as the world looked for signs of tension following the change of leadership in North Korea in 2012, we facilitated a trip for Korean and Western press to the Demilitarized Zone separating the two countries to show that operations were normal. We demonstrated resolve through the professionalism of our troops and by allowing the media to independently verify that we were continuing to provide the same level of security as any normal day. We successfully increased the stories that downplayed tension on the Korean peninsula and more accurately described the posture of the U.S. and Korean armed forces.

In the nonprofit space, organizational goals often include informing and influencing Congress. Generally speaking, if Congress cares, the media will care. And, conversely, if the media cares, Congress will care. A strategic approach can garner valuable congressional attention to core nonprofit or association issues.

In government, the goals often include increasing awareness or understanding of a policy or issue. The first story on an issue can frame the narrative. While government public affairs offices generally avoid giving exclusives, placing the story in advance under an embargo allows the media time to digest the complex information, clarify any points, and prepare their editorial schedules. Once the embargo is lifted and the information is released, outlets that had the information early can file immediately with more accurate stories.

Determining the attribution is a strategic decision, not a tactical one. In my opinion, senior leaders should always speak on the record. Your strategy may involve having a subject matter expert speak on background to afford more open dialogue. I prefer to avoid off-the-record conversations because if it is worth arranging engagements with subject matter experts or senior leaders, it should be worth communicating our story, not to mention—nothing is really ever off the record.

Finally, I have learned that evaluating media outcomes is just as important as planning and implementing strategies. Always monitor stories for fairness, accuracy, and balance. Years ago, inaccuracies that went unchallenged for more than 24 hours became the truth. Today, it happens much faster, so you must correct the record in real time. Since many outlets file content online before going to print or broadcast, you must be on alert to get corrections made before the copy gets fully published.

If you don't tell your own story, someone else will do it for you. The strategy should result in a narrative that reflects the truth and one that allowed your organization to provide context. To build brand awareness or increase public trust and confidence, organizations must pursue a media strategy that leads to increased exposure. However, success hinges on preparation, setting expectations and sound planning of goals and objectives before stepping to the podium or blasting out a news release. I think former Secretary Gates would agree, not engaging the media is a strategy, but it is generally a self-defeating one.

(Continued)

> **Jonathan Withington Biography**
>
> Jonathan Withington is chief of the Plain Language Division at U.S. Citizenship and Immigration Services (USCIS) where he leads the agency's program to ensure quality, consistency, and clarity in all USCIS communications. Previously, he served as the chief of the Media Division at USCIS. Before entering federal service he was VP for communications for the Military Officers Association of America (MOAA) where he was responsible for public relations, communication strategy, and publishing.
>
> Withington retired from the U.S. Army in 2014 as a public affairs officer after 28 years of active duty. He served as a communicator at all levels, including division, Department of the Army, joint command, and the Office of the Secretary of Defense. He built almost 20 years of experience leading integrated communication strategies in complex and fast-paced environments, both domestically and overseas. He has a master's degree in integrated communication from the University of South Carolina.

The basic series of questions for which we usually need to discover the answers are

1. Where does the organization, product, or situation; the problem, challenge, or opportunity about which you need to communicate stand right now, today? Depending on the type of organization or the situation that could include additional questions such as: Is it successful? Just starting/being introduced? Losing or making money? Buying or selling? Has there been an accident or death? Are publics, stakeholders, or constituents involved? Is there a management problem or change? Is this a new or recurring situation? Is there something new happening? Is a new idea being attempted?

2. What has historically happened with the organization, product, or situation? Is there a history you can look at to get some background to what's happening?

3. How significant is what they're facing in terms of the overall organization?

4. What else do you need to find out before you're comfortable communicating about the problem, challenge, or opportunity?

It is at this point in defining the problem when it should become clear to us, or to our managers who are coordinating the preliminary fact finding, whether this is a situation in which media relations can help. If you, or they, believe it can, it's time to take the next step into primary research.

Once we recognize what we don't know, we can move on to additional research such as collecting background information we don't have immediately at hand, conducting a management or client interview to get more details, or doing some secondary research to see how other organizations might have handled a similar situation. From there we can determine if we need additional data that can only be obtained through surveys, or more insight that could come from focus groups or interviews with those in the affected departments or constituencies. Whatever the case, you will be working in conjunction with your managers and usually in cooperation with other communicators in your department or unit who will be focusing on additional aspects of the campaign, plan, or communication that needs to take place.

Determining If Media Relations Can Help

We all want what we do to matter to our organization. When it comes to media relations we seem to work for one of two very different types of organization. One type is an organization whose leaders want nothing to do with the media, and count on us to buffer them from reporters, and keep a low profile about both the positives and the negatives that go on in the business. Or we may work for an organization in which the management is looking for all the traditional media and digital attention it can possibly get, as long as it's positive. Of course, they're not too fond of negative media or online attention and look to us to protect them from reporters when something bad is happening.

Given those very different viewpoints, deciding whether media relations is called for in a particular situation can be a challenge. Thinking back to earlier chapters where we defined media relations, we know that media relations is about relationships with journalists; we know it involves using earned or shared media; we know that understanding why journalists consider a story newsworthy is essential, as is making sure your story is newsworthy, and you are being aware of the needs of various journalists and their media; and we know that there are a number of theories that can help guide us as we write the story.

Information from a chapter by Lynn Zoch and Juan-Carlos Molleda in the book *Public Relations Theory II,* which uses the principles of framing, information subsidies, and agenda building to determine the need to initiate media relations, can be useful in your thinking. It is set out in Table 3.1 in the theory chapter. Based on their literature review and previous research, the chapter tells us there are four situations where media relations is called for.[7] We have updated them here to take social media into account. The situations are (1) when the organization recognizes that it is taking some action that will affect one or more of its stakeholders or constituents; (2) when a public—see Chapter 4 for a discussion of publics—reacts before the organization does about an issue or situation that affects that public; (3) where a real-world or online event creates negative consequences for the organization; (4) when media, either online or traditional, report a problem or issue that involves the organization before media relations within the organization is able to send the information out themselves.

As with other topics we have discussed in this chapter, making a list of what is facing the organization in a specific situation can be useful. Because we're trying to be general here, and are not writing about any one particular situation, thinking of the questions you need to answer will work as well. Below is a general list of questions to use to determine if media relations can help address a problem that has affected your organization. You can make your list of what to do next based on your answers. If you find yourself answering YES to the questions that indicate this is a problem or opportunity that will interest or affect a broad audience, then you should move forward with a media relations plan. If it appears the situation only affects a limited number of stakeholders or constituents who can be reached in another way, then you need to talk with your supervisor about other alternatives.

Making the Most of Media Relations

Once you've decided, or your manager has decided for you—a point we will discuss later in this chapter—that it is appropriate to use media relations as part of the solution to your current issue or situation, another question is raised—*How and where can media relations be helpful?*

As a media relations practitioner, our job is to build relationships with journalists and other information disseminators so that we become trusted sources of information for them. We become trusted over time once we prove again and again that we can provide newsworthy information that is interesting to the journalist's audience, in a timely manner and in a form that fits the medium in which they're working. Therefore, the *how* of the question above is fairly easy to answer. As we discussed in Chapter 7, "Assessing News," part of our jobs is knowing the style and the newsworthiness values of the media we are targeting. We can be helpful by reaching out to journalists we have cultivated over time, who write in media our audiences pay attention to, and who have come to trust us to provide them with communication they can rely on to help them fulfill their jobs.

The major decision we have to make in terms of *how* we can be most helpful is to determine the form of communication we use. Do we call or email journalists first to pitch the story? Is the information in the form of a straightforward news story, a feature story, or even a news feature? Does it warrant a letter to the editor or should it be an opinion piece in the newspaper? Do we need to provide sources to be interviewed, or photos, maybe audio or video? Is the situation serious enough to call a media conference—in person or online—to reach

---

How to Determine If Media Relations Can Be Useful for Communicating

1. What type of situation are you facing?
   a. Is it a problem? A crisis? Something negative that will get out anyway, and it will be better if the organization gets its position out first?
   b. Is it something positive and new? Something that will build the organization's reputation, help the community, or in some way enhance a group of stakeholders or constituents?
   c. Is it a regular occurrence about which upper management likes to get news out into the community?
2. Does it involve only one or two groups of constituents or stakeholders who can be best reached through direct or owned communication?
   a. Is there a more efficient and personal way to reach these groups?
   b. Does your organization want to establish a dialogue with stakeholders or constituents, or simply inform them about something?
3. Is it an issue or situation that is directly related to the organization's mission and goals?
   a. Would this be a strategic use of media relations or a tactic used because it's there, so why not use it?
4. Do you know from previous research what media your target audience pays attention to?
   a. Would shared media be better to use than earned?
   b. Do you have time to do the demographic and psychographic research necessary if you don't know the audience's media choices?
5. Is this an issue or situation that involves or would interest a broad enough audience to justify outreach to media in areas where you do not currently have relationships?

---

all our media contacts—or even those outlets we seldom work with—all at one time? Depending on the situation, any of these forms of communication, or a mixture of several, might be the answer that achieves the widest or most targeted coverage.

The question of *where* media relations can be most helpful may be the complicated part of the question. It depends on the size, type, and variety of audiences that are involved in the situation we're facing at the time. And, as discussed above, it also depends on the type of situation with which we're working.

If we cooperate with sales or marketing in publicizing new products, then we'll be targeting media broadly as potential customers can be almost anywhere. We might even find ourselves working with a brand or product influencer, or a blogger who writes about the kind of products our company produces.

If we work for a nonprofit that does fundraising events, the answer would be similar. We will want to reach out to potential donors or event attendees no matter where we can find them. The only concern in this case might be taking into consideration the geographic area from which we pull most of our clients, donors, or attendees.

Are the important audience members in a specific geographic region or a local community, or would the information be better suited to a professional or trade publication targeted toward our organization's purpose? If the issue involves a financial change within the organization, do we announce the situation broadly or reach out to the financial media?

Is our audience mainly on the Web? Then using social media might be the best way to go. No matter what the final decision is, we are best served by making certain we know the makeup of our ultimate audience prior to reaching out to our media contacts.

Helping Ourselves by Writing Useful, Targeted, and Measurable Objectives

Objectives will only help us if we write them early enough in the media relations process that they can help us to focus and direct our activities. The best time to set your media relations objectives is immediately after you, or other colleagues in your department, complete any research that needs to be done to better define the situation you're facing. You can then place the situation you're currently facing within the framework of the already established organizational and departmental goals. It is also important to remember that the most useful objectives to us as we move forward are the most specific. There are two kinds of objectives we should think about using.

Outcome Objectives are the first type, and have been termed "ultimate," "outcome," "final," or "impact objectives." They can help us measure our success with our final audience: the consumers, investors, volunteers, government officials, or other constituents we want to reach. They can also help us in measuring our success with our most *important* audience, the journalists we are targeting with our information.

Outcome objectives are generally used to measure whether we are able, through our media relations outreach, to inform or persuade our targeted audiences, *including the journalists with whom we work*, about something. Outcome objectives are commonly considered to have one of three purposes: (1) to inform, or seek learning in our constituents about an organization, an issue or a product or service, called knowledge objectives; (2) to seek to change or to reinforce how constituencies think about an issue or an organization, called attitude objectives; or (3) to try to change or reinforce how people actually act, called behavioral objectives.

These three purposes build on each other, and become a continuum, with information dissemination being the most basic: People need to know about something before they can have an attitude about it, either positive or negative. It's important for us to get our organization's point of view out there to its constituents. Quite often, media relations' role in moving our constituents along this continuum toward an action encouraged by the organization ends once we have disseminated information to the targeted media outlets. But media relations has also proved itself to be helpful in keeping topics or issues on the media's agenda, and that sort of repeated coverage may reach the point that attitudes or behaviors of targeted constituents begin to change. Unfortunately, as will be discussed in Chapter 11, it is almost impossible to know if it was media relations that caused any changes to occur to the ultimate audience.

When dealing with journalists, however, we are looking for a different kind of outcome or impact. The outcome we seek is publication, and for those of us in media relations it implies knowledge, attitude, and behavioral change. To achieve media placement, we are wise to set what are called output objectives for ourselves.

Output Objectives are the second type of objective used by communicators. They are also called process or action objectives and describe the actions or steps we will take to achieve our impact objective. Media relations, remember, is a process. We will take dozens of steps to build the trust and credibility that will persuade the journalist to consider our story or information for inclusion in their media outlet. These are the actions we take along the way to reach our ultimate goal of publication and they are specific, relevant, time bound, and easily measurable. They keep us on track.

To keep us on track in the fast-paced environment of media, our action objectives work best if they include specific dates, specific reporters or outlets, and specific actions we are going to take. They should tell us "who does what, when, and with which results,"[8] similar to the requirements for a simple lead in a story. What is it that you have to do, to achieve a particular result within a hard time frame? Using one of the goals we discussed earlier in the chapter, several examples of SMART action objectives would be

- By Tuesday, April 7, I will discuss with the three sergeants [fill-in names] of the precincts involved in the community policing initiative about having them talk with local reporters to describe the project and answer questions.
- By Friday, April 10, I will pitch the story about the new community policing initiative to the community reporters [fill-in names] at the local newspaper [list name] and the two local television stations [list call letters].

Being realistic is also essential when writing your output or action objectives. As we discussed earlier in the chapter, be certain that what you're setting out to accomplish is truly doable. Don't think you can do five interviews in a day when you already know you have three in-person meetings scheduled and a deadline to complete an update of the organization's online newsroom.

Managing Organizational Expectations

Another component of media relations is being able to work within the expectations of the managers and leaders in your organization. Earlier in this chapter, when we were discussing how to make the decision about whether to use media relations, we indicated that you often don't get to make the choice yourself. You are told by your manager, or even upper management, to reach out to the media. This can occur even when you are not convinced this is going to be productive in a specific situation.

To be successful in media relations, it is important for you to be proactive about educating your manager and other leadership about your job from almost your first day with the organization. Everyone in an organization doesn't automatically understand what is required to achieve media coverage, or what they can expect from media coverage. It's essential to your success as the liaison between the media and your organization that your leadership *does* understand. As we mentioned earlier, few CEOs and other upper managers have an accurate view of what media relations can achieve. The first expectations you will face are the ones built on an inaccurate idea of what media relations is and what it can accomplish for an organization. Leaders at this level tend to believe that media relations will either solve all their problems, or that dealing with reporters will cause more problems for the organization. Few managers, except those in public relations, have any idea how much work goes into developing a relationship with journalists and other information disseminators. Nor do they realize how difficult it can be to get news covered, even when you are providing the journalist with everything they need. The news cycle is as uninteresting to most upper managers as the lunar cycle, and social media can be something to be feared rather than leveraged because of how quickly information, particularly negative information about an organization, travels.

Setting up expectations about what having an active media relations program means for an organization, and then educating upper management as well as your direct superior about those expectations, is a good place to start. As Zoch and Molleda pointed out in their chapter that builds a model of media relations,

> Although the media relations practitioner may not, herself, be part of an upper management team, she must have open access to those in upper management and keep direct communication open with important

sources such as the CEO, CFO, president, or vice presidents of important divisions or functions with the organization. . . . [E]mployees such
as media relations practitioners who are expected to interact quickly and
accurately with important external publics must be accorded direct access
to the sources they need to accurately explain the organization's stand on
issues of concern.[9]

When you are gathering information to write your media releases, update the
organization's online newsroom, or respond to a reporter's questions, you may at
times need the cooperation of upper management. They need to know that to the
journalists you work with *they* are the most credible sources, not you, the media
relations practitioner. Upper management also needs to know that you will lose
your own credibility as a representative of the organization if you can't get information from them quickly, or you aren't able to schedule one of them with a
timely interview requested by a reporter. None of this will benefit the organization or its ability to work with the media in the future.

Key Concepts

During the media relations process it is essential to always remember that what
we do works to support and fulfill our organization's mission, goals and objectives, and to support its strategic plan. Overall, the emphasis in this chapter is
about how media relations professionals must connect the many pieces of what
we do to the whole—the organization. Even if you are the sole media relations
person in the organization, you will work in a team with others to help the organization fulfill its mission.

We define the concepts of *goals* and *objectives*, differentiate between them and
discuss *outcome* and *output objectives*. We discuss the importance of writing objectives that are SMART—*specific, measurable, attainable/achievable, relevant,* and
time-based—and give the reader a chance to critique some objectives.

The concept of a *strategy* is defined and the importance of *thinking strategically* is explained and discussed.

We take the reader step by step through preparatory stages in the media relations process, starting with determining if media relations should even be a part
of the particular communication outreach you are considering, through writing
your own objectives and making the most of the media outreach.

The chapter ends by briefly discussing the need to deal with preexisting attitudes about media relations among management in the organization. We also
address the necessity for you to make clear to organizational leaders that you have
expectations of them that they must fulfill for the organization to successfully
achieve relationships with journalists.

Challenge Case[10]

In May 2019, New York City's city council proposed a ban on selling products made from fur, keeping in line with other cities such as Los Angeles and San Francisco. New York, however, is the largest fur market in the country so the protests were much larger and louder than in the other cities. Both sides of the ban issue held protests. Each side has at least one celebrity to help them gain attention. What was unusual, however, were two of the groups that opposed the ban: Black pastors and Hasidic rabbis.

The pastors, all members of a group called Mobilizing Preachers and Communities told the *New York Times* that "in our culture, fur is a sign of status, achievement, that we've made it against all odds." They also said that to ban selling fur in NYC but to have it available in stores in Westchester County, just north of the city, would be culturally insensitive.

Hasidic rabbis also reacted to the cultural insensitivity as many Hasidic Jewish men wear fur hats. A Jewish councilman expressed concerned that those men who continued to wear their old fur hats might become victims of hate crimes.

You have been offered a freelance opportunity to conduct media relations for the group Mobilizing Preachers and Communities.

1. Using the information in this chapter, write an overall organizational goal for this group.
2. Now, think—and write—about the sorts of research you would have to do to learn more about both the organization and this particular issue they've become involved in. This will help you define the issue you've been hired to help with.
3. Develop three SMART media relations objectives for the organization.

REFERENCES

1. Nager, N. R., & Allen, T. H. (1984). *Public relations management by objectives.* New York, NY: Longman; Grunig, J. E., & Hunt, T. (1984). *Managing public relations.* Fort Worth, TX: Harcourt Brace College Publishers.
2. Nager & Allen, p. 60.
3. Doran, G. (1981). There's a SMART way to write management goals and objectives. *Management Review, 70*(11), 35–36.
4. Nager & Allen, p. 60.
5. Anderson, E. (2010). Being strategic: Plan for success; Out-think your competition; stay ahead of change. http://erikaandersen.com/books/being-strategic
6. Smith, R. D. (2002). *Strategic planning for public relations.* Mahwah, NJ: LEA.

7. Zoch, L. M., & Molleda, J.-C. (2006). Building a theoretical model of media relations using framing, information subsidies, and agenda building. In C. H. Botan & V. Hazleton, (Eds), *Public relations theory II* (p. 297). Mahwah, NJ: LEA.

8. Nager & Allen, p. 60.

9. Zoch & Molleda, p. 296.

10. Information developed from a story in the *New York Times*, May 15, 2019, titled "Proposed fur ban in New York pits animal rights advocates against black ministers." Downloaded May 15, 2019. https://www.nytimes.com/2019/05/15/nyregion/fur-ban-nyc-sales.html?action=click&module=Top%20Stories&pgtype=Homepage

TOOLS OF THE TRADE

In Chapter 3 we introduced you to *information subsidies,* the name for the source-delivered news products that we share with journalists and other disseminators and influencers of information. In this chapter, we will explore the various written tools that act as information subsidies, and also some of the tactics that we use as part of an overall strategic media relations program. Many people consider these tools and tactics to be the heart of media relations, and while that may not be entirely accurate—because the center of media relations is the relationship between the practitioner and journalist—they are the building blocks for forming working relationships with journalists.

Many blog articles, professional advice columns, and industry articles discuss working with tools and tactics in media relations. Entire books are dedicated to the various types of public relations writing. To examine each written tool and explore the broad range of tactics available to media relations practitioners would take far more pages than are in this book. This chapter is designed to be a starting point in which we examine some of the most used and fundamental tools and tactics, with the hope that you will use the information to come up with creative and effective ways to share information with journalists.

Thinking About Writing

In its 2019 "Global State of the Media Report,"[1] Cision states "it's more important than ever to write for the end consumer." So far, we've been discussing the journalist—or other information disseminator—as the end audience. After all, they are the ones we are trying to build a relationship with. But when it comes to writing, there are high expectations for the media relations practitioner. Not only must we be adaptable to the needs of multiple journalists—we must also be able to write for a variety of journalists' publications and audiences. In the days before the explosion of media outlets and content, media relations practitioners could rely on a single style guide for print, and industry standards for broadcast. Today, with increased competition and nearly unlimited web-based platforms and outlets, publications have increasingly sought to differentiate themselves to audiences by providing different perspectives and approaches to information. Thus, the key to effective writing in media relations is to understand the nuances and expectations of each publication and its audience.

The goal for the media relations practitioner is to balance effective writing with strategic relationship building. Another way to look at it is the need to produce written subsidies that balance the organization's messaging goals with the goals of the journalist and their outlet. Most of the time this is fairly simple; but as more outlets seek to gain traction in a saturated information world, they have adopted a unique "**voice**" for their outlet. The voice of a publication refers to the tone and style used by a media outlet to connect with its audience. Often, journalists will have their own style, or voice, as well. Success in creating subsidies often depends on the media relations practitioners' ability to meld the organizational voice with that of the journalist and the outlet.

Think about it—have you ever been in a place with people who speak a different language than you and you needed to ask someone for directions? If you're insistent, and the native speaker is willing to work with you, eventually you will probably figure out where you need to go. If you have information for a journalist that holds great value, then you might find success no matter what, but good media relations practitioners know their chances of success are greatly increased when they speak the language of the journalist.

Look at the next page for two examples of voice in an outlet. Each of these stories addresses the same topic, and each was written from the same social media announcement. See if you can differentiate the voice in each story.

As you may have discerned from the stories, one outlet reported on this unexpected news in a straightforward, though light-hearted way; the other, a more cynical approach. Ultimately, the embassy office in Vienna was able to generate media coverage of its announcement, though clearly, the voice of the organization (the embassy) was more present in one outlet than the other.

The ability to be able to write clearly, succinctly, and with an audience and purpose in mind are essential to becoming an effective media relations practitioner. Writing for media relations is not an innate characteristic, it must be learned and nurtured. You may have even had the experience of taking a writing exam as part of a job or internship interview. Often, these exams are not designed to see if you know the specific styles and technical aspects of writing, but rather whether you are aware of some of the most basic aspects of media relations

McDonald's in Austria Will Double as Mini U.S. Embassies for Tourists in Need of Help

American tourists will soon be able to get more than a Big Mac at McDonald's in Austria. The U.S. Embassy in Vienna announced on Facebook that Golden Arches restaurants in Austria will serve as mini embassies for American tourists, starting Wednesday. "American citizens traveling in Austria who find themselves in distress and without a way to contact the U.S. Embassy can enter—as of Wednesday, May 15, 2019—any McDonald's in Austria, and staff will assist them in making contact with the U.S. Embassy for consular services," the announcement read.

Consular services include reporting a lost or stolen passport or seeking travel assistance.

The post featured a picture of United States Ambassador to Austria Trevor Traina and Isabelle Kuster, managing director of McDonald's Austria, shaking hands over the signed agreement and a cup of McCafe coffee.

In a statement to Independent.co.uk, McDonald's spokesperson Wilhelm Baldia said the U.S. Consulate selected the fast-food company because of the "brand's great fame among Americans."

Although employees at the restaurants will not be able to issue passports, they will be trained to help U.S. citizens contact the embassy 24/7 for such services, Baldia added. Naturally, social media users poked fun at the new collaboration.

"Can I get a vanilla shake with my visa please?" one user joked, while another added, "I will have small coffee, egg mcmuffin and a passport, on the side please."

USA Today reached out to McDonald's for comment.[2]

Fries With That? In Most American Move Ever, US Outsources Austria Consular Service to . . . McDonald's

Distressed American tourists who are not lovin' their time in Austria will soon be able to seek urgent assistance at the nearest McDonald's, thanks to the US Embassy in Vienna signing a deal with the iconic fast food joint.

Yes, you read that right.

The US embassy in Austria recently announced via its Facebook page that Ambassador Trevor D. Traina had signed the agreement with the McDonald's Austria boss Isabelle Kuster.

As part of the deal, McDonald's restaurants across Austria will be granted permission to offer consular assistance to Americans who are *"in need"* and unable to reach the embassy by phone, starting May 15.

I have some questions.

Firstly, why would one not be able to contact the embassy by phone? Surely most American tourists have both phones and access to the internet (to check the number) via those phones? For those who do not have a phone or internet access, couldn't they simply ask a travel companion or nearby stranger? If they are in the vicinity of a McDonald's anyway, there's probably already someone around who could help.

Then there's the logistics of how this would work at McDonald's itself.

Do you go in and stand in line, as if you're planning to order a Big Mac like everyone else? Or will there be a separate line especially for distressed Americans?

What about the staff? Will they need training for this, or are they literally just going to be making a phone call to connect people to the embassy proper? Even if that's all they are doing, isn't it a bit odd to have random Austrian citizens essentially working as intermediaries on behalf of the US government?

I mean, there's upskilling and then there's really upskilling—and it's probably fairly unlikely that Austria's McDonald's employees bargained for this when they signed up. There's a big difference between apologizing for a messed-up burger order and dealing with a panic-stricken tourist who just had their passport stolen.

Also, why Austria? Do US citizens find themselves in distress in Austria at a higher rate than other countries?

So, so many questions.

McDonald's spokesman Wilhelm Baldia told the Independent that the company had been chosen to attain mini-embassy status due to *"the great fame of the brand"* among Americans and because there are a lot of branches of the fast-food restaurant in Austria. Americans will be able to report lost or stolen passports or seek travel assistance at the restaurants, he said.

I can't help but imagine that iconic scene at the end of "Not Without My Daughter," when an exhausted but determined Sally Field finally arrives at the US Embassy in Ankara and sees the American flag flying above its gates . . . only this time she's arrived at the nearest McDonald's and is gazing up at those iconic yellow arches instead. Doesn't quite pack the same emotional punch.

Unsurprisingly, the news was met with mixed reaction on Facebook, with some feeling the McDonald's–embassy deal was a genius idea, while other Americans (quite understandably) felt rather mortified by the whole thing.

"Introducing the McVisa," one wrote sarcastically, while another wondered if her fellow Americans were *"too incompetent"* to contact their embassy without assistance from McDonald's employees. *"...can we be more of a meme in the world?!"* she wrote.

Anyway, there is a perfect aptness to the fact this deal happened in the era of Donald Trump—well-known for his own love of McDonald's fast food. If nothing else, he's probably fairly happy about it.[3]

writing, namely, the ability to convey information in a persuasive form. Brody and Lattimore,[4] writing in an era before the Web, social media, and the proliferation of voices across the information landscape, gave five points (which hold true today) to consider when preparing to write:

1. The audience or group to which the message is to be addressed;
2. The objective or result that the message is designed to accomplish;
3. The benefit or primary reason that the audience will be given to behave as the writer desires;
4. Support in the form of information that will convince the reader that the promised benefit will materialize; and
5. The tone or manner in which the information will be presented.

If you, as a writer in your media relations career, can identify, understand, and execute on these five considerations, you are likely well on your way to success.

Thinking About Written Tools as Subsidies

Perhaps an even greater challenge to the media relations practitioner is choosing among the variety of written tools and tactics to communicate with journalists. Public relations, as an industry, has multiple tools, tactics, and strategies for various audience—but for those engaged in media relations, the various types of information subsidies are integral to relationship development.

In thinking about information subsidies and their use by media relations practitioners, we can classify them by how they are used. **Primary subsidies** are those that are meant to be directly communicated to journalists, with or without a preexisting relationship. Those subsidies include pitches and media alerts. **Secondary subsidies** are tools that are designed to be used to augment a conversation, to provide additional background information, or to otherwise act in a supporting role to the relationship between media relations practitioners and journalists. Secondary subsidies include such tools as backgrounders, biographies, FAQ sheets, b-roll footage, or canned audio. The final type of subsidies are **focused subsidies**, which are used as part of a specific media relations tactic. Focused subsidies include such tools as speeches, op-ed columns, letters to the editor, and white papers. We will address each of the types of subsidies later in this chapter.

The Press Release

Many readers of this book probably read the previous paragraph and thought, *where do press releases belong?* It's a valid question, with a not-so-simple answer. The truth is they can be classified as any of the types of subsidies, depending on how they are being used. So the best way to categorize press releases is to put them in a category of their own.

The press release has been called many things: the workhorse of public relations, the engine that drives media relations and, by your authors, the single most-used and misused tool in the public relations toolbox. In fact, in a dissertation published in 2008,[5] interview respondents stated their doubts that press releases would even be "a thing" in a decade. Turns out, press releases are still very much "a thing" today. So what is a press release? It is a brief announcement of information, written in the style of the targeted media outlet, used to announce information from an organization. The ultimate goal of a press release is that it could appear, as written, beside another story in a media outlet and not stand out as being decidedly different. In the past, the press release was used to provide journalists with a story that was "ready for print." Public relations practitioners would write the release, send it off to a media outlet and, hopefully with very minor editing, it would appear in the newspaper. Generally speaking, this only happened rarely—though it did happen!—and still happens today with very small weekly newspapers with little staff.

While press releases are still very much in use, that use varies greatly. There are times when a press release should be used for each of the subsidy types. As such, press releases today do not necessarily always use the traditional format taught in many writing courses—but the elements of the traditional format are as important now as they have ever been. While we, generally, no longer print and mail—or fax—press releases, many organizations still rely on the elements of traditional print releases in creating their own press releases. This has both positives and negatives. On the positive side, journalists are used to the traditional elements of releases, as they are devised in a way to mirror a story that would appear in a publication. Press releases are, traditionally, written using a headline, a dateline, and follow the inverted pyramid style of writing (putting the most important information at the beginning). Most releases use what journalists refer to as a "nut graf" as the first paragraph, that is, a short paragraph of six lines or fewer that contains all of the pertinent information to relay the basic elements of the information contained in the release. Many still attempt to use a quote in either the second or third paragraph as part of additional information and use the concluding paragraph as a call to action.

Some elements of traditional releases have fallen by the wayside in the world of modern media. The embargo date (the date on which the intended recipient can use the information) seldom appears. In Chapter 6, we looked at ethical concerns surrounding media embargoes. Today, distribution dates are often used. We are seeing less use of mailing addresses and increased use of cell phone numbers, emails, and social media handles as points of contact. And while many journalists may recognize the use of an endmark—the traditional ### that appears at the bottom of releases—there are a substantially increasing number of traditional and nontraditional journalists who do not recognize the significance of an end-mark, and more organizations are leaving them off their releases.

So while press releases have undergone some minor transformations, they generally have not changed substantially in the past 40 years. As we noted, this can be considered a positive because it allows media relations practitioners to share information with journalists in a format that is recognizable and easy to work with. However, using the same format nearly without change could also be considered a negative. Modern platforms, design, and interactive elements should allow media relations practitioners to create news releases that are compelling and can provide all of the information a journalist might need in a single release. Some organizations are starting to incorporate these types of elements into their releases, but they are far from the mainstay.

Instead the news release has, in many instances, been transformed into the **social media release**—that is, a social media post that contains many of the traditional elements of the news release. Earlier in the chapter, you read news stories from two different outlets, each of which was based off a social media release that appeared on an embassy's Facebook page. Social media releases are easy ways for organizations to include video, sound, links, and other elements that are otherwise cumbersome in a traditional print release. Social media releases also guarantee the release is published in its entirety, and all of the organizational messages are present. However, it does not mean that external media will necessarily link to the social media release or include the entirety of its content in any stories they disseminate.

Using the Press Release

Earlier, we discussed that press releases, as an information subsidy, can be used in a variety of ways. The best use of press releases is as a secondary subsidy, background information that can be sent if a journalist expresses an interest in more information about a story idea. Many organizations collect their press releases and archive them in their **online newsrooms** (a tactic that we will address later in this chapter). By archiving organizational news releases on a website, organizations are able to provide a repository to multiple audiences, but particularly journalists, who might be interested in learning more about the organization. Done well, usually using links embedded within the body of the release, news releases have the ability to increase the **search engine optimization (SEO)** of an organization. News releases, then, have the ability to serve the organization, and its journalistic audiences, in multiple ways as secondary subsidies.

News releases can, occasionally, also act as a primary subsidy. Many organizations utilize wire services, such as Cision PR Newswire, Business Wire,

	Business Wire — A Berkshire Hathaway Company	Nasdaq GlobeNewswire	NEWSWIRE	CISION — PR Newswire	CISION — PRWeb
Pricing - U.S. National Release	• $795 - First 400 Words • $220 - Additional 100 Words	• $580 - First 400 Words • $190 - Additional 100 Words	• $999 - First 400 words • $225 - Additional 100 Words	• $805 - First 400 Words • $245 - Additional 100 Words	$369
Distribution Network	• 89,000+ Outlets • 193 U.S. Industry and Trade Categories	• Global Newslines • Trade Media • Specialty Media	• 2 Distribution Networks - Newswire and PR Newswire • 4,500+ Site Distribution Network	• 10,000 Traditional and Online Media Points • Trade and Industry Publications are Included Based on Content	• Premium News Sites • Premier Outlets
Multimedia	Color Logo with Link	• Company Logo Included • Images/Video/Audio are Available at an Additional Cost	• Up to 4 Images • Embedded Video	Images, Video, and/or Logos are Available at an Additional Cost	• Images • Video • Links • Attachments
Analytics	• NewsTrak Report (Release Views, Traffic Sources, Multimedia Views, User Engagement) • Social Media Monitoring and Analytics	• Reach • Access • Social Media Engagement • Visibility	• Detailed Analytics Report • PR Newswire Visibility Report	PR Newswire Visibility Report	• Impressions • Reads • Shares • Traffic • Engagement • Keyword & Search Engine Referrals
Links	No Follow	No Follow	• On Newswire - Do Follow • Distribution Network is Majority No Follow to Adhere to Google Guidelines	No Follow	No Follow
Editorial Review	Included	Included	Included	Included	Included

FIGURE 9.1

GlobeNewswire, and others to reach journalists. Media relations practitioners pay a set amount, usually based on word count, for distribution of their releases to media outlets. Christine Slocumb, founder and president of Clarity Quest Marketing, put together the information presented in Figure 9.1, that represents the costs involved in popular wire services.[6] The costs for each of the services found in the figure were accurate as of January 2018.

By using a wire service, the press release becomes a primary information subsidy. As journalists will have access to the release even if they don't have a preexisting relationship with the media relations practitioner, the wire service provides an opportunity to start a relationship. Wire services also provide an opportunity to have analytics accompany the distribution of the release, an important element we will address further in Chapter 11.

Finally, press releases can also serve a purpose as a focused subsidy. Press releases can be written with the intention of distributing them as a stand alone or as part of a **press kit** for a specific event. These releases are usually written to be used as a subsidy unique to the event, such as a **speech** or a **press conference** (we will address each of these tactics and tools in greater detail later in this chapter). As a focused subsidy, the intent of the press release is to provide a baseline story for journalists who are covering the event, with the hope that journalists might adopt the story frame the organization is advocating, and then supplement that frame with additional information or quotes. While journalists will often not tolerate being asked to write a story using a particular frame, the news release as a focused subsidy allows the organization to plant the seed of a story idea in an acceptable format.

Overall, when thinking about how and when to use a press release, particularly through a wire service, the key is to be strategic in their use. Writing many releases and sending them over the wire *might* result in *some* media coverage, but that coverage may not be meaningful to your organization. Putting a large number of releases in an online newsroom *could* help a journalist discover information about your organization, but if it is unorganized or overwhelming, the journalist may decide to move on. Social media releases *can* serve as effective tools for communicating with multiple audiences, but if journalists are only engaged with you on social platforms, then you are not maximizing the releases' potential.

The press release remains the workhorse of media relations. It is an integral subsidy that is dynamic and has many uses. But the key to effective news releases can be found in the considerations brought up earlier—*Who is the audience? What is the purpose? Why will the audience care? What other forms of information are you providing?* and, *How are you presenting the information?* If you cannot answer each of these questions about your release *and* relate them back to your overall media relations objectives, then you may want to reconsider whether the press release is the right subsidy for you.

Primary Subsidies

For the most part, we don't use subsidies in the traditional sense, as a means of reaching out to journalists. That is, we should not plan on sending a journalist a subsidy for the purpose of establishing a relationship. The goal for media relations practitioners is to establish effective and mutually beneficial relationships with journalists, and simply sending them some information will not usually accomplish that. There are three general exceptions to this axiom. The first was covered in the previous section, where a press release sent via a wire service acts as a primary subsidy. The second primary subsidy is the **media pitch**. The media pitch, while not normally considered an information subsidy, does relay information intended to be used by a journalist in creating a news story. Therefore, we can consider them information subsidies—though they are also much more than that. Media pitches are such an integral aspect to media relations that we are going to spend the entirety of Chapter 10 addressing them.

That leaves us with one more exception where we can use an information subsidy as a primary contact tool, though most good media relations practitioners know that primary subsidies—outside of the media pitch—will nearly always have more impact with journalists if there is an existing relationship. There will be times, though, that a media alert will serve as a primary subsidy.

A **media alert** is information that is meant to let the media know about an upcoming event or a news item of significant importance—this is the rarer of the two uses. It usually contains a brief description of an event, the time and location, and any other pertinent information that a journalist would need to know to cover the event, such as whether a press pass is needed, if parking is available, and whether there will be an opportunity for interviews or photos. An example of this type media alert is below.

As you can see, the media alert is purely an informational subsidy, but it can be used as a primary subsidy. For example, you may be holding an event such as the one in our example. You will likely have already let journalists you work with on a regular basis know about the event, but you may also have an entire media list full of journalists with whom you have not yet established a relationship, but that you know cover your industry. A media alert sent to these journalists as an email blast might encourage some of those journalists to reach out to you with questions, requests for press passes, or even come to the event. Any of these potential interactions is an opportunity for you, as a media relations practitioner,

---

MEDIA ALERT—GOVERNOR TO ATTEND GROUNDBREAKING OF NEW UNIVERSITY GREENHOUSE TO ANNOUNCE NEW GREEN INITIATIVE

WHAT: Governor Christine Johnson will attend the groundbreaking of the new Randolph State University Greenhouse to announce her new state initiative and incentive program for sustainable farming subsidies.

WHEN: March 27, 2019. 2:30 p.m.

WHERE: 1740 Border Lane, on the Randolph State University campus, between the law school and administration building.

WHO: Speakers will include Randolph State president Robert Matthews, Governor Christine Johnson, Randolph Mayor Tess Woods, Drs. Mary Smith and Mark Johnson, NASA Engineering Corps.

BACKGROUND: The new Randolph State University greenhouse is a state-of-the-art structure designed to allow for year-round, sustainable farming. The greenhouse is designed for use in multiple climates, and is a working model of the structures NASA has in the works for farming on Mars. The governor will be announcing a new tax incentive for state farmers who plan to incorporate sustainable farming practices. Following the ceremony, all speakers will be available for Q&A.

IF YOU GO: Media passes not required. Designated media parking will be located behind Merrill Quad complex. On-site hookups available for live feeds. Please call Kim Fernandez at 242-764-7811 if you require special broadcast accommodation.

ADDITIONAL: Please visit www.randolphgreenhouse.edu for background information and downloadable photos, graphics, and video.

to begin to establish a relationship with those journalists. Sending out a media alert should be the only time that you ever use an email blast.

However, just because you can do a thing doesn't mean that you necessarily should. If you decide to use a media alert, you should ensure that the event you are inviting journalists to attend is truly newsworthy. Or, in the rarer situation, if you issue a media alert and accompanying email blast to make an announcement, it is exceptionally important that the information is truly significant, and it is important to get it out to the media quickly. For example, if you are working at an organization that produces a food product and you need to issue an immediate recall of the product due to contamination, then a media alert would be appropriate. On the other hand, if you are using media alerts to blast out information about regional manager promotions at retail stores, you will likely be considered to be the media relations practitioner who "cried wolf," and the next time you send out a media alert, no one is likely to pay attention.

Some organizations are able to use media alerts to announce events that will draw journalists out whether they have preexisting relationships or not. Imagine if Apple were to send out a media alert announcing an event to introduce a new product line. You can probably imagine nearly any journalist, influencer, or blogger who received that alert would want to go. The same might be true for the mayor's office in a small town with just a few media outlets. For those of us who fall somewhere between the largest of corporations and the smallest of towns, we need to think strategically about when and how to use the media alert to ensure that journalists will pay attention. Our goal is to be able to capitalize on that attention to develop new relationships.

Secondary Subsidies

Secondary subsidies consist of those types of information that are most traditionally thought of as information subsidies. This is the information that truly provides the background knowledge about organizations, people, and events that journalists use as part of their research. Traditionally, secondary subsidies were printed documents that a media relations practitioner would have on hand to give or send to journalists who requested more information. These subsidies generally have a longer "shelf life" than other types of subsidies, that is, they are often constructed and only updated when the information they contain changes, so they can be used for an extended period of time without substantial rewriting.

Many organizations still use secondary subsidies in a format that is similar to the traditional printed version, though they are put on web pages or stored in some other electronic format, which is often referred to as the **online newsroom**. We will be discussing the online newsroom as a tactic later in this chapter—suffice to say, some organizations are beginning to use more advanced graphic and video formats for their secondary subsidies. As we discuss each of the following subsidies, we will explore ways to make them more interactive.

One of the most used secondary subsidies is the **backgrounder**. A backgrounder can be used to provide information about an organization, an event, a product, or nearly anything for which a media relations practitioner may need to provide further information. The information in a backgrounder usually follows either a chronological, or reverse chronological, approach, but it should always try to answer the *who, what, where, when, why,* and *how* questions for journalists. The goal of the information in a backgrounder should be twofold—first, the backgrounder should provide the information that a journalist would *likely* need in writing an article. Therefore, when constructing the backgrounder, media relations practitioners should take care to pay attention to elements of newsworthiness and to the general principles of journalism.

The second goal in providing information in the backgrounder should be to provide content that may not be *readily* available to journalists. As backgrounders should generally be limited to 250–300 words (about the length of a double-spaced page), space is at a premium, and therefore media relations practitioners need to carefully choose what information they present. If the backgrounder includes commonly known facts or information that is easily obtainable via web search, then it becomes less effective as an information subsidy.

Backgrounders, in their traditional format, are exceptionally useful to media relations practitioners as they provide ready-made information to send to journalists. However, practitioners should also ensure they are useful for journalists. One way to do this is to take advantage of organizational websites and social media channels to make sure you have information available in several places in multiple formats. Creating content that augments written communication serves the purpose of engaging more with journalists. For example, if you are handling the media relations surrounding the opening of a new building on a campus, there are many additions to written information you could provide. You might create a video tour of the building, a time-lapse video of the construction, recorded interviews with builders and administrators, floor plans, or photos. All of this content can accompany a written description and could be used by the journalist in their story. Ultimately, the goal of all information subsidies is to make journalists' jobs easier, so anything you can do that helps attain that goal is time well spent.

In addition to backgrounders, media relations practitioners use **biographies** as secondary subsidies. A biography is basically a backgrounder for a person. Most biographies, in their static format, are about a page long. They too can be formatted in different ways according to the organization's style and to the preferences of the person being featured. A common use of the biography is to provide information about those people journalists most often write about: the organization's leader—or CEO—or founder, members of boards of directors, or senior leadership. More commonly, the **profile** is used on organizational web-sites. A profile is a shorter version of a biography, usually two to three sentences, that highlights only the most important aspects of an individual. However, the terms "biography" and "profile" are often used interchangeably, depending on the organization.

Biographies, and profiles, are also ripe for interactive content on web-based platforms—either organizational sites or social media channels. Examples of interactive content include video interviews, downloadable photos, and timelines. Once again, any information that might be useful for a journalist writing an article should be included with biographies.

A **visual** subsidy has the ability to play an important role in developing relationships with journalists by providing them with information that is easily digested and can be used for a variety of purposes. This could take the form of an infographic, which is a visual representation of data; a headshot, a chart, a video; interactive graphics; or some other form of visual representation of information. These are usually sent with the permission of the journalist ahead of time. As news consumption becomes increasingly visual, more journalists are incorporating these elements into their stories. Whereas space was once at a premium in printed outlets, the Web allows for increased use of visuals, thus creating an opportunity for media relations practitioners to share their stories in ways beyond the written word. Media relations practitioners today should take the time to determine if it is possible to tell their story using visuals, or to at least supplement their information with a visual, and to also ensure that they let the journalist know that such visuals exist.

The final secondary subsidy we will address in this chapter is the **Frequently-asked-question—FAQ—sheet**. Done well, this subsidy can be of great assistance to journalists, as it should contain a list of questions and answers that would typically be asked about the organization. Much like the biography and backgrounder, care should be taken when constructing the FAQ sheet to ensure the questions are not common knowledge or easily answered with a simple web search. Media relations practitioners should ensure the questions are journalistic, and the answers should be substantive. An idea some organizations employ is to hire a journalist as a consultant to help construct the questions on the FAQ sheet.

Traditionally, FAQ sheets are about a page long, or contain between eight and 12 questions and answers. Because the Web allows us to create pages of any length, this is no longer a hard limit in electronic format, but practitioners should attempt to keep the number of questions to fewer than 15, no matter where they appear. The only substantial difference in using FAQ sheets online versus in print is the potential that answers to questions can include links to other parts of the website, or perhaps include downloadable content as part of the answer.

If the press release is the workhorse of public relations, then secondary subsidies are the cart that is being pulled. They provide much of the information that journalists require to write a story, and by crafting the subsidies in an accessible and usable format, media relations practitioners are better able to provide value to the journalist. This, in turn, will—or should—help the relationship between the practitioner and journalist.

Focused Subsidies

Sometimes an information subsidy can have an initial non-media purpose, and then be repurposed later to provide information to journalists. This is the case with focused subsidies that are created for a specific reason but are then archived so that journalists who are following up or are seeking additional background information on a specific aspect of the organization might be able to use them. Focused subsidies, by their very nature, are usually time sensitive and therefore do not always hold up well over time. But they are good for historical purposes, as they can tell the story of an organization for a given topic at a given time.

Speeches are an example of a focused subsidy. It is likely that senior members of an organization will, from time to time, be invited to give speeches at community events, trade associations, graduations, or some gathering of stakeholders—volunteers, employees, shareholders, and so forth. When appropriate, media relations practitioners should take advantage of these opportunities by inviting media to attend the speech. However, in all cases, a recording of the speech and a copy of the speech should be captured. The video and the speech can then be retained, and in the event a journalist is interested in the material, it can be shared.

Another example of focused subsidies is an opinion-editorial, or the opposite-the-editorial, mainly known as an **op-ed column**. The op-ed column is a contributed column to a media outlet that traditionally appeared on the page opposite the editorial page in print newspapers. They are usually columns seemingly written by opinion leaders, organizational leaders, or experts. Many print newspapers carry on the tradition of high-profile op-ed columns, and many organizational leaders use the space as a platform to make statements of corporate philosophy, respond to crises, or get involved in social causes.

While the op-ed carries the byline of an organizational leader, they are often ghostwritten—though not always—by media relations practitioners, and usually go through multiple edits before being submitted for publication. The op-ed article is most commonly used as a response to a specific situation, which is why they are considered a focused subsidy. However, unlike many other types of subsidies, they are published with little, if any, editing by the outlet. They are also not the result of a relationship with a particular journalist, but rather a relationship with an outlet or with an editor, as the columns are generally planned in advance and are even sometimes written at the request of the media outlet. Like speeches, they have a great deal of archival value, and are often considered the official position of an organization when written. A **position paper** (or white paper) is the final type of focused subsidy we will address. A position paper is a document that is put out by an organization, often as the result of research or an internal thought exercise; it is written to examine a particular issue and to offer a stance, or to make a recommendation. Many trade associations, or membership organizations, use the position paper to make announcements on particular issues in which they are involved. Corporations, nonprofits, and nongovernmental organizations also use position papers.

The position paper, in terms of media relations, can be used as a subsidy because it acts as background information for an organization. However, as position papers can be lengthy, media relations practitioners will usually only share the executive summary of the paper, and then direct journalists to the full paper. It is vital that the media relations practitioner be thoroughly familiar with the contents of the position paper and, at a minimum, have the opportunity to review it before it is published. Like all focused subsidies, position papers are often developed to address a particular issue, but as they are usually based on research of some sort, their shelf-life tends to be longer than other types of focused subsidies.

As a whole, the focused subsidy is an effective tool for the media relations practitioner, particularly if the practitioner is able to link current or trending events in media coverage with preexisting subsidies that were produced by an organization. For example, if a topic such as urban farming is trending on social media, and your organization's CEO gave a speech on urban farming last year, then you as the media relations practitioner have the opportunity to bring that speech to a journalist's attention. By doing so, your organization might be viewed as a thought leader or early adopter about the topic. Therefore, the focused subsidy can have a positive impact for your media relations efforts, particularly if your organization is creating focused subsidies aligned with organizational goals.

The Boilerplate

A boilerplate paragraph is a short paragraph that was, in the past, often used at the end of every information subsidy that was sent to a journalist. Commonly they were found on press releases and secondary subsidies, but they could pop up just about anywhere on written materials. The purpose of the boilerplate paragraph is to provide a brief background about the organization on whose behalf the subsidy is being sent. If two organizations were announcing a joint venture, then sometimes two boilerplates would be used. One of your authors recalls a time in an earlier career where a short press release was distributed sharing news about an event that involved four organizations. Because of this, the release contained four boilerplate paragraphs—though the entire body of the press release was only three paragraphs. Talk about overloading a press release!

The boilerplate paragraph still exists today, though its use has waned greatly. The fact is, if media relations practitioners are doing their jobs, there should be no need for a boilerplate paragraph, outside of their possible use in press releases that will be sent via a wire service. Most journalists today who want to see a press release will either ask for it directly from the media relations practitioner, or they request a link to an archived release that is accessible from the organization's website. In other words, the boilerplate paragraph has become a redundancy, much like the embargo date on a subsidy.

The Media Kit

The media kit is also a subsidy, though it is more accurately described as a collection of subsidies that are meant to give journalists a complete picture of an organization. Traditionally called a press kit, they would often include such subsidies as news releases, backgrounders, biographies, FAQ sheets, print-ready photos, and perhaps copies of previous newspaper articles about the organization. These would all be gathered into a folder, and then mailed to journalists. Later on, as information was able to be stored, press kits often included CDs or flash drives with the material in digital format, or sometimes the entire press kit would be digitized and the mailing to the journalist would include only the data storage device. Press kits were often costly to produce and mail, but most organizations would keep a few dozen at a time on hand to send out as needed. The cost of mailing a press kit is one of the reasons public relations people often asked a journalist, "can I send you more information?" instead of just mailing one to all journalists they contact.

In today's digital world, media kits, as press kits have become known, are nearly all web-based. In fact, if an organization has a media kit at all, it is likely only available via download from the organization's online newsroom. But since all of the material that would normally belong in a media kit is already available in the online newsroom, most organizations are no longer using media kits in the traditional sense.

However, the traditional printed and mailed media kit is still occasionally used—although its purpose is no longer just to get information subsidies out to journalists. When used today, media kits are frequently elaborately produced, often using high-end printing and glossy photos, and they may even be packaged uniquely. In fact, today's media kits may cost upwards of a hundred dollars each to produce and mail. They are often only sent to journalists who routinely cover organizations, not so much as a media kit, but as a souvenir and as a brand-building exercise. Clearly, these types of media kits are less about information subsidies, but are instead a tactic to keep the organization prominently in the minds of these often-contacted journalists. This is but one of the many tactics media relations practitioners have at their disposal.

Traditional Tactics

In Chapter 6 we discussed some of the less ethical tactics media relations practitioners have used in the past—at least, tactics which belong in the past. Today, public relations practitioners can use multiple, ethical tactics to achieve a variety of objectives with a variety of audiences. Many times, the same tactics can engage a variety of audiences, though they are generally created with a specific audience in mind. In this section we will examine the tactics media relations practitioners traditionally use alongside written tools to disseminate information to journalists.

> **Media Pitching**: Media pitching is perhaps the most commonly used tactic in public relations. Its objective is to provide the journalist information directly through targeted, one-to-one communication. We briefly examined the media pitch as an information subsidy earlier in this chapter. As this is one of the most important skills in terms of executing media relations, we will examine media pitching in depth in Chapter 10.
>
> **Press Conference**: This is an event where the media are invited to a location to gather and hear information in the form of an announcement from an organization. Press conferences are effective at getting information out to a wide variety of journalists quickly, and they are often used by government bodies during crisis situations, or by organizations to announce new products or significant structural changes. The list goes on. People are perhaps most familiar with White House press briefings or postgame media availability of professional athletes, which are regularly scheduled press conferences, although outside of these briefings, most press conferences are not planned with such regularity.
>
> Press conferences are effective because they allow for journalists to receive information directly from an organizational source. Journalists are generally allowed a period of questions and answers, which allows them to gather more details to work into their particular story frame. Most organizations should take care when choosing to hold a press conference to ensure that media will be interested enough to show up. Usually, a media alert is used to announce a press conference.
>
> **Media Tour**: This is a tactic that involves traveling to different journalists so that they may conduct interviews with people working within your organization. In practice, this can be referred to as "doing the rounds" or "going on the circuit" to different outlets. This is most commonly seen in

promotion of new films or television shows where the star or stars may make guest appearances on late night talk shows, or a CEO will appear on each of the network morning news programs to discuss new initiatives or respond to a crisis. Media tours also occur outside of television. For example, a media relations practitioner may arrange for an out of town client to meet with multiple outlets throughout the course of a day or two, including print, broadcast and radio. The purpose of the media tour is to quickly disseminate information to a variety of journalistic audiences in a short period.

Satellite Media Tour: This is a variation of the media tour, but instead of traveling to different journalists, the organizational representative stays in the same place with a camera feed that outlets can access. A more modern version of the satellite media tour might involve a form of video conferencing, using a platform such as Skype or Zoom. The goal of the satellite media tour is the same as the traditional media tour, to engage with multiple journalists in a relatively short time.

Press Trips (or media trips): These are a traditional tactic used primarily in the travel and tourism industry, but can also be used for things such as factory tours, new building openings, or for events or clients that are difficult to access. This tactic involves inviting journalists, arranging transportation and lodging, and providing information so that journalists are able to engage with an event or organization. Press trips can range from highly elaborate and expensive—opening a new resort in Southeast Asia that you want American tourism journalists to write about—to very simple—arranging a tour for local journalists of a new LEED-certified building. The idea behind the press trip is to give journalists special access to something and make it as simple as possible for them to cover it.

Product Trial/Demonstrations: These are meant for journalists who generally write about specific product segments to allow them to sample a product for sufficient time to produce a review. Generally, the journalist will receive the product for a period of time to use/test/review it, and then return it to the company. While many media outlets have moved away from accepting free products in return for writing reviews, in some industries such as automotive and high-tech, product trials are still the norm.

Online Tactics

The Web and the ease of interaction via online platforms has allowed for a variety of new media relations tactics that further assist media relations practitioners to build effective relationships with journalists. Some of the traditional tactics can be adapted to use in online environments. For example, you might decide to hold a virtual press conference rather than a traditional, in-person one. You could also create virtual product demonstration through the use of interactive video, or you might create a virtual reality tour of a new facility that journalists could take via their personal devices. While these ideas are certainly creative and would likely increase journalistic interest in your organization, this section will examine several tactics that are unique to the modern media environment.

Online Newsroom: We've talked about the online newsroom several times throughout this book because it is one of the most important tools of the modern media relations practitioner. The online newsroom is a section of your organizational website dedicated to providing information to journalists. In the early days of the Web, these online newsrooms were sometimes password protected and, to gain access, you needed to request permission from the organization. Today, most are open, though some information, such as high-resolution images or video, may only be accessible to those who are verified journalists.

The online newsroom is an opportunity to gather all your organization's information subsidies in one place. Ideally, the online newsroom should contain all of the information needed for a journalist to write the "story of your organization." Effective online newsrooms include principles of dialogic communication,[7] meaning they ensure that there is useful information, an opportunity for journalists to leave comments or ask questions, a simple and easy to navigate interface, limited links to outside sites so that journalists are kept in the online newsroom for the information they're seeking, and that journalists are encouraged to come back to the page. The last is usually done by clearly showing the online newsroom is frequently updated with new information, an important component in an effective online newsroom.

The online newsroom is an integral tactic to the modern media relations professional. Practitioners should ensure that it provides for the needs of journalists. This might include a searchable database for organizational press releases; accessible logos, photographs, and video produced at a quality suitable for print, online, or broadcast; contact information so journalists are able to reach practitioners with questions—you might be amazed to know that many online newsrooms make it difficult to find a phone number or an email for a journalist to send an inquiry; and other content that provides background information. Effective newsrooms will also likely have links to other organizational content, though the links should either open a new window or guide the journalist to a branch of the organizational website or social media pages.

Branded Content: While the purpose of this book is to examine the relationship between media relations practitioners and journalists, to ignore branded content as a tactic in that relationship would be impossible. The online world allows for organizations to act, in a way, as a publisher of multiple types of content that can be geared toward a variety of audiences. While this content is generally designed to serve more as marketing communication than for the purpose of media relations, in an integrated world of communication, we know that journalists are often drawn to information that is outside the scope of material that is specifically sent to them. As a rule, media relations professionals need to remember that *any* information that is produced by an organization, whether a blog, social media page post, or even influencer partnerships, are subject to scrutiny by journalists.

Media relations practitioners should be part of the conversation when an organization is creating branded content. Journalists, and the public, often view much of this content as the authentic voice of the organization. While it is clearly owned media, and therefore not media relations, there are very real implications for media relations. Like any organizational public presence, branded content must be integrated into the overall media relations plan—lest the proverbial right hand will not know what the left one is doing.

Key Concepts

Media relations practitioners rely on multiple written tools and tactics to disseminate information to journalists. Some of these are traditional but are being adapted in new ways in order to find a place in today's connected world.

Practitioners should be mindful that information subsidies are meant to provide journalists with the background information needed to write a story. Practitioners can often suggest story ideas, but ultimately the journalist will make the choice in the way information is presented—therefore it is vitally important that the subsidies created for the journalist are accurate and up to date.

In the age of information, organizations are producing increasingly more content on their own, and for multiple audiences. It is imperative that the media relations practitioners have some input on that content, because without question, it will also be used by journalists who are covering the organization. Some of the biggest media relations crises in organizations today are caused by an errant social media post.

Challenge Case

On page 167 in this chapter, you were given a sample media alert for the opening of a university greenhouse. This event was designed to host journalists in a very traditional format, with photo opportunities and speeches by university and government officials, with time for questions from journalists. How would you turn this event into an online-only format? Go beyond simply creating a video of the event. What subsidies would you create to support a comprehensive, interactive and immersive online event designed for journalists who wanted to cover this program?

REFERENCES

1. Cision's 2019 State of the Media Report. (2019). Retrieved from https://www.cision.com/content/dam/cision/Resources/white-papers/2019_Q2_SOTM_report.pdf

2. McDonald's in Austria will double as mini U.S. embassies for tourists in need of help. (2019, May 14). *USA Today*. Retrieved from https://www.usatoday.com/story/travel/news/2019/05/14/mcdonalds-austria-double-mini-u-s-embassies-tourists/3672262002/

3. Fries with that? In most American move ever, US outsources consular service to . . . McDonald's. (2019, May 14). RT News. Retrieved from https://www.rt.com/news/459355-us-austria-embassy-mcdonalds/

4. Brody, E. W., & Lattimore, D. L. (1990). *Public relations writing.* New York, NY: Praeger.

5. Supa, D. W. (2008). Maximizing media relations through a better understanding of the public relations–journalist relationship. Open access dissertations, p. 144. Retrieved from https://scholarlyrepository.miami.edu/cgi/viewcontent.cgi?referer=https://scholar.google.com/&httpsredir=1&article=1143&context=oa_dissertations

6. Slocumb, C. (2018, January 29). Press release wire service comparison. Retrieved from https://www.clarityqst.com/blog/press-release-wire-comparison/

7. Kent, M. I., & Taylor, M. (1998). Building dialogic relationships through the world wide web. *Public Relations Review 24*(3), 321–334.

10 REACHING OUT, MAKING CONTACT, EARNING A RESPONSE

Understanding the strategy behind a media relations campaign is an important first step in finding success. But translating that strategy into action is often where public relations practitioners seem to struggle. This is frequently the case because expediency and results take precedence over strategy. Or sometimes it happens because your client—or your boss—is more interested in clicks, page views, or column inches than in impact. And sometimes, strategy gets left at the door through a faulty or outdated measurement metric—we'll discuss some of the problems with measurement in Chapter 11. No matter the reason, the execution of media relations must rely on the overall organizational strategy, objectives, and goals. We hope that, after reading this chapter, you'll be ready to implement effective media relations tactics that are aligned with your overall media relations plan.

Who to Target?

In Chapter 4 we looked at how to understand our multiple audiences. Now is the time to put that understanding into action. The whole time you have been developing your media relations plan, you've been thinking about your ultimate audience, that is, the consumers, investors, volunteers, government officials, and others who you want to reach. Now is the time to start strategizing about how you're going to reach them. You have a message that you want those audiences to pay attention to, a story to tell. Now you need to determine who's going to help you tell that story, your penultimate audience and, we always hope, your partner in information dissemination—a journalist. To do that, you're going to need a **media list**, a document comprised of the names and contact information of people who are likely to be interested in your story.

In the past, constructing a media list was a fairly simple and straightforward exercise, with little strategy involved. All you had to do was identify a geographic market and pinpoint the newspaper and maybe the handful of local radio and television stations and who worked there. You would then put together a document with their names, their beats, phone numbers, addresses, and the outlet they worked for. You might have a hundred or so names on your list in a bigger market, decidedly fewer in smaller markets. In those days, journalists tended to work for an outlet for a long period of time, so you might only need to make sure your list was updated once a year, if that often.

If you had to reach national audiences, your agency or company might invest in a series of media guides that did the initial work for you. These tomes contained virtually every professional journalist in the United States, broken down by state, with separate books for daily newspapers, radio stations, television, magazines—basically whatever you needed. All you had to do was find the correct listing in the right volume, and you would have access to all the information you needed. These yearly publications were available on a subscription basis and were considered the bibles for constructing media lists.

Why bring up the past? The point here is that getting your hands on media lists used to be a fairly simple proposition. If you knew where your ultimate audience was located, you could be fairly sure to find the contact information for the journalists who would reach that audience. Generally, the public relied heavily on their local media outlets, and perhaps a few national sources. Successfully constructing a media list wasn't dependent on strategy; it was primarily dependent on knowing who your audience was.

Putting together a media list today still relies on knowing your audience. But simply knowing their geographic location is probably not enough. People are accessing information from around the world literally from their fingertips via mobile devices, and may ignore their local, traditional media. Understanding your audience today means knowing where they seek information. Uses and gratifications is a theoretical perspective that helps us understand why people seek out and use various media, assuming the audience is actively seeking information. The theory indicates that audiences will utilize various media or media technologies based on whether the media fulfills certain needs, or gratifications. Broken down simply, the theory tells us that audiences may seek to fulfill their differing needs through a variety of media sources. Why is this important to know? It shows us that, particularly in the modern age of information, identifying how people seek information and the type of media they engage with, is more fluid than it has ever been—consequently, making the need for strategic decisions in constructing media lists more important than ever.

So how do we go about strategically constructing a media list? It seems the simple answer would be to gather as much contact information as possible, put it all on a giant list, and simply try to reach out to every possible journalist on the list every time you have a story idea . . . except this is likely the worst way to practice effective media relations. In Chapter 1, we discussed the hitchhiker model of media relations, and this is a very clear example. By attempting to contact large numbers of journalists every time you have a story you want to share, you are likely establishing relationships with few—if any—of them. What you are more likely doing is spamming email inboxes, and showing that you have little regard for the journalists you are reaching out to. This is not a good way to build relationships.

If, however, you put the time into understanding who your audience is and what media outlets they are exposed to or regularly seek out, then you have a good starting point for putting together your media list. The more specific you can get, the better. Let's work through an example of how you might practice basic through advanced audience understanding. Let's assume you work for a company that offers innovative products for tropical saltwater fishing.

> **Basic**: You know most of your sales come from South Florida, so you create a media list with journalists from major outlets in the Miami, Fort Lauderdale, and Palm Beach areas.
>
> **Better**: You realize that most of your consumers aren't permanent residents of South Florida, and they only travel there for fishing excursions, so you create a media list of national magazines and websites dedicated to saltwater fishing.
>
> **Advanced**: You find out that most of your consumers and potential consumers get information on new products by reading a once-weekly fishing column that is produced by a journalist working out of the *Naples Daily News* in Florida. You also discover that many of your consumers follow several fishing-boat captains on Twitter who regularly tweet fishing condition updates for popular fishing areas.

Having an advanced understanding of your audience, in this case, means that you've been able to narrow down your media list from several hundred journalists to a handful of key influencers. This doesn't mean that you shouldn't have journalists from the major news outlets in South Florida on your media list, nor that you should delete the journalists from the national outlets either. But, if you understand which media and influencers your primary audiences pay attention to most, you can seek to develop stronger relationships with those journalists. In this way, when you construct your media list, you may find you want to develop three separate lists.

By using multiple media lists for your organization or your client, you are more likely to set clear expectations for your media relations campaign. We recommend that you set up primary, secondary, and tertiary lists. The **primary** list contains the contact information of journalists who are most likely to be interested in your organization's stories. In the case just described, the journalist at the *Naples Daily News* should be on your primary list, as might be the contact information for the boat captains whose Twitter profiles are most followed. You might also include journalists who have covered your organization before. Your primary list should be fairly specific and might be limited to only a few to several dozen journalists—depending on what your organization does and the types of stories you have to share. Though your primary list may not be huge, this is where you'll spend the bulk of your time building relationships. Ultimately, you will want those journalists on your primary list to know you and, more importantly, believe that you are a valued/trusted source of information for their audiences.

Your **secondary** media list is composed of journalists who are likely to be interested in your information but are less likely to cover your stories. In the case above, they might include websites and magazines dedicated to all types of fishing, not just saltwater or tropical fishing. These folks are likely to be interested in your information and stories, but they have limited space and your information may be competing with stories from a wide variety of fishing-related topics. However, it is also possible that you could have a journalist from one of these outlets on your primary list, while others from the same outlet could be on your secondary list. Remember these are media lists, likely Excel files or some other computer document, and the contacts are not set in stone. You may move journalists from list to list over time, particularly as you successfully establish and build relationships.

Your **tertiary** list is made up of journalists who *might* be interested in your information given a certain set of circumstances. These could either be large national outlets—think *CBS Evening News* or the *New York Times*—or they may be journalists who are writing on a special topic that, for this one circumstance, involves your client. You might have several clients or projects that share a tertiary list. These are the journalists you are less likely to form a relationship with, but with whom you might occasionally engage.

While there are no hard and fast rules with regard to how much time you will spend cultivating relationships with the journalists on your three media lists, if we were to break down the percentages, we might say you will spend about 75% of your time working with your primary list, about 20% working with your secondary list, and 5% working with your tertiary list. The more time and care you spend in constructing your media list, the more likely it is you will be able to divide your time effectively.

One additional note to remember about media lists: Journalists today are no longer bound by the tradition of working for the same outlet for their entire careers. Nor do journalists necessarily only work for one outlet. These are important factors. For one, it means you must keep your list updated. In the case of your primary contacts, you should strive to develop strong enough relationships with the journalists so that if they do move, they will reach out to you. However, when it comes to those on your secondary and tertiary lists, you may not have as strong a relationship, or one at all, and therefore it is important to maintain current contact information. In terms of working with journalists who may work for multiple outlets—known as freelancers—it is important to remember that they may report on different topics for different outlets. As such, it looks unprofessional if you are to contact them via one outlet with a story that would be more appropriate for another. However, the better organized you are, the more likely you are to avoid these situations.

The Importance of Relationships

If you've learned one thing so far in reading this book, it should be that the multiple relationships you have with journalists form the foundation for your media relations activities. Now that you have put together your media list, it is time to start thinking about those relationships. Let's start with your primary list, since that's where we should be spending most of our time.

Your media list should, realistically, be a list of journalists with whom you would like to create and foster a relationship. But just because a journalist is on your media list does not mean that they will suddenly respond to your emails and look at you as a valued source of information. Your media list, at this point, is your road map toward building your media relations program. So where do you start?

Let's look at relationships developed from your daily interactions with people. Say you've never met someone before, but all of a sudden they email or call you and they want you to do something for them. Does that sound like an email phishing scam—or even someone you want to respond to? Likely not. So put yourself into the shoes of a journalist. Someone whom they've never met wants them to write a story or to report information based on a fact sheet or a press release they have sent you. Often the best-case scenario in this situation is that the reporter actually *opens* the email before they delete it. Remember, just because you spent a lot of time coming up with a story idea and writing a press release or a fact sheet, doesn't mean that it is important to a journalist.

Now think about this—someone who you've been introduced to and perhaps even met with sends you an email with information that might help you with your job. Would you open that email and perhaps appreciate this effort on their part? It's the same way with journalists. If you have successfully started to form a relationship with a journalist prior to sending them information about your organization, then it's more likely your message will be received. The effective media relations practitioner knows that the likelihood of success increases if the journalist knows who you are.

So how do we do this? In the old days, we might invite the journalist out to coffee or to lunch, or perhaps send a gift basket introducing ourself. These tactics still *might* work occasionally—depending on the journalists with whom you are trying to establish a relationship—but nowadays journalists are either not ethically allowed to be taken out to coffee or lunch, can't accept gifts, or otherwise are just too busy to meet with you. But that does not mean that you can't establish a relationship. For example, if the journalist is a blogger, you could begin by becoming a regular and thoughtful commenter. If they use social media in a professional setting, you might like, follow, or retweet them. Or, you might simply send them an email introducing yourself, who you work with, and asking a simple question related to what they might be looking for in terms of story ideas. Does this mean you've done all the prerequisite work to now send them your story ideas? No. What you have done is started to build a relationship.

It's important to keep in mind there is a fine distinction between building a professional media relations relationship and, for lack of a better term, "stalking" a journalist. This is especially true in the age of social media. It is simple, for example, to find someone—a journalist—on Facebook and notice they post pictures with their children. If the journalist often mentions their children in their professional life, as in they write about their families in a column, then it may be okay to introduce yourself as a fellow parent—if in fact you are. However, if you only know that the journalist is a parent because you found their personal social media page, then it would be best to not engage with them on the topic of parenting. In other words, if there is a characteristic that is part of their professional life, then its fair game. If it is a part of their personal life, leave it be and connect on something else.

Probably the most important element to remember as you begin to form relationships with journalists is to remain genuine. If you begin your relationship with false expectations, empty promises or—worst of all—lies that you think will advance your opportunities, you are only setting yourself up for failure. As in life, not every media relations connection will be fruitful. You may find that there are conflicts that do not allow for a strong professional relationship—perhaps your organization's stories and information don't align well with the journalist's needs, or maybe the journalist already has a source for your industry. These conflicts are not personal; rather, the journalist may have an established way of doing their job that doesn't align with your efforts. If your attempt is made as a good faith effort, the journalist will likely not be offended, and may even provide you with some direction as to where to go next.

As you form your relationships with journalists, the final element to keep in mind is the idea of the professional relationship. Even if you have worked with a journalist for years, and the two of you have truly become partners in the dissemination of information, they may still reject one of your story ideas. Always remember that each of you has a job to do, and no matter the nature of the relationship, neither of you ever becomes subservient to the other. The most effective media relations relationships have clear expectations, and even if you eventually become friends with the journalist, they are under no obligation to you or your organization. Successful working relationships can be irrevocably damaged in the same way an interpersonal relationship can, so managing expectations is vitally important in the media relations relationship. The most effective media relations practitioners know that good working relationships are invaluable to a successful media relations campaign.

Crafting a Pitch

For many media relations practitioners, sending a **pitch**—a short story idea—is often the initial step in the media relations interaction. This is not a good idea. Whenever possible, you'll want to have formed, or started to form, a relationship with a journalist prior to sending them a story idea. But the way you construct your pitch is the same whether you are using it as an initial contact or as a continuation of the relationship. So what exactly is a pitch, and how do we craft them in a way that journalists are willing to receive them?

A media relations pitch is a brief introduction to a potential story the journalist might decide to share with their audiences. It is akin to a proposal of sorts. You, as the media relations practitioner, have an idea for a story that the journalist, or their publication, may find of interest to their audience. A pitch can be transmitted via email, by phone, or in-person—though overwhelmingly the most popular method is by email. It is important to remember that a pitch is not the final product, it is the introduction to the story idea that you are hoping to share.

Any pitch, no matter the mode of transmission, should be carefully crafted as an individual message to a specific journalist. You've taken the time to put together a media list for your campaign, to learn about the journalist and, you hope, set the groundwork for a successful working relationship—so why send a particular journalist the same pitch you're sending to a dozen—or more—other people? Learning to craft a successful pitch is an art that may take years to get right. And no one has ever had a 100% success rate. But there are some tactics that may increase the odds in your favor.

Your authors recommend a fairly simple and straightforward series of steps in crafting your pitch. The steps are the same, with some slight variations, no matter the medium you are using to transmit your pitch. Those steps are (1) Establish a connection, (2) pique an interest, (3) provide information, and (4) elicit a response. Let's take a closer look at each of these.

Establish a Connection

Journalists don't want to be a face in the crowd of a media relations practitioner's efforts. Remember, we should treat relationships with journalists the same way we would treat our other relationships. Most of us do not like receiving emails when we are clearly one of many on the distribution list. The same goes for journalists. The idea of establishing a connection is to let the journalist know that the pitch you are sending was crafted *only* for them. This can be done in a variety of ways. First, your pitch should be addressed to the journalist by name. While seemingly simple, you might be surprised to know just how many pitches a journalist receives that are generic in nature. On the same note, you will want to make sure that if you are sending your pitch via email, that there is a clear, personal "from" address. Sending out your pitches via some automated mechanism—like a distribution service—may result in a return address that is blocked by a media outlet's spam filter.

The next step in establishing a connection is to somehow show that you are familiar with the journalist's work. You may start off by letting the journalist know how much you enjoyed reading their last article, or that you appreciate their work in reporting on your industry—some means of showing that you have done your homework and that you're familiar with what they generally report on. Of course, you must make sure that you are in fact familiar with their work—establishing a connection is not an excuse to be deceitful or insincere.

Pique Their Interest

Consider this the beginning of your pitch. This is your opportunity to have a "hook" for your information. There are no firm rules for creating interest—except, of course, not lying. You might provide a key piece of data, or you might ask a question, or it might even be a quote relevant to your information. Perhaps you have just heard some breaking news related to your topic or maybe there was a hyperlocal story that is relevant. No matter how you go about creating interest, it should be related to information you are reasonably sure the journalist is interested in and that it is related to your story idea.

Provide Information

This is the heart of your pitch. You have made a connection and gotten them interested. Now is the moment to share your story idea. A few things to keep in mind, though, at this integral step: *You are not selling something.* Your pitch is not an advertisement, it is a story idea. If you've effectively done your research, you can be fairly certain that it is information the journalist *could* use. Superlatives—best, newest, cutting-edge—seldom have a place in a pitch. This is the point in the pitch where you show the newsworthiness of your story (see Chapter 7). If you can't determine why your information is newsworthy, why are you bothering to pitch it to a journalist? If you don't know exactly what your story is—then how can you share it with someone? Here is an excellent opportunity not only to get your story idea across but also to show why it's important for the journalist's audiences to know the information.

Elicit a Response

As you wrap up your pitch, what do you want to have happen? Ninety-nine times out of a hundred, your goal is to have the journalist follow-up with you and to eventually turn your story idea into information that is then disseminated to their audience. But what action do you want the journalist to take? First, you want the journalist to respond. If you've done your job with research and establishing a relationship, and you have written an effective pitch—most journalists will respond— even if it is to say they're not interested. A standard final line to a pitch is "May I send you more information?" While this may be a direct question that might elicit a response, it is really quite vague and is fairly easy to ignore or say no to. A more effective solicitation of a response should involve something more specific. Extending an invitation to the journalist to interview a key member of your leadership team or suggesting they visit a particular website to watch a video on the topic might be a better way to garner a response and sustain interest in the story.

While there are no rules in pitching, there are a few things that journalists generally don't like and should be avoided as a closing solicitation of a response. For starters, the phrase "I think your readers will enjoy this" is problematic. It presupposes that you know more about the journalist's audience than they do. In addition, many journalists don't want to see the direct "please write this story"—or some variation, line. You are a media relations practitioner sending an email to a journalist with a story idea. They know what you want. You know what you want. Asking a journalist to "please" cover a story is not professional. Finally, you want to be cautious about how aggressive you are in eliciting a response. Offering an interview opportunity for a journalist can be a good way to garner a response, but scheduling a journalist for an interview in your pitch is likely to result in a negative reaction. As an example:

> AGGRESSIVE: I've scheduled our CEO for an interview with you next Tuesday at 10 a.m.
> BETTER: Our CEO will be available for interviews next Tuesday from 9:00–11:00 a.m., could I pencil you in for a time slot?

More Thoughts on Crafting a Pitch

Keep in mind, your pitch should be brief and to the point. Think in the classic terms of the elevator pitch—where you only have a short ride to get your idea out before folks get off. As a rule of thumb, a journalist should be spending a minute or less receiving your pitch and deciding whether your idea is worth pursuing.

That means short interactions in person, on the phone, or via email. We'll discuss the social media pitch later in this chapter—where you have even less time. In terms of an email pitch, this means you might have four or five lines to get your idea across—maybe a maximum of six sentences, though achieving it in three or four would be even better.

The pitch is where the art of persuasive and concise writing coincide. Your goal should be to get the journalist interested in contacting you for more. Ideally, they will ask you for the exact details they need. However, sometimes a story idea calls for more detail up front. You might end up with a few added sentences to show the value of your story idea. In this case, you may want to consider several additional key elements—or you may be able to effectively work them in to your original four to five sentences.

For instance, you might include a relevant quote in your pitch. This may be from someone within your organization, likely the CEO or a leading expert, or it may be from a prominent individual, which could help draw attention to the relevance of your story. For example, if a major politician or some other well-known thought leader has made relevant comments on your story, organization, or product, then it might be appropriate to include this in your pitch—assuming it flows logically and does not detract from the information you are providing within your pitch.

You might provide additional information to highlight the impact your story will have on the journalist, or more importantly, on the journalists' audience. In other words, can you show why your story idea is important? Once again, it is not sufficient to tell a journalist that their audience "will appreciate this" or "find this interesting," but if you can show in a clear way why your story is important for the journalist's audience, it may be more likely that the journalist would be interested in disseminating your information. However, it is essential to keep in mind that just because information is important to you or your organization, it may not necessarily be impactful to a journalistic audience.

By way of example, let us say that you are pitching a story idea about a new fast-food restaurant opening in an area of the city that already has multiple types of restaurants. This sort of "news" is not likely to have much impact or to be considered important by a journalist. Therefore you may want to rethink how you frame your story idea. On its own, the information of a restaurant opening may not be important for an audience to know, but if that new establishment is going to provide reduced price meals for low-income residents or hire a large number of locally unemployed persons, then the story may have a greater effect on the audience. Knowing what is important to a journalist's audience is a key component of a successful pitch. And realistically, if you don't know why your information is important to a journalist's audience—why are you pitching the journalist in the first place?

Another element you may want to consider is the use of empirical research to show the value of your story idea, or to add weight to its importance. If you're paying close attention to media—and if you are reading this book, it means you likely are—then you've probably noticed that many news stories these days contain mention of some sort of statistical information. This is a common element that exists across multiple platforms. From a journalist's perspective, the use of empirical data within a news story provides a solid grounding for their audiences, and often shows the importance of a topic. By the same token, presenting your story idea alongside highlighted research may show the journalist that your story idea has merit. Empirical research might be research that your organization has conducted, or it might be data that you have found elsewhere. While many organizations lack the ability to conduct research on their own, there is a wealth of data from public information sources that can be found and adapted for your organization's purpose. Whether it is primary or secondary data that you are utilizing, using research—where appropriate—may show the journalist that you are willing to put some thought and work into developing story ideas they might want to use.

A final aspect you may consider is the use of an interactive element as a part of your pitch. An interactive element is a component that engages the journalist to spend more time with your story idea but is not necessarily a persuasive tool on its own. Often, an interactive element can be found via an embedded link within the body of your text. This is an effective alternative to an attachment, which is often static. An interactive element is most often produced ahead of time to coincide with a media relations campaign. Examples of an interactive element are a link to video, perhaps an interactive infographic; or if your story idea is the introduction of a new product or service, it might be a demonstration of that. The reason for using an interactive element is to keep the journalist engaged with your story for a longer duration. The purpose is that the longer a journalist is engaged with your information, the more likely it is that the journalist will remember your story idea, and may be more likely to use it in their outlet. By their nature, interactive elements take time and money to produce, so it is important to utilize them in a way that makes sense for your organization. Also, if you are pitching multiple stories over time to a journalist, you will want to be careful to only use the interactive element once, otherwise it may look like you are recycling the same product over and over, which will take away from the individual nature of your pitch. And keep in mind—your organization's website doesn't count as an interactive element. Save the link to your website for your signature line.

So there it is, four simple steps in crafting a pitch, with a few added ideas to enhance its effectiveness. Any introductory student in a media relations class can craft a pitch using these guidelines, but the ability to create pitches that consistently receive responses is a skill that can only be mastered over time. The success or failure of your pitch is highly dependent on you as the media relations practitioner doing your homework about the journalist, their audience, and their area of interest. It is also highly dependent on your ability to identify the newsworthiness of your story idea. And finally, effective pitch writing is essentially reliant on the skill you develop as a practitioner who can combine the art—in terms of creativity and persuasive writing—and the science—the ability to research and determine what the journalists' needs and expectations are—of media relations.

Just following these tactics doesn't guarantee a good pitch. Let's assume you are managing a media relations campaign for a nonprofit organization in Seattle that provides services to the homeless population. Your current campaign is to try to persuade local lawmakers to budget for police to carry Narcan—a drug used to resuscitate those who have overdosed on opioids. Your organization's goal is to increase awareness within the city about the debate that lawmakers are having, with the intention of garnering public support for the legislation. Assume you have done your research and identified a journalist who writes about homelessness in the city and whose audience in both the print newspaper and online seem to care about the issue—for the sake of argument, we will say it is a journalist named James Smith. You've determined that email is the best method to reach Jim, and you've already laid the groundwork for a relationship by commenting on his blog and sending him an introductory email several weeks ago. In other words, you've done everything correctly up to now, and you're ready to send Jim your first pitch. It might look something like this:

> Hi James:
> I recently read your article on the homeless in Seattle, and thought it was very good. Did you know that many homeless people are in that situation because of drug addiction? We here at the Seattle Homeless Coalition are lobbying local legislators to finance police officers to carry Narcan to help overdose victims. Can I send you more information on this project?

This pitch includes all the required elements: an attempt to establish a connection; a question to pique interest; information; and last, a call to action. The only problem is—it is a pretty terrible pitch. Our journalist, Jim, would likely receive this and, because there's no real news story here, probably delete the email and move on. This is a classic example of knowing and using the guidelines, yet failing to execute them well. Let's look at how a more seasoned media relations practitioner might craft the pitch.

> Hi Jim,
> I wanted to write and thank you on behalf of the Seattle Homeless Coalition for all your coverage on this growing problem facing our community, particularly your latest blog post discussing drug use among the homeless population. The post seems to be generating a lot of commentary.

While the Department of the Interior says that nearly 80% of homeless persons end up in their situation because of drug use, we've found the majority of people we work with haven't become drug users until they've been displaced. As we're trying to help the homeless in the city, we're also lobbying legislators to provide funding for police officers to carry Narcan, with the hope that we'll be able to prevent nearly 50 deaths among the homeless population each year. We're holding a campaign rally next Tuesday, the 15th at 11:00 a.m. in Central City Park, and our director, Janette Jones, will be available afterward to talk about the Coalition and its campaign. Can we schedule a time for you to talk with her?

In this example, we see the same basic elements of the pitch, but they're elevated to clearly show the practitioner's understanding of the journalist's interests, and we made the call to action more concrete. While the basic story idea is the same as the first pitch, the second pitch does a more comprehensive job of presenting it and would be more likely to receive a response from the journalist.

How to Reach Out and Stand Out

While the most common way of pitching today is email, there are certainly a lot of options available to make connections with journalists and to share information. It is important that, as you build your media list and your relationships, you attempt to identify how journalists wish to be contacted. While media list management programs, such as Cision, can sometimes provide information on how journalists prefer to be contacted, it is essential for you as a media relations practitioner to do your own research as well. Some journalists will include an email in their published work; this is generally a sign that they expect feedback in this manner. Some include other methods of contact, such as a Twitter handle or some other social media contact. We'll discuss social media pitching in the next section, but if a journalist includes this contact information, then it is likely that would be their preferred method of communication.

So, the journalist likely has expectations in terms of how media relations practitioners will reach out, and most of the time it is best to honor and follow those expectations. However, if a journalist is openly sharing contact information, then it is likely they are receiving hundreds, if not thousands, of messages on a regular basis. Therefore, sometimes it is better to contact journalists in an unexpected way. Of course, doing so may be taking a risk, and it is therefore important to weigh the potential payoff against the potential cost. While some journalists may view a nontraditional contact as creative, others may be put off by such attempts.

Therefore, creativity and risk should be calculated. Creatively contacting a journalist need not be intrusive. For example, while traditional mail may be out of fashion, a hand-addressed letter sent to a journalist's place of work will likely be opened and read. Or, perhaps a courier-sent package might elicit some interest. Clearly, these tactics cannot be used all of the time, and should only be used once you've already established a working relationship with a journalist, but given the appropriate story idea and situation, you may want to think about various ways in which to contact the journalist.

Often in media relations, the initial hurdle to overcome is the hardest when it comes to reaching out to journalists: getting the journalist's attention. So how do you make yourself stand out? As we've discussed repeatedly, the formation of effective relationships is the most important element. Once you have established a good working relationship with a journalist by consistently providing valuable information and story ideas, it is likely that any contact you initiate will be met with a positive reaction.

In the beginning stages, though, you'll need to work to get journalists' attention. Often, this will be initially accomplished by your email subject line. There are a couple of schools of thought on subject lines with regard to pitching the media. Some practitioners suggest creating a catchy headline that summarizes the story idea in a short statement. Other practitioners think it best to ask a compelling question, or to create a headline with humor (when appropriate). Some practitioners will create subject lines that are reminiscent of "clickbait" headlines. Other practitioners will start off their pitches with a clear indication of what the email is, such as starting the subject line with "STORY IDEA." As with all things media relations, often these decisions are dependent on the story idea, and the type of relationship you are hoping to establish with the journalist.

However, it is important to remember when writing your subject line that you are not selling something, nor are you sending a direct mail piece to thousands of people; you are attempting to share information with a journalist and hopefully their audience. Your goal, most of the time, is not to get a journalist to open a single email, but rather to consistently open your messages.

The Social Media Pitch: When and How to Use It

One of the most popular areas of media relations, and an area that has received generous attention, is how to best use social media to develop relationships with journalists. As people are becoming increasingly reliant on social media to develop interpersonal relationships, and the new generation of media relations practitioners grew up utilizing social media to build relationships, it makes sense that media relations would also transition to social media. And it is likely, as the adoption of social media for business purposes continues to grow, that increasingly more media relations will be taking place in the realm of social media.

But to assume that all journalists are ready for social media pitching is problematic at best, and more realistically, wrong. While research has shown that nearly 88% of journalists[1] have developed a story idea based on information they saw on social media, not all journalists are ready to develop social media relationships with media relations practitioners. In fact, nearly 75% of journalists have stated that they never, rarely, or only sometimes engage with public relations professionals on social media.

However, some journalists do in fact actively encourage media relations pitches through social media, and social media is the third most desired form of communication about a story idea, following email and phone. So there is certainly a value in using social media to contact journalists, but that value is best maximized when used as either a follow-up or as a means of maintaining a relationship, rather than as the initial contact. Research shows that journalists perceive a significantly higher level of source credibility with public relations practitioners with whom they have an "in-person" relationship as opposed to an "online-only" one. Perceptions of competence, goodwill and trust are all increased for public relations practitioners who have these real-world relationships, and therefore it is more likely that subsequent online interactions will achieve a carry-over effect from those perceptions.

In examining the best practices for the social media pitch, first and foremost, it is important to think about the relationship you have with the journalist currently. Have you worked with the journalist before—or will social media be your initial interaction? If you've worked with the journalist in the past and maintain a good working relationship, then your social media interaction may be more "professional friendly" than if you are engaging with a journalist for the first time.

Another question you need to ask is whether you currently have a social media relationship with the journalist. Are you following, friending, or linking to the journalist already? If so, you should have a pretty good idea whether the journalist is using social media professionally. A warning here—journalists may not use social media for their work. If you are engaged in a social media relationship with the journalist, and it's clear they only use particular platforms for work and others for personal relationships, it would be very bad form to contact them using the platform that is reserved for personal use—even if you are "friends" with the journalist. Respecting boundaries is as important a step in media relations as managing expectations.

So when is the appropriate time to use the social media pitch? Basically, it is if you know the journalist wants to get story ideas from social media. Otherwise, you may be infringing upon a space that is considered personal. And how do we best use social media to pitch stories? By following the same tenets as we would in any other pitch situation. Remember, just because social media is faster does not mean you have an excuse for letting your standards slip. Maintaining professionalism and, most of all, remembering the needs of the journalist remain paramount.

Professional Commentary

Michael Holley
Television Host, Podcaster, and Faculty Member
NBC Sports Boston, "The Michael Holley Podcast," and Boston University

I was a teenager, probably 16 or 17, when I first considered and called myself a journalist. I knew then that there were many ways to be in the field, but I was drawn to the vast range of stories contained in daily newspapers. The thought of being a story*teller* who would share what I learned with the public was exhilarating. That's when I decided to study the business in college and, from that day—let's just say it was a little while ago—to now, the "Good Journalist's Warning" has been seared into my conscience:

Beware of spin.

Every journalist, regardless of platform, has been told that a good BS filter is necessary to do the job well and with authenticity. We are constantly on the lookout for those who are pushing half-truths, contrived, and agenda-ridden story angles and, worst of all, lies.

Since my first introduction to the industry that I love, I've reported on high schools, colleges, and professional sports teams for newspapers. I've written features on education and business, columns on the Olympics, and books about managing people. I've been a radio and TV host and podcaster, too. In every position, on every story, that warning has been there, a firewall with which every reporter is familiar.

Why do I begin with that preamble? Because if one is going to approach a journalist to gauge interest in a potential story, being knowledgeable about journalistic instincts is essential. There are exceptions, of course, to everything. But in my career, I've found the most successful journalists to also be deeply skeptical. It's a personality trait that's a foundational part of the skill set, and your understanding of this will ultimately help you perfect your pitches.

For example, most good reporters who are assigned to a beat are constantly seeking story ideas. They are getting them from their previous reporting, their sources, their editors, their family members. So the good news is that the "story pitcher" and "story executor" are generally after the same thing: compelling stories that engage the public. While there is inevitable tension between journalism and public relations, that's not to suggest that the relationship must be adversarial. On the contrary, I've found it refreshing when I've met PR professionals who have quickly gotten to the intersection of how the publication, or broadcast, of a story can help both of us.

A commonsense exercise, one that will also help you perfect your pitches, is one in which you routinely ask yourself a couple of questions:

If I were this reporter, why would I be interested in this story?

If I were this reporter, how would I describe it to my editor in one or two sentences with the hook included?

The ability to answer both of those questions means that there is keen awareness of the invisible bridge linking the PR professional's interests to the reporter's. Conversely, if those questions cannot be definitively answered, it might indicate that either the pitch is too unwieldy or that there is no viable pitch at all.

Each story has special quirks and challenges of its own, but there is an unmistakable commonality to the best experiences I've had with PR professionals. A couple of them truly stand out and our relationship has gone from months to years to multiple decades. I've switched jobs several times in that period and so have they. The bond, then, is based on mutual trust and respect. I give them all the credit for the lifespan of our connection. From the beginning, they both effectively used approaches that I believe will hold in any media atmosphere. When I worked for newspapers, they both were familiar with my work at the *Boston Globe* as well as my competition at the *Boston Herald*. As a result, on the way to the ask of the story pitch, a line might read something like this: "I thought of you and your readers for this one; I'm honestly not sure if it works for the *Herald* . . ."

The brilliance and transparency in that short line is amazing. To write it, a professional has to know about the intensity of journalistic competition. Notice, there is no promise that the *Herald* won't be contacted; rather, the implication is that the *Globe* writer will have the first opportunity to accept or decline the opportunity. There are some stories where the professional cannot deliver the coveted exclusive, but in the situations where it's possible, I believe that it should be included in the pitch. It brings urgency and additional relevance to the story idea.

I've also found that the most beloved and trusted PR types don't always check in only when they need something. Well, they do and they don't. Let me explain. I have a friend who works in real estate. Part of her routine, every three weeks or so, is to make phone calls. That's it. She's making phone calls. She's not calling to say that a new house has gone on the market or that interest rates have gone up or down. She calls to say hello, ask about the kids, hear vacation plans, or gossip about the neighborhood. The check-ins are brief, conversational, and memorable. She remembers names, birthdays, and other important milestones. And, of course, she is always ready—when necessary—with a real estate nugget or to answer an inquiry.

The same approach can be taken with journalists. When I was covering a particularly dysfunctional pro sports team, I would occasionally hear from one of my PR contacts from another sports team. He would call to comment on something weird that happened in a game, and we'd exchange anecdotes. It let me know that he was paying attention. I'd also ask him to give me some

(Continued)

educated guessing on inside information about his team, something that I wouldn't write for my audience, and he'd tell me the info. When I'd actually see it happen a few days later, it let me know that he had credibility.

As often happens with corporate reshuffling, that contact wound up moving and working for a team in my coverage area. The dynamic of our relationship had to change. Yet, due to his willingness to be a quick study (his new market was a lot different than his old one) and his knowledge of journalism, the connection was preserved.

I believe that there is an artistic-scientific hybrid to doing media relations well. I can say that with confidence. But I also believe that within that successful art-science mix are the timeless qualities of intelligence, efficiency, and awareness.

Michael Holley Biography

Michael Holley is a Pulitzer Prize winner, *New York Times* bestselling author, and current *NBC Sports Boston* television host. He has worked for three daily newspapers, the *Akron Beacon Journal, Boston Globe,* and *Chicago Tribune,* and cohosted a daily radio talk show for 13 years. He currently hosts "The Michael Holley Podcast," which covers a variety of topics including pop culture, sports, music, politics, food, and more. In 2019, Holley was named Associate Professor of the Practice of Journalism at Boston University.

Being a Steward to Your Story

So you've done all your research; you've come up with a great story idea that a journalist would likely be interested in; then, you found a journalist and an outlet that you're fairly sure will want to work with your story and you; and you've crafted your pitch effectively and sent it off in a manner the journalist will want to receive it. At this point, because you've done everything right, the journalist is likely to receive your pitch and immediately start working on publishing your story. It will include all of your key points and showcase your client organization in a favorable light—leading to increased reputation for your client organization and accolades for all of your brilliant media relations acuity . . . until you wake up.

All the research, planning, and effective execution you put into your media relations efforts to produce an effective pitch adds up to the first step in the life of your storytelling process. Once you've made your story pitch, the hard work begins.

If you've constructed your pitch well, even if the journalist you're pitching isn't interested in using your information in a story, you will likely get a short response acknowledging your pitch, and letting you know they're not interested. While disappointing, this type of response lets you know you've done everything well, but that the timing of your story wasn't right for that journalist or that media outlet. This should give you confidence that another journalist may be interested in your story. Receiving a "no, thank you" email should not be considered a success, but shouldn't be considered a total failure either. In fact, it may be possible that this particular "no" could leave the door open to future "yeses."

If the journalist is interested, you will likely receive a response thanking you and seeking some sort of directed follow-up information or a specific request—an interview or media passes to the event, for example. Any such response should be addressed as soon as possible, and hopefully you've already got the information the journalist is seeking close at hand.

Either situation makes it relatively easy to be a steward to your story. In the first, you know that the journalist has closed the book on that particular story idea, and you can move on. In the second situation, you've received clear direction from the journalist, and you can follow up accordingly.

Unfortunately, what often happens is you send out your pitch, and . . . nothing. Maybe a day or two—or three—passes without a response from the journalist. This could mean one of several things. It could be that the journalist saw your pitch, didn't like it, and deleted it from their email. Or maybe it means they're working on another story, and even though they like your story idea, they just don't have time for it right now. Or it could be that your pitch is in their junk folder. Or it could be any number of other reasons. The bottom line is, no matter what the reason for the nonresponse, it puts you into a holding pattern, and it can be very frustrating.

In this case, what do you do? If you've read this far into the book, you probably know the first question to ask yourself is, "Did I have a relationship with this journalist before I sent the pitch?" Think about how easy it is to ignore or delete an email from someone you don't know. Then think about how guilty you feel about not returning a friend's phone call or email. It works the same way in the media relations relationship. Being a steward to your story means not only following up after the pitch, but establishing a relationship before you even send a pitch in the first place.

So let's assume since you didn't hear back from the journalist that you didn't have a preexisting relationship. If you've sent a pitch and you haven't gotten a response, there are a few factors to consider. First, consider the nature of the story idea and its time sensitivity. Were you sending a pitch about a product launch or an event that would require a journalist's immediate attention? If that's the case, determine whether you gave enough lead time for the journalist to effectively cover the story. If not—you should have! Perhaps the journalist figured they missed the opportunity to cover the event. You might want to consider a short email after the event summarizing the key points and offering an interview or a product demonstration.

Assuming your pitch was not time sensitive to an event but rather a story idea that could have a longer window of opportunity, you will likely want to think carefully about when you want to follow up. A good rule of thumb to consider is 48 hours. If you've sent a pitch on a Monday morning, and haven't heard back by Wednesday afternoon, you will probably want to start thinking about your follow-up: That should occur either Wednesday afternoon or Thursday morning. It should be simple, reminding the journalist what the story idea was, and ideally, should contain something new that wasn't in the original pitch. Perhaps there is some additional information you left out in the first pitch that you were hoping to share when the journalist followed up—now is the time to share it. The idea is that you're not simply resending the pitch, but that you are actually following up and providing novel information. The follow-up is not a time to be snarky or attempt to "blame" the journalist for not immediately responding to you or your idea. Doing so is a surefire way to not get your story covered, and it will likely create acrimony for any future interactions.

Of course, your follow-up needs to be timed thoughtfully. If you are pitching a journalist who is writing for a magazine with a long lead time, following up after 48 hours would likely be too soon. Alternatively, if you are pitching a producer at a local news station, 48 hours could be too long. Knowing your journalists, their deadlines, and the basic practices of their outlets are all important to helping you determine when you should follow up.

And if, after your initial pitch and a follow-up you still don't get a response, move on. Again, perhaps the timing just isn't right for this particular journalist and your story idea. We all get busy, so don't begrudge a journalist just because they didn't respond to your pitch. Hopefully it will work out the next time.

A Few Dos and Don'ts for Being a Steward to Your Story

DO:

Provide additional information in a follow-up.
Respond to any requests for information quickly.
Make allowances for journalists being on vacation, working on other stories, or anything else that may make a response to your pitch difficult.
Vary the time of your contact—if you sent the initial pitch in the morning, try following up in the afternoon. You might also vary your contact method if you're unsure about how journalists like to receive information.

DON'T

Hound or harass journalists—one pitch and one follow-up.
Ask when you can expect to see your story "published."
Overpromise what you can deliver or exaggerate your story.
Expect a journalist to give your story idea as much interest or attention as you do.

Key Concepts

We've said it before, and we'll keep saying it—success in media relations depends primarily on establishing good working relationships with journalists. When it comes to building your media list, you need to be realistic for your client organizations. It is important to seek journalists working in outlets that are most likely to be interested in your stories. This doesn't mean it's not worth "taking a shot" occasionally at a large national media outlet but managing both yours and your client's expectations is important; and finding journalists and outlets that share information with your key audiences is always a better path to success.

Pitching is a skill that takes an hour to learn and a lifetime to master. Being strategic and purposeful with your pitching activities is a better path to success than trying for quantity. Remember, a pitch is an opportunity to begin a relationship with a journalist, or to build upon an existing one. You've taken the time to come up with a strong story idea, make sure a journalist isn't turned off by a subpar pitch.

Challenge Case

You're new to a public relations agency, and you're placed on a team working to securing media coverage of a longtime client of the agency, a successful local construction and property management company that specializes in building and managing adult—55 and over—communities. During your initial research, you realize that the client receives four to five mentions a week, and over the past year, has been featured in local print, online, and in broadcast outlets. They have a strong reputation in the community, primarily due to their quality properties and engagement in civic and corporate social responsibility activities.

The challenge? Your research has shown that coverage has stabilized in local media, and the client wants to gain a larger profile in both the state and across the country. First, what strategies will you use to identify new journalists, and second, what are some stories that you will pitch, knowing that while your client is a fairly large organization for your community, there are much larger competitors?

REFERENCE

1. Supa, D. W., Zoch, L. M., & Scanlon, J. (2014). *Does social media use affect journalists' perceptions of source credibility?* Presented to the Public Relations Division of the Association for Education in Journalism and Mass Communication, Montreal, Canada, August 6–9.

A PROACTIVE APPROACH
TO MEASUREMENT AND EVALUATION

There are few terms in media relations that can create the sheer terror—or at least eye rolls and heavy sighs—as do measurement, evaluation, and data. Many of us are excited by the *idea* of "proving the worth" of our media relations efforts, but few of us have a strong understanding of how to go about doing it. One of the biggest challenges is that there is no single way of showing the value of media relations, nor of measuring its effectiveness with audiences. Oftentimes, media relations practitioners use measurement tools that are not specifically designed for their organizational purpose or are inappropriate for their audiences. Even more troublesome is when clients or senior executives demand the use of a particular type of measurement that will not accurately evaluate media relations efforts.

By the end of this chapter, you should have the confidence to set up your own evaluation system for your media relations efforts and the ability to measure both internally and externally, formally and informally. And while it may seem intimidating, there are many simple methods that you may already be using that can be a part of a strategic measurement and evaluation plan.

We should point out here that there are several excellent books and how-to guides that go deeper into measurement and evaluation than we cover here. Our goal is to give you the basics required to evaluate your media relations efforts, which is your starting point in this process. Following the discussion, if you want further information about measurement and evaluation, we've listed a few books at the end of the chapter that you may want to seek out.

Before We Begin

When it comes to measurement and evaluation, there are a lot of terms that get tossed around. Some are simply buzzwords designed to make the process sound complicated—or used to make you feel as though you *need* to hire an outsider to handle your measurement. What follows in Box 11.1 is a brief glossary of terms that you may have already come across, or that you may read or hear in the future, and that are important as you read this chapter. These include only a few of the terms out there—and there are some good resources available that go into substantial depth about each of these topics, but what we want to present in this chapter is what you need to know—with a few of the more popular terms thrown in . . . just in case you find yourself in a high-level meeting and want to throw out some impressive terms about how you intend to prove your media relations strategy is working.

As we mentioned above, these are only a few terms that are used when discussing measurement. You've probably encountered many more, or perhaps your organization has different terms to describe the same thing.

At this point, it's probably only fair to mention that both of the authors of this book hold PhDs and have published research articles and presented conference papers using a substantial amount of the complicated statistics that journal article reviewers like to see. And complicated statistics do have a place in measurement and evaluation. But our hope here is not necessarily to train you on the ins and outs of *how* to measure, although we will share some ideas, but rather, we are hoping to show you *why* you measure, *what* you can measure, and *how* to incorporate simple methods of measurement into your media relations efforts.

BOX 11.1

Research Asking questions and taking steps to find the answers to those questions. The basis of all measurement and evaluation.

Method Whatever steps you decide to take to answer your research questions. This can range from the very simple (observation) to the very complicated (experiments).

Measurement Conducting research to establish a benchmark point and comparing it to where you end up, so you can determine whether or not you have been able to "move the needle."

Data The information you collect during your research.

Evaluation Determining how well you are doing based on your measurement.

Informal research Doing research without a predetermined plan or structure.

Formal research Doing research with a predetermined plan or structure.

Outputs The steps you, as a media relations practitioner, take to foster a relationship with a journalist. This includes phone calls, in-person meetings, emails, story pitches, social media—basically all of your tactics to develop a relationship.

Outcomes For the purposes of media relations, an outcome is the journalist sharing your story via publication.

(Continued)

Impact The result of an outcome, usually what attitudinal, perceptual, or behavioral changes occur in the audience that has viewed the story.

Analytics A noun, often used incorrectly, to describe some combination of measurement and data.

Dashboard A tool that is used to analyze a specific aspect of a campaign, usually set up specifically for a client or organization. *Also,* where you left your sunglasses.

Data visualization A modern-day term for "charts." Usually very nice ones.

Big data This is information that is often collected through coding software and reflects the information for a massive number of people. Big data is usually gleaned from social media.

ROI (Return on investment). In terms of media relations, how much time or money is being spent on something relative to the value it brings back to your organization.

Media monitoring Sometimes called media listening. This is a process whereby a specific piece of information, an organization, an industry, or a cause is tracked in the media.

Trend tracking Also known as trend watching. This is a long-term look at the media and how they cover, or don't cover, specific events. For example, we might track media coverage of a particular industry over time to determine how different media cover that industry and how that coverage has or has not changed.

Clips These are the stories that appear in the media about your organization that you likely had a hand in helping bring to fruition. They're called clips because we used to cut them out of the newspaper and put them in a book. Today, clips are more likely to be a list of links to stories.

Sentiment analysis An analysis of how a large number of people are thinking about, or behaving, regarding a certain topic. This is usually done by analyzing big data sets.

Initial Steps Toward Media Relations Measurement

Media relations and measurement have, seemingly, always gone hand in hand. Done well, traditional media relations resulted in a physical manifestation of effort—namely an article in the newspaper or coverage on the news broadcast we were targeting. It would only make sense that these artifacts would be collected by media relations practitioners as evidence of their efforts. These early clip-counting efforts were a form of measurement, one which continues to this day. For all of the metrics, analytics, and dashboards available today, there is still something about presenting your client or your CEO with a collection of articles from media outlets. The reason we use these clips is the same driving force behind all of our measurement—we want to show the value of our efforts.

Over time, media relations practitioners learned that showing clips would be enhanced if a monetary value could be associated with the collected clips (sometimes called clip books), after all, even now, clients and executives generally like seeing how money is being maximized. Thus, the **advertising value equivalency**, or AVE, was thrust into popular use. Initially, the AVE was calculated for print articles by measuring the column inches of the article and comparing that to the cost of an advertisement of an equivalent size in the same publication. Later, it was determined that because people were more likely to pay attention to articles than to advertisements, a multiplier needed to be added based on the publication. This multiplier was—is—usually a number between 1.5 and 3 and was based on numerous factors including the type of publication and its publication frequency. Further iterations of the AVE included more measures, including circulation, number of clicks online, and other factors that were added into the mix depending on the medium and what your client was concerned with.

An example of an AVE would look something like the following. A media relations practitioner works successfully with a journalist and a story that mentions the practitioner's organization is published in a daily newspaper. Let's say the article mentions the organization along with several others as part of a relief effort for a natural disaster. The article is 12 column inches, and an equivalent ad in that newspaper would cost $1,000. But because the article was on the front page, a higher multiplier is used, let's say 3.5. So now, the AVE for that article is $3,500. If the media relations practitioner spent 10 hours to secure the placement, and they make $40 an hour, then the cost of the article was $400. So, with an AVE of $3,500, the return on investment for that article is $3,100, which isn't too bad at all.

Except, is that article actually worth $3,500? What if the article is on the same page as a story about a local family impacted by the same natural disaster, or if another story of great interest is on the same page? Or perhaps the article appeared in the publication on the day after Thanksgiving? Either of these placements could negatively influence the overall audience effect of the article. Or conversely, what if that article is picked up online by hundreds of blogs, or is shared on social media across thousands of audience members? Suddenly the impact of that article appears to be worth much more than $3,500. Unfortunately, the bottom line when it comes to AVEs is that they just don't accurately reflect the value of media relations. Multiple research studies have shown problems with AVEs[1] though they remain in moderately popular usage today, primarily due to their ease of use and that they remain one of the only measurement tools that equates a dollar amount with the results of media relations efforts.

AVEs do show us that there is a conscious desire to measure the impact of media relations efforts—and that has been the case for many years, although the importance of tying financial incentives to those efforts has been continuously questioned. In his 1958 book, *Corporate Public Relations*,[2] John Hill, chairman of the board of Hill & Knowlton, wrote about the confluence of public relations and the financial investment of an organization in that public relations.

> The increasing hundreds of millions of dollars annually that American corporations spend on their public relations programs would not be so invested if the economic return had not become wholly clear to properly cautious management. . . . The strides made by public relations indicate a healthy trend not only in the development of broader public relations facilities by industry, but also in the growing recognition of the policy implications of the activity. Experience has shown us that it is not enough for the corporation to have good policies, perform good deeds, and then keep its own counsel.
>
> The successful modern business must make sure that people—all kinds of people—*know* what it is doing and approve of its actions. There is more than a grain of truth in the old admonition that if you refuse to tell your own story, somebody else will—and probably will tell it wrong.

Mr. Hill is referring to the ability of public relations to impact the overall *reputation* of an organization, and reputation is a difficult concept to measure effectively. Why? Because reputations are based on attitudes, and what contributes to an attitude can be any number of factors. Without getting into the litany of research and theories that have examined attitudes and attitude formation, it is sufficient to say this—the measurement of how humans seek out, perceive, and then produce attitudes about something is fundamentally flawed, because human beings do not always act rationally in the process.

Why We Should Measure

This is not to say that we shouldn't attempt to measure the efforts of media relations. It is just that we should do so with the understanding that even the most well-placed, significant, informative, and audience-driven piece of information may only get a fraction of the attention of a keyboard-playing cat—though there is a theory to explain that as well. But if we should measure our media relations efforts, and the AVE is overly faulty, then what other methods are available to us? The next section explores some of the methods of evaluation, and the advantages and disadvantages of each. Before we look at some of those forms, though, there is the lingering question as to *why* we should measure our media relations efforts.

The answer is both simple and surprisingly complex. Simply put, we measure media relations as a way of showing its value to our organization. The more complex answer lies in that every organization has different goals for its media relations efforts, thus different reasons for measurement. In Chapter 8, we discussed goals and objectives. When you establish the goals and objectives for your media relations program, you are, in essence, defining your purpose and reason for measuring. In other words, measurement should not exist as separate from your overall media relations program. Rather, measurement is an integral component, even when done informally.

Traditional and Nontraditional Forms of Media Relations Measurement

When it comes to measurement, specifically *what* we measure, the first decision we should make is whether we are trying to measure our *internal outputs* or our *external outcomes*. In our list of terms above, *output* refers to the actions you take—the things you have some measure of control over. The *outcome* is the result of your output. In the case of media relations, the outcome we are seeking is that our information is shared by the journalist with their audience. And here's a hint: you should be actively measuring *both*.

It is important to note that many public relations texts, which do not focus on media relations, will refer to a published story as an "output" and will refer to an "outcome" as the result of the story. This approach is problematic, as it does not account for the effort put in by the media relations practitioner to achieve the publication, and it assumes that the media relations practitioner has control over whether a story is published or not. For media relations professionals, **impact** is the result of your outcome—which we hope is the result of effective output. We will discuss evaluating impact at the end of the chapter when we examine measuring ROI.

Tracking Output

Why the difference? Keep in mind we are focused on the practitioner–journalist relationship, and that relationship is a *process*. We may need to have a series of information exchanges—outputs—to garner the trust and credibility needed with a journalist to produce a published story—the outcome. Measuring outputs in this way holds several key benefits for media relations practitioners. First, it allows us to see what information we are sending to journalists, how often we are sending it, and when we have followed up. Recall in Chapter 9 when we talked about having multiple frames surrounding how we construct our information. By tracking our output, we can see if certain frames work better with particular—or groups of—journalists, and can identify frames that are just not working at all. We can also determine if different means of contacting journalists work better or worse than others.

Measuring our output also allows us to gauge how much time we are spending on a project. If our goal is to measure the value of media relations to an organization, then it is important to know how much time we are putting into the effort. One of the most effective tools for keeping track of our media output is the **media log.** As you can probably envision, this is a record of each output a media relations practitioner creates. It can also be referred to as a "contact" log, though each output may not be a specific contact to a journalist, as we will see shortly.

A media log is best set up as a file, either individual or shared, that contains room for date, time, type of output, recipient—if applicable, frame, response, follow-up, and result. An example is given below.

As you can see, the output log helps us to keep a record of our daily activities in terms of media relations. This helps us to stay organized, but it can also help us from a measurement perspective. For example, if you start to notice that certain story frames are consistently getting responses, whereas other frames do not, it might be worth revisiting both to see what is going on.

Did you also notice in the last entry that the output wasn't directed toward anyone in particular—and in fact wasn't even really trying to get the attention of the media? Remember that journalists are also active on social media, and if you know that journalists who cover your organization are following the various social media accounts you have, then—in this example—a tweet may reach them. Therefore, even though you haven't specifically messaged them, they are still an audience. So, in essence, any organization's social media message can be considered a potential message to the media.

Date	Time	Output	Recipient	Frame/ Story	Response	Follow-up	Result
Jan.23	9:30 a.m.	Email	Jane Smith— *Washington Post*	Legislation affecting non-profit entities	Phone call requested	Interview with CEO scheduled —1/27	CEO quote in 1/28 story
Jan.23	10 a.m.	Press release	Business Wire	New store opening	None	Need to send individual pitches— in-progress	
Jan.23	10:15 a.m.	Tweet from customer service account		Change in return policy	32 retweets	No journalist RT, follow-up with trades	Need to meet with Sales VP to prep media questions

Maintaining a media log helps us track and measure our efforts in media relations. But the media log is also helpful in determining what journalists think about our efforts. Remember back to Chapter 3 and the *expectations management* theory. In the final stage, there were two potential results—message acceptance and message adoption. *Acceptance* means the message you have sent may not be used by the journalist immediately, but it may either be used later or might spark an idea for a future story. It means that the journalist hasn't immediately deleted or ignored your information. In other words, you need to attempt to evaluate whether your message resonated with the audience—the journalist. We can't always know this with absolute certainty, though if the journalist responds to our outreach, we can be confident that the message was accepted, even if they don't use it in a story. However, if you don't get a response, it may be that the message was never received, or that the message was received and the journalist didn't have any questions or need a follow-up. Interpreting why you haven't received a response is a challenge for media relations practitioners and can be a source of great frustration. However, by establishing effective relationships with journalists, and by planning your message as we outlined in Chapter 10, it can often be avoided.

Your media log may have other uses as well, or it may serve as a foundation for the next stage of your measurement. Once you train yourself to keep a media log, it will become an invaluable tool for better media relations practice.

Tracking Outcomes

It's a pretty simple job to keep track of the things that *we* are doing with information about our organizations; it's completely different when it comes to what *others* are doing with that information. When we think about **outcomes** in media relations, we are talking about whether the information you sent to the journalist is being adopted, that is, being used in a story that is disseminated to a larger audience. The adoption of information is a very important step in the media relations relationship. It is the result of having established a relationship with a journalist—often over time—and having provided them with information that they found valuable. In the best-case scenario, one adoption will lead toward greater source credibility for future information, thus providing journalists with information they can use—and do use—and can elevate the relationship between you and the journalist.

It used to be a simple process to figure out whether your information was adopted for use in a publication or electronic medium. You could send the journalist information, and the next day you could open the newspaper to see if your story idea was published or turn on the television to watch the evening news, or even listen to the radio drive time reports on your way in to work. Today, with the quantity and speed of information, it is decidedly less simple to see if journalists are adopting your information. Today, to know if your messages are adopted, you will need to set yourself up for measurement success.

Looking back to your output in preparation for adoption, before ever sending a piece of information, make sure that

- You are following the journalists you're sending the information to on social media—including their outlets' social media accounts;
- You have set up appropriate news alerts for your organization, or for the subject about which you are sending information; and
- You have some form of analytics set up if you are also directing journalists to your website or social media accounts.

A journalist may not always contact you if they are engaging with information about your organization, particularly if you have not previously established a relationship. But, with the various analytics tools available, you should be able to tell fairly quickly if journalists are adopting your information.

Let's assume your information has been adopted. What's next? From a very traditional media relations perspective, you have achieved your goal. You have earned a "clip," and you have something to show either your client or your boss. Congratulations.

Except . . . for someone who is trying to show the value of media relations to an organization, your work is just beginning. Now, we need to spend some time figuring out *how* your information was used, where it was used, and whether audiences might have even seen it. And of course, you're probably pressed for time and need to go to your next meeting. So, let's look at three different ways of evaluating that clip, from the quick and straightforward to the more complex. We'll show you where each type of evaluation might be useful but remember that you can pull together any of the following ideas to create a more personalized approach to measurement.

Type 1: Manifest Attributes—Your Entry-Level Evaluation

Start with your placement. Beyond just clipping it out of a publication or linking to its web home on a list, we need to do some basic evaluation. This evaluation, over time, will lead to measurement. The simplest way of evaluating the placement is to examine its **manifest** attributes. These are the attributes of the placement that are easily counted without further analysis. For a print publication this would include word count, placement on a page or the section in which it is found, number of times your organization is mentioned, and whether a graphic element—such as a photo—accompanies the article. This evaluation will change depending on the medium where the message appears. In an online article, for example, you may want to include such things as how many other elements appear on the page, how many shares/likes/pins the article has, or the number of comments. For a magazine, you may want to include whether the article is teased on the front page, or whether the name of your organization appears in the table of contents. For television, you might include the length of the story, the time it appeared in the program, and which reporter gave the information.

Evaluating adoption in this way is a form of **content analysis**, though it does not constitute measurement on its own. In larger organizations, evaluating manifest content is sometimes "hired out" to media monitoring companies. In those cases, the organization defines the search parameters and which attributes are required, and the service provides a report at regular intervals. Smaller organizations might use interns or entry-level employees to do this.

The use of some form of manifest content analysis is fairly common for a variety of reasons. First, it's often simple and straightforward yet can be used for a variety of measurement purposes. For example, an organization might provide a weighted score for each of the attributes, and then give each adoption an overall score based on whether the story contained certain elements. This "scorecard" approach allows for media relations practitioners to grade the value to the organization of each information adoption and is easily customizable for individual organizations or clients. An example of a scorecard for a story adoption appears below.

Obviously, a scorecard such as this can be adapted for different media and story types. The goal for the media relations practitioner is to garner as high a

Attribute	Score
Article on front page/website splash page +50	
Article on section front/sidebar head +25	
Article is elsewhere in publication/more than one-click +10	
Article contains more than one photo +50	
Article contains one photo +25	
Article contains direct quote from CEO +50	
Article contains name of CEO +25	
Article contains core message +25	
Article has more than 50 comments +50	
Article has more than 50 shares/likes +50	
Article has 10–49 comments +25	
Article has 10–49 shares/likes +25	
Article has link to home site +50	
TOTAL	

score as possible. This approach is mainly beneficial to internal audiences, as the scores can be assigned arbitrarily—though the more comprehensive the scorecard, the better. The trick is to decide in advance what is important to your organization and your media relations activities and make sure you measure those aspects of the adoption.

Type 2: Taking the Next Step—Latent Content

While examining the manifest content is an important first step, it doesn't give us a lot of information about the media relations process. In other words, manifest content allows us to examine the end product, but if we want to take a closer look, we need to examine how the adoption has incorporated the information we want it to contain. What is the impression we assume people get when they see or hear the information? To do this, we need to go deeper into the content.

The second step is to examine the **latent** content of the adoption. Latent refers to the aspects of the article that cannot be easily counted, and therefore can only be evaluated by reading the actual article. This is most often done by assigning a value of "positive, negative, or neutral" to an article that is published. For example, if an article appears that talks about how employees of an organization are giving back to the community, then we would likely assume "positive." An article talking about the closing of a production facility due to rising costs would be classified "negative." This is a common, but simplistic, approach that can be easily expanded.

When looking at latent content, you can still use the scorecard type of tracking, though your categories will obviously be different. As with the previous scorecard focusing on manifest content, you will want to customize what you are looking for depending on your goals. The following are some potential items you may want to track when examining an article for latent content.

- Does the article include our key messages in a way that conveys our organizational goals?
- Is there information included about our company that we did not transmit during the output process? Did the reporter do additional research beyond the information we provided?
- Are any of our competitors also featured within the article? Are they more prominent than our organization?
- Is there a mention of our upcoming event? Does it include information for people who want to attend?
- If the article is an opinion column, does the writer seem to have a positive opinion toward us?

As you can see, questions like this cannot be answered simply by counting, but are attempts to garner a better understanding of the overall article and, in an indirect way, help us better evaluate our own outputs. For example, if information about your organization is included that you did not share with the journalist directly, it may indicate that you did not know enough about what the journalist needed or wanted for the story. Or it could mean that you have a good relationship with the journalist, and they had a quick question that was answered via a simple web search and thus didn't feel the need to contact you. This is the challenge with **indirect measures**—you can never know for sure what occurred. However, knowing what your output was, the status of your relationship with the journalist, and the overall article that was written or shared can usually allow you to make inferences based on looking at the manifest content.

You can also use the latent content to start to get an idea about the *impact* of the article. If the article is web based, this can easily be determined by examining audience reaction that includes comments, shares, and retweets. While not everything published online offers these, stories that are interesting and newsworthy generally include some interaction with the public. You can use the same techniques in examining comments from the public as you did for the article.

Type 3: If We Have the Time and Budget

Measurement can be time consuming, expensive, and involve a lot of statistics. Hopefully, you have found the first two types of measurement to be straightforward and realize that we can effectively measure media relations efforts in a way that allows us to understand our outputs and our outcomes without representing a significant drain on resources. The third type of measurement is decidedly less simple, takes quite a bit of time, and may require significant financial resources—though there are ways to do it for less money as well.

You may be asking yourself why you would do something complex when something simple would suffice. The answer is that sometimes indirect measures cannot give us a broad enough picture of our media relations efforts, and we want to see what the overall impact is on the public. Conducting a more comprehensive measurement allows us to get the most accurate picture. This is usually accomplished by using survey research methodologies, focus groups, and possibly interviews with key consumers—or influencers. Starting on the next page we will walk through an ideal measurement and evaluation scenario—keeping in mind the ideal is very rarely the reality.

Taking these steps allows you to directly measure your media relations efforts as compared to the overall success of your organization. Unfortunately, it is often not realistic to be able to establish a "zero baseline" of public engagement with your organization—as in the example above, most of the time we start our work long after an

Imagine that you have been appointed the director of media relations for a well-known stereo systems company that has previously only sold its products to car manufacturers. The company is now getting ready to launch into direct-to-consumer sales. Your first duty will be to hold a press conference to introduce its first commercially available stereo system. Before doing so, you want to establish a baseline against which you can evaluate your media relations efforts. Your company has given you a substantial budget of $250,000 and six weeks to conduct your initial research. While your company is fairly well known among consumers, all of the previous efforts in media relations have been put toward trade and specialty publications.

Your first step is to outline the communication goals, objectives, and strategies as were discussed in Chapter 8. Once you've done all your internal organizational research to collect this, you will need to get a sense of what the public and journalists think about your company's industry, its competitors, and the products that are currently available. You might conduct a content analysis of media coverage of the stereo industry, and pair that with a nationwide survey of consumers. To conduct the survey, you will construct the survey **instrument** based on the questions you want answered, pretest it with colleagues and friends, and then likely use a survey company to gather a representative **sample** of consumers. After the outside company distributes the survey and sends you the findings in either the form of raw numbers and percentages or, depending on what you paid for, tables and graphs, you will analyze its results based on what you wanted to know. You probably wanted to measure what consumers attitudes toward the stereo industry are, what products they currently purchase, and how they feel about those products. You will also want to find out about where consumers get their information about the industry, and what drives their purchase decisions for products.

While you're doing this, you are also conducting your media analysis, to see what journalists have written about the industry and associated products. You will likely want to discover whether there are tendencies in coverage and tone, and the type of media that generally covers your industry. It is likely you will also be looking at what online communities and influencers have written about the industry.

Once your research is completed, you will have a baseline to work from. Now, you hold your press conference and, if you've followed the other steps in this book, you will begin to see media coverage of your company and product. During this time, you will be tracking social media coverage, traditional media coverage, and analyzing as much as you can about the coverage.

Assuming you have tracked your output with a media log, and you have garnered outcomes in the media with coverage of your information, in six months you will conduct another national survey to see if public awareness and perceptions about your company and its products have changed. Specifically, you will want to see if the messages you have shared via the media have resonated with the public. You will also try to determine where people are hearing about your company and its products. You will then use this information to help you determine if your key messages or output attempts should be modified.

You repeat this cycle every six months to, we hope, show that your media relations efforts result in positive interactions with journalists and positive perceptions among the public. You also may start to organize focus groups with specific categories of consumers to get greater detail about their media habits so that you can better target your output efforts, or even change your key messages if necessary.

organization has established some reputation with both journalists and the public. However, in this scenario, the initial baseline for media relations is established before the media relations campaign begins. Even in a long-standing organization, establishing a baseline prior to the implementation of a campaign is integral to directly measuring the impact of the campaign. For example, if your organization is about to launch a new initiative involving the community, you could certainly gauge public perception before you begin to reach out to journalists with the information.

Realistically, many organizations will not provide the resources needed to effectively measure media relations using multiple surveys and focus groups. However, organizations will often engage more traditional marketing research, particularly if the organization is sales driven. If you are aware that your organization conducts consumer research from time to time, then it may be possible for you to include a few questions that could serve as a direct measure of media relations efforts.

Most organizations that do conduct market or consumer research often rely on outside vendors to conduct the study. In addition to attempting to get some key questions added onto an existing survey, it would probably also be useful to get to know these vendors. They might have additional data regarding their survey respondents that could be useful to your media relations measurement. For example, they could have a strong idea of the media habits of the respondents, or they may have other information that would be valuable.

While you may never have the opportunity to conduct the "ideal" media relations measurement campaign, it is certainly valuable to know what that ideal project would be for your organization's measurement goals. If, at a minimum, you can identify what you *should* be looking for, then it is more likely that you will find components that can better help you assess the impact of your media relations efforts.

Some Common Mistakes in Measurement

Today's public relations environment is moving more toward integration of data into all aspects of campaign and organizational management. In fact, the move toward increased use of data is affecting organizational practices across the board.

This is generally a good thing for measurement and evaluation. Organizational leaders are often making data-driven decisions, and the media relations practitioner who can provide data on her or his efforts is much better positioned than one who cannot. Although research and evaluation are integral to the modern media relations environment, mistakes and errors can easily happen along the way. Let's look at some common mistakes in media relations measurement.

1. **Not measuring**. This common mistake is, perhaps, too common. But it's also understandable. Media relations can be a time-intensive, results-driven field where the headline in the newspaper or the interview on a national morning show is enough to satisfy the client. However, even if you have a demanding client and are constantly working to garner great placements, you should still be doing some form of measurement.

2. **Measuring too much**. Yes, this can happen too. Remember that public relations is both a science *and* an art. So is media relations. Sometimes you have to step back from strictly using the numbers to see the reality of a situation. For example, let's say you get your client an interview on a television show that will be repeated eight times over the course of a day. You could evaluate all of the official averages for the show—reach or viewership, for example—and then determine how many "impressions" the interview will generate. Using data, you might be able to claim that your media relations efforts have resulted in vast numbers of viewers. One of your authors, for example, was once able to determine that nearly every person in the state of Florida had been exposed to a particular media message. Relying solely on the numbers to drive your evaluation—and not using common sense—can be a mistake. Did 11 million people really get exposed to that message? Maybe, but probably not.

3. **Measuring the wrong thing**. When we engage with measuring our media relations efforts, we sometimes fail to show the value because we are looking at the wrong thing. Let's go back to our media log. What if our log shows that we are consistently failing to get a story idea adopted? We might assume that we are not telling a compelling story or that our outreach is not particularly strong. But what if there's another reason why we are not able to get to the next step? Perhaps our story idea is strong and our outreach is done well, but we're working to get information into a market that is dominated by another organization. Or we discover that we have put the wrong names onto a mail-merge email. When we become overly focused on measuring certain aspects of our campaign, we can get tunnel vision and not see where the obvious problems are.

4. **Generalization**. This is a common mistake, even among academic researchers. When we measure something, we are often looking at human responses.

Professional Commentary

Marianne Eisenmann
Managing Director of Public Relations and Analytics
Syneos Health

The intangible nature of relationships, the mainstay of the public relations profession, often leaves practitioners a bit daunted when it comes to measurement. In my experience, the primary obstacles are lack of knowledge about how to measure and fear that (1) the cost will be high, diverting resources away from programs, or (2) the results will not impress. But, as the authors point out, *not* measuring is a mistake and burying your head in the sand is not a strategy. You need to measure something that is meaningful to the organization and this chapter will get you started thinking about how to approach that and what makes sense.

In the agency environment, measurement of our media relations efforts for clients is essential to help demonstrate value and keep or grow budgets. A lot of resources are invested in building relationships with journalists, understanding the media landscape, and developing the right story lines. Ideally, we want to keep this momentum moving—but we need to give our client data to justify ongoing budgets for media relations. That's why my mantra is "get it right from the start." Defining objectives and putting a measurement plan in place right from the start sets you on the right course and reveals the way forward.

For example, if the business objective is to educate key audiences, we identify the top tier media targets in trade, business, and consumer outlets based on how their readership aligns with the client's stakeholders. That forces us to prioritize outreach to those outlets, track placements and message penetration, and show a direct link between outcomes and business objectives—which can help justify our future budgets.

Outputs (what we did) are a valuable measure of efficiency and how well we utilized resources for outreach, and they can also be an indicator of what we can expect. As examples we can ask, *When does our story align with the editorial calendar?* or *What breaking news has temporarily bumped our feature?*

Getting it right from the start also makes the tracking of outputs and outcomes more manageable. It can be done as we go along, as part of

(Continued)

the overall media relations process, and be built into the budgets for that. Measurement is a moving process, not a one-shot deal. It is far too painful if you wait until December. You need to do it continuously to show progress, to identify barriers and to change course, if needed. Measurement provides insights that inform your media relations strategy and, if you follow the advice in this chapter, set yourself up for success. Who doesn't want to do that?

Marianne Eisenmann Biography

Marianne Eisenmann, MBA is Managing Director of Public Relations Research and Analytics at Syneos Health. She is also a member of the Measurement Commission for the Institute for Public Relations (IPR), was chosen for the 2015 *PR News* Measurement Hall of Fame, was voted one of 2012's "100 Most Inspiring People" in the life sciences industry by *PharmaVOICE100*, and was the 2012 Healthcare Businesswomen's Association "Rising Star."

Even when we look at whether our information is being *accepted* by journalists, we are in essence measuring one journalist's reaction to something. Data is a collection of single responses. In media relations, we *should* focus more on the single response and less on the whole collection of responses. And while obtaining a large number of data points is valuable, the mistake of assuming that all humans will respond in the same way is a problem. It doesn't matter if you've created a thousand relationships with journalists, the next one you contact is going to be unique. We need to be on guard against generalizations, particularly if we are concerned with relationships.

5. **Big data as the solution**. There is a move in organizations to aggregate lots of information into large data sets from which information can be extracted. There can be value in this, particularly if we want to see what consumers are saying about our organizations on social media, or if we are attempting to determine how strong of an influencer a particular journalist is. But, extracting information from large data sets cannot always give us the answers we need to evaluate our media relations effectiveness. Keep in mind that big data is often aggregated individual social media data. While this *might* be valuable from the perspective of understanding consumers, it may not necessarily be valuable from a media relations perspective. Big data is a tool that should be used when appropriate, but it is not the appropriate tool for every instance.

6. **Measuring without a plan**. While not engaging in measurement is a serious issue, measuring haphazardly may be even worse. In the next section, we will discuss what goes into an effective measurement plan, and how to set yourself up for success.

Setting Yourself Up for Success

Planning for measurement is one of the best ways to be successful in your efforts. Knowing what elements are important to your organization, what the overall goals for media relations are, and your goals for evaluation will help ensure you avoid some of the common mistakes in measurement. Keep in mind—the effective media relations practitioner has a plan before first reaching out to a journalist. Similarly, effective measurement requires thoughtful consideration and research prior to putting measurement to work.

The best way to accomplish this is to integrate measurement into your overall media relations plan. For example, you have likely already planned your story ideas, your outreach, and the various strategies you will use to establish and maintain relationships with journalists. Chances are, you have also established a timeline for certain events to occur in your media relations program. As part of this timeline, you should seek to integrate measurement and evaluation at multiple stages.

As you begin to think about your measurement plan, you will want to consider the following questions:

1. What is the overall goal of your organization's media relations efforts? This question is deceptively complex. The simple answer will usually be that the goal in media relations is to garner press coverage. However, if this were truly the only goal, then we would have stopped talking about measurement at counting placements. A more nuanced approach to this question should answer whether or not your organization is, as examples, trying to build awareness, change or create a reputation, support sales, or drive donations. In other words, your media relations goals must always be aligned with your organizational goals. These goals should drive your decision on what to measure and when to measure it.

2. How will you define success? While this is similar to what your goals will be, success can also be defined by a number of other factors. For example, if you have a client who defines success as being featured in national media, then your measurement plan should speak to that. Or, if your organization's managers believe social media mentions are the primary source to use to gauge audience interest in a story, then you will need to plan for that as well. Each media relations project will likely have different definitions of success, but to create an effective measurement plan *those definitions must be developed in advance.*

3. What will you do with the results of your measurement? This is an important consideration when putting together your measurement plan. It is one thing to collect information and to measure your

efforts, but it is quite another to know how you will use that information to change course as needed. Having an idea as to how you will use the data you gather, as you gather it, will save you from having to try to figure it out as you go.

4. What is your plan for managing expectations?
   Your measurement will undoubtedly show that you are doing well in some aspects of your media relations efforts. Similarly, it will probably show some weaknesses that need to be improved upon. It is a good idea to understand what limitations your media relations efforts, and the associated measurement, will have. For example, if your organization is primarily connected to one region, or a community, then it is unlikely that you will garner national media coverage. Therefore, it wouldn't make sense to create a measurement system where national media coverage is the most important element. Another limitation would be the nature of your measurement. If you are not going to conduct surveys of the public, it will be impossible to know what the perception of the public is, based on media coverage of your organization. Knowing these limitations and expressing them to your organization ahead of time may help you avoid unrealistic expectations once your media relations efforts are underway.

Your organization, and you as a practitioner, will benefit greatly from having a predetermined measurement plan for your media relations efforts. In putting your plan together and then executing that plan, one important element to keep in mind is the need to be flexible. All good media relations plans should have the ability to adapt and change course as need. Your measurement plan must also have the flexibility to change as your media relations program changes.

Defining ROI in Media Relations

To this point in the chapter we've discussed various methods for measuring media relations. In the beginning of the chapter, we also discussed how return on investment—ROI—was once envisioned in monetary terms using advertising value equivalency (AVE). But a simple problem remains for many current media relations practitioners—without using advertising equivalency, how do we show the return on investment for media relations?

Organizational leaders, particularly corporate leaders, often have backgrounds in business, where ROI can be measured in terms of sales, investments, or some other form of tangible—read: "monetary"—engagement. With media relations, we are often more concerned with creating and maintaining relationships and affecting attitudes and perceptions, which might result in monetary relationships, but can also be a decidedly nonmonetized commodity. In an organization that is only concerned with monetized outcomes, media relations is often relegated to the role of being simply a tactic, rather than a strategic function of an organization. It is usually up to the media relations practitioner to show the value associated with media relations, and the goal of this chapter has been to give you the basic tools needed to start that process.

In thinking about how to address your organization in terms of the value of media relations, being able to show your output efforts will be a key first step. Your media log will be helpful in this regard. As part of this, you will need to be able to show *why* the journalists and publications you are attempting to engage with are valuable to your organization. Here again, research is vital. For example, if you are operating within a small community where the public has high trust in its local media, then there may be a greater value in reaching out to those journalists, as opposed to national media.

The media relations practitioner needs to have a strong understanding of the audiences that each journalist serves, and in turn, the value of those audiences to the organization. Effective practitioners should be able to show the value in reaching out to certain media and, particularly, how audiences will or will not engage with the information. For example, while many organizational leaders will "feel good" about a national media mention, it may not have a strong return in terms of public engagement, whereas a more directed engagement with small outlets may create more movement within targeted publics within those audiences.

The value of media relations, and the return an organization can seek from investing in strategic media relations, often comes in terms of **knowledge, attitude, and behavior.** Knowledge refers to what people *know* about your organization; attitude is how people *perceive* your organization or product; and behavior is how people *act* in regard to your organization. Media relations efforts should create an **impact** on all three of these key areas, the sum total of which is able to show the ROI of media relations efforts.

Measuring Knowledge

Creating name recognition and awareness of an organization is often one of the goals of media relations. We certainly want journalists to have knowledge about who we are, but ultimately we want the journalists' audiences to recognize us. Our hope is to create **salience**, or top-of-mind recognition among the public. This is obviously important for newer organizations, but is also valuable for longstanding organizations as well, particularly if there is a new aspect about which the public should be aware.

There are various ways to measure knowledge as it relates to media relations. For example, have you ever received a comment card or short survey when you've purchased a product? One of the questions is often "where did you hear about us?" The options are generally related to hearing about the organization or product from a friend or relative, or media of some type. These consumer responses are usually recorded in some way to capture the impact of media relations outreach. While these point-of-purchase measures are valuable, they are limited in that they only collect information from people who have previous knowledge of the product or organization.

We can also gather data on knowledge of our organizations from consumer surveys and focus groups. These methods often are more costly in terms of time and money, but they provide a direct measure of our efforts with consumers. A less costly approach might be to use social media to determine if people have heard about your organization. Looking at articles that have been published and the resulting comments or shares might also give you some indication of how many people are aware of your organization, though these are indirect measures and may not give the most accurate picture.

When looking at the impact of media relations on audience knowledge, it is important to decide whether direct or indirect measures are most important. Many times, organizations are more concerned with other impact measures, and assume that attitudinal or behavioral measures are also capturing knowledge. This is likely the case in terms of marketing measures such as sales, but it may not be sufficient in determining the value of media relations. When we are looking at the impact of media relations on knowledge, we should seek to measure directly whenever possible, and to tie it directly back to our media relations outcomes. For example, if we want to know the ROI of a particular published article based on its impact on knowledge, we would need to link our measurement to the article in question, usually through direct measures.

Measuring Attitude

Attitude, or perception, about an organization among the public should be one of the key goals for media relations. After all, we've put a lot of time into developing our key messages and working with journalists to attempt to make sure those messages are part of their articles. We also often share our good news with journalists, whether it is to tell them about a special event we are having as part of our corporate social responsibility efforts or to tout a better-than-expected earnings quarter. We share this good news because it reflects positively on our organization. When we share bad news—as we learned about in Chapter 6—we hope to do so in such a way that the public still perceives our organizations in a positive way.

Attitudes are essential to our efforts. Unfortunately, they can be difficult to measure. Of course, we can go back to our direct measures—surveys and focus groups—which are the most reliable methods, but, as we noted previously, the time and costs associated with these measures may not allow us to use them as often as we would like. Here again, indirect measures are used to help us get the "pulse" of the public with regard to our organization. Examining the content of social media mentions, a form of *sentiment analysis*, can give us at least some idea of what the public is saying about our organization, and the prevailing attitudes associated with us. Unfortunately, these snapshots are not generalizable to all our audiences (as not all audiences are on all social media), but they can often be quickly obtained with relatively low costs.

Ideally, we would measure the change in attitude among the public over time. This is where establishing a baseline is vitally important. As with knowledge, we would prefer to link our media relations outcomes with attitudes. This can be done only if we measure those published articles in addition to audience measures. For example, if a journalist writes an article about your organization that contains your key messages, you will want to be able to see if those messages are resonating with your publics. You can only do this if you have determined that the article contains the key messages in the first place. It's not necessarily a complicated process, but you may be surprised how often it doesn't happen.

Measuring Behavior

Behavior is likely the most impactful aspect of media relations efforts. Constituents who are knowledgeable about an organization and have a positive attitude toward it are most likely to behave in a way that is consistent with those perceptions. Admittedly, positive attitudes do not always lead to positive behavior—but media relations outcomes can often be linked to behavior. Sales are the most consistently used measure of behavior, but other behavioral aspects can also be tied to media relations outcomes. Attendance at events, increases in donations or volunteers, and sharing or liking on social media are all examples of behavior that can be shown to link to media relations.

One example that you will be familiar with is a blood drive, particularly those drives surrounding events that have affected large numbers of people. Often, media relations efforts are used to create knowledge about the event, generate a perception within the public about the importance of donating blood, and ultimately, to produce a behavior that results in people donating blood.

Changing or reinforcing behavior based on attitudes and knowledge can be considered one of the primary goals of public relations, and the same is true in media relations. Behavior is always measured directly, either through measuring the actual behavior—*How many people came to the event?*—or through directly asking—*How many times in the past month have you . . . ?* The challenge in measuring behavior as part of media relations is the ability to directly relate it to the media relations efforts, which is part of the reason that those point-of-purchase surveys ask where you heard about the organization or product.

Ultimately, you will measure the ROI of your media relations efforts based on audience knowledge, attitudes, and behaviors. Usually, this will be done in a combination that makes sense for your organization. You *may* be able to determine the impact of a single outcome—for example, if you are trying to get people to attend an event and information about that event appears in multiple media sources the day before. But most often you will be looking at ROI as a longer-term process. In thinking about ROI, it is best to consider your media relations efforts as a whole. In other words, it will be far easier to measure the return on your overall media campaign rather than it is on the impact of a single story. In the end, if you can establish an effective system of measuring your media relations efforts that is supported by your organization, you will more likely be able to show the impact of your efforts because everyone is starting with the same understanding of success.

Key Concepts

Measurement in media relations ranges from the very simple measurement of output to ultimately looking at the impact of the media relations efforts. It is important to establish which measurements will provide the most value to you as a practitioner, and to your organization.

Measurement of your own efforts—output—is equally important to your success with media vehicles—outcomes. The added benefit of measuring ourselves is that it helps us to stay organized. Measuring media relations need not be an arduous task, but it is a necessary one to ensure we are consistently being strategic in our approach to media relations.

Plans for measuring media relations should use a highly personalized—to our organization—approach. While standard measurements exist, they may not always reflect our organization's goals. Similarly, each campaign should establish a new measurement plan to ensure the correct things are being evaluated.

Ultimately, our goal should be to show the overall impact of media relations for our organization. This contribution to the "bottom line" does not need to be monetary, and likely shouldn't be. But, if we want to be involved with the overall strategic communication efforts of our organizations, showing the impact we've achieved is key to media relations success.

Challenge Case

Think back to earlier in the chapter when you were the director of media relations for a hypothetical stereo system company that is about to launch a product line for direct-to-consumer sales. In that example, your company gave you substantial resources for your media relations measurement that allowed you to conduct national surveys.

Assume the same situation but cut your time down to two weeks and take your budget down to $2,500. You no longer have the time or resources for a national survey, but you still need to get a sense of what the consumer and journalist mindset is surrounding your company and industry. Your analysis will need to include both traditional and social media.

Using what you've learned to this point—how would you conduct your research to prepare for the press conference and to allow for continued evaluation of your media relations success?

Resources for Public Relations Research and Measurement

Eggensperger, J., & Redcross, N. (2019). *Data-driven public relations research: 21st century practices and applications.* New York, NY: Routledge.

Michaelson, D., & Stacks, D. W. (2014). *A professional and practitioner's guide to public relations research, measurement, and evaluation* (2nd ed.). New York, NY: Business Expert Press.

Paine, Katie. (2011). *Measure what matters: Online tools for understanding customers, social media, engagement, and key relationships.* New York, NY: Wiley.

Stacks, Don W. (2016). *Primer of public relations research* (3rd ed.). New York, NY: Guilford Press.

Watson, T., & Noble, P. (2014). *Evaluating public relations: A guide to planning, research and measurement (PR in practice)* (3rd ed.). Philadelphia, PA: Kogan Page.

REFERENCES

1. Watson, T. (2012). Advertising value equivalence—PR's orphan metric. *Public Relations Review, 39*(2), 139–146.
2. Hill, J. W. (1958). *Corporate public relations: Arm of modern management.* New York, NY: Harper Brothers. 169.

12 ADAPTING YOUR MEDIA RELATIONS PROGRAM

Thus far in this book we have addressed media relations from a broad perspective and have discussed commonalities that exist no matter the organization for which the media relations program is being conducted. For the most part, the concepts, tools, and tactics we have covered are applicable across a broad range of areas where media relations is commonly practiced, including public relations agencies, corporate communication departments, nonprofit organizations, and government entities. However, when it comes to the actual execution of media relations, including the development of relationships with journalists, each situation is unique, and applying a formulaic approach may not result in optimal results.

Becoming a Flexible Media Relations Practitioner

Before you begin any media relations program, or are brought into an existing program, it is necessary to take the time to research and understand the specific nature of your position. Each industry, client, workplace, and relationship will have specific challenges and intricacies that will require you to adapt what you know about media relations to fit that given situation. In the case of working in a public relations agency, where you may have multiple clients, the flexibility to adapt to multiple situations is a must.

Any number of blog posts, books, organizations, and how-to guides offer characteristics that are necessary to become an effective media relations practitioner. This book is no different, and the following are offered as important qualities to adopt for any media relations professional, no matter the industry, client, or workplace.

Understand the value of relationships. If you've gotten this far in the book and you don't understand the importance of developing relationships in media relations, you may have skipped a page or two. As with any relationship you have in your life, each relationship you have with a journalist will be unique. The same goes for working on teams, with supervisors, or clients. The field of public relations is a relationship-driven field, and in media relations those relationships are even more important. Remember, you don't have to be a "people person" to be good at media relations, but you need to understand the value of relationships with people and know how to strategically and effectively cultivate them.

Be flexible. No two situations are the same, and the unexpected should constantly be expected. You could plan an entire media relations campaign utilizing a drip-drip tactic surrounding the launch of a new product, and before you have a chance to execute, the product information is leaked to a journalist who tweets or posts or writes about it with accompanying pictures. You will need to change gears quickly, as your slow-release plan has now turned into a full product launch.

Be respectful. Paramount to any relationship, media relations practitioners must show respect for journalists and their roles in information dissemination. Show respect for clients, even when they demand to be featured on the front page of a major national newspaper for an announcement that is better suited to be mentioned on the page 12 news brief. And most importantly, show respect for the relationship between you and the journalists with whom you are working.

Be indispensable. Media relations practitioners need to "own" the value they are bringing. This means you will need to take ownership over showing the impact of your efforts to multiple audiences, including your organization, your clients, and most importantly, to journalists. An effective media relations relationship is one that is mutually beneficial, but if you are not providing value to the journalists you are working with, then they will seek out someone else who will.

Be creative. To effectively share information with journalists, you need to break through the clutter. That is, journalists will need a reason to pay attention to your message. This could mean a unique method of delivering a message, a creative approach to a story, or maybe even reaching out to a journalist who is unlikely to cover your organization by giving them a reason to do so. As in any relationship, sometimes it's good to shake things up a bit. Your relationship with the media shouldn't be any different.

Be proactive. In Chapter 1, we talked about proactive media relations programs, versus reactive or passive. But when thinking about how to conduct media relations and your relationships with journalists, it is important that you, as the media relations practitioner, be the one who reaches out and serves as the cultivator to the relationship. Relationships, by definition, are two-way. However, it is your job to act as the steward to those interactions.

Remember that it's business, not personal. Yes, a trite and overused quote ripped from *The Godfather*. And yes, establishing connections with journalists means that you will likely get to know them, thus making the relationship somewhat personal. But, the meaning here is to remember that if a journalist doesn't cover your event, want to interview your CEO, or simply doesn't respond to your email pitch, it's likely that it wasn't of interest to their audiences at the time; or, you failed to cut through the clutter; or you missed their deadline; or, they were out of town on vacation; or, any number of reasons that have nothing to do with you as a person. Always remember that you are doing your job, and journalists are doing theirs. And even if you develop a strong personal relationship with a journalist over time, they still may need to reject your story idea. It's not personal.

Maintain a sense of humor. You are not perfect; you will mess up. You will send a pitch meant for a food writer to the financial journalist. You will leave the "l" out of public. You will schedule a press conference for an animal shelter and one of the dogs you have brought out will do his business next to the speaker. These things will happen, and they will not be funny at the time. The good news is, no matter how badly you mess up, the sun will probably rise the next morning. Keep a sense of humor, and also keep things in perspective.

Be a student. Perhaps the most important characteristic of being an effective media relations practitioner is that you must constantly be open to learning. You will need to learn about journalists, new media outlets, messaging platforms, trends in the industry, client interests, the list goes on. As a media relations practitioner, you must constantly be ingesting new knowledge about a variety of things. One of the reasons people love working in media relations is that every day has the *opportunity* to be different— but that will be true only if you're willing to constantly learn and adapt.

If you can maintain each of the qualities listed above in any media relations scenario, you are setting yourself up for success. However, within some fields of media relations practice, there are particular aspects that are slightly different—and perhaps unique—which are important to consider. In the following sections, we will examine several industries where media relations is commonly practiced in a slightly different fashion than what you might encounter in agency or organizational settings.

Sports Media Relations

Imagine a situation where an entire journalistic industry exists just to write stories about your client, with standing-room-only press conferences nearly every night, and an opportunity to directly address your ultimate audience because they have paid money to be close to your employees. Does this sound like the best job in media relations? This is the world of sports media relations, and though it sounds as though it would be a fairly easy thing to do, it is one of the toughest jobs in the media relations world.

In most areas of media relations, we start at the ground floor in terms of relationships with journalists, and the more work we put into the relationship, the more value we provide, the better our relationships become. Journalists will, hopefully, come to see you as a valuable resource who can speak with authority as the voice of your organization. The media relations practitioners who fail to accomplish this are often the ones who view journalists as a "necessary evil" and who treat them simply as a means to an end. In sports media relations—at least at the professional level—the tables are turned. Journalists view the media relations staff as a potential hindrance to the people they want to talk to, namely the players, coaches, and team executives.

Working in sports media relations means you will need to work with the players and other team personnel in coordinating their media interviews; training them for interviews and press conferences; finding translators for athletes or journalists who need them; deciding who to allow into the locker room, in press conferences, or on the field; and handling media inquiries when someone doesn't "feel" like talking to journalists. Oh, and those journalists you're managing are trained to be aggressive and to get information that none of their competitors have, and they also expect well-catered media boxes during the game. In other words, you are the liaison between a group of people who are not trained to work with the media and journalists who know how to take advantage of that situation—and who may have high expectations when it comes to the ancillary benefits of being a sports journalist. Still sound like the best job in media relations?

In addition to managing these relationships, there will be the expectation that you provide journalists with the data and statistics they need for every game, background information on each of the players, and be able to provide unique insight and story ideas for every member of the team. On the plus side, you will be working in a fast-paced environment that puts you around a sport every day. But, you will need to work a regular nine-to-five workday, and also pregame, in-game, and postgame. You may be on the road for up to eight months a year, and you will need to know journalists in every city.

Overall, working in sports media relations can be a lot of fun, but it is also a lot of work, both to get into the field and once you're in it. Being strategic in sports media relations may mean playing a part in the organization's overall strategy, such as downplaying a player's injury so as not to give opponents an advantage, helping players to increase their popularity to help apparel sales, and helping to build international fan bases. And while the nature of the job, and the nature of the relationships with journalists may be different in sports than in other areas of media relations, many of the principles remain the same, particularly the value of the relationship between your organization and the journalists who are covering it.

Entertainment Media Relations

The entertainment industry is large and runs a gamut of multiple businesses, organizations, and people. When most people think about the entertainment industry, they are thinking about the music they listen to, the movies or television shows they watch, and in particular, the celebrities with whom they are familiar. In other words, people tend to think of the end product, and pay less attention to the "back-of-house" goings on in the industry. Think about it, when was the last time you stayed to watch the entirety of credits of a movie, unless you were confident there would be additional content?

In reality, the entertainment industry employs thousands of individuals who are not celebrities and who work in various facets, including media relations. In this section, we will explore the interaction between the media and the entertainment industry, which share a long and storied history.

In Chapter 6, we introduced you to P. T. Barnum, who once wrote in a letter to his partner James Bailey—"I am indebted to the press of the United States for almost every dollar I possess and for every success as an amusement manager which I have ever achieved."[1] Of course, as we examined in Chapter 6, many of the tactics Barnum and others used to achieve media coverage would today be considered too outrageous and unethical to be used in any form of media relations. Throughout the course of this book, we have sought to establish media relations as a strategic, mutually beneficial relationship between practitioners and journalists based on mutual respect of the others' role in dissemination of information. "Publicity," a word that often holds a negative connotation, is a term used to describe any and all information that a public receives about something. To *publicize* something usually does not mean that you are working to establish relationships, but instead trying to blanket the public with information through whatever means are needed.

The entertainment industry relies heavily on publicity. Commonly referred to as *buzz*, publicity is meant to keep events, people, or things—such as movies—top of mind with the public at large. The phrase "there's no such thing as bad publicity" originates within the entertainment industry. Of course, there very much *is* such a thing as bad publicity, but the idea that the entertainment industry relies heavily on constant exposure to the public within the media is very real.

In looking at how media relations operates within the entertainment industry, there are two areas we need to explore. The first is more aligned with the type of media relations that we have addressed thus far in this book, which is working to establish strong and strategic relationships with journalists. This is primarily found in the aforementioned "back-of-house," or support aspects of the industry. The second is more aligned with dissemination of information via publicity, an approach used more often when looking at media relations for celebrities.

Much of the more standard media relations in entertainment often involves industry trade media, though some involves mainstream media as well. For example, a production company may decide to shoot a movie involving a new technique or use a new type of camera. This might involve the production company's media relations team preparing a series of press releases for both types of media. For the trade press, the media relations team would need to know the technical specifications, perhaps including quotes from the cinematographer or camera operators. The media relations outreach might also include outreach to mainstream entertainment media, where the technical specifications would be less important but quotes and interviews with the producer and director would be more impactful. Either targeted approach would utilize many of the skill sets we have outlined in this book.

For the same hypothetical movie, there may be another team working to publicize the film through a variety of tactics—including various marketing tools—to generate publicity. This method *might* include some media relations tools and tactics, such as media tours and interviews, but will likely also include other tactics unrelated to media relations, such as cross-promotion marketing and advertising. While there may be some media relations components, this aspect of publicity is usually separated from the traditional role of media relations and is instead handed off to a specialist known as a *publicist*.

Publicists also generally are behind handling the "media relations" for celebrities. Much of the work between celebrities and the media operate similarly to the manner we discussed sports media relations working earlier in this chapter. There are a large number of journalists and outlets that are actively seeking information from celebrities, and similar to sports media relations, the practitioner often acts as a gatekeeper of information and access. In other words, instead of pitching media and attempting to earn coverage, the role of the gatekeeper is to control the flow of information that journalists are constantly attempting to obtain.

And though these publicists are generally not practicing media relations in the manner that a practitioner working in a corporation, nonprofit, or agency setting would, there are similarities. Celebrity publicists, perhaps, are even more skilled in some areas. For example, their job is all about managing expectations for journalists, a skill they must master, lest the media create a story based on speculation or flat-out false information. Unfortunately for celebrity publicists, this is not an uncommon occurrence.

One way that celebrities have sought to control some of this misinformation is by seeking to change the information flow to the public by taking journalists out of the equation and communicating directly to fans, followers, and friends on social media platforms. Similar to how organizations use social media to attempt to create an "authentic" organizational voice, many celebrities use social media to attempt to tell their own story. Most of the time, these social media accounts are managed by a small group of people, or a public relations agency. And while they are seemingly meant to share information with their fans, oftentimes the media or other social influencers are the targeted audience. The best examples of celebrity use of social media are when they are attempting to use their platforms to work in concert with media, fully cognizant that the information they are sharing will be used in media outlets and in social media.

Professional Commentary

Karen Freberg, PhD
Associate Professor and Author
University of Louisville

Social media has become an integral part of current strategic media relations practices. In many cases, social media plays a fundamental role in how reporters gather news stories or share updates with the community in real time, and it may be the first place where audiences look to find the latest news about a crisis, a new development in an ongoing story, or breaking news. In addition, the rise of influencers as a media source has made them a dominant group of individuals to  include in a growing number of media relations practices (Chapman, 2019).

In fact, for influencers in particular, social media has been the chosen vehicle for big announcements and statements rather than going directly to the traditional media. The shift over control and ownership of stories and brand narratives are constant factors in the diverse profession of media relations. Social media has in many ways allowed individual users as well as organizations to own their news and content, breaking down the barriers of exclusivity and newsworthiness. For example, when the Duke and Duchess of Sussex announced the birth of their baby boy, they went to their official Instagram account with the breaking news, not to the traditional media ("Meghan Markle, Prince Harry," 2019).

By sidestepping the traditional media outlets with the royal news, Prince Harry and Meghan Markle clearly understand their own channels serve as the digital front door for their brands. A *Telegraph* article reported the decision to break from royal tradition and create their own presence online on Instagram is about having direct access to their fans, rather than going through other channels. The article states, "The decision gives the Sussexes and their staff much greater control over the public's interaction with their posts, with Instagram—unlike other social media platforms—granting the ability to filter and delete unsuitable or unwanted comments" (Furness, 2019). It is a common practice among influencers to have a consistent presence across all platforms to share relevant news with everyone, yet in the case of Harry and Meghan, they have decided to focus on Instagram as the only channel through which they share their news with fans ("Inside Meghan Markle," 2019). While the Royal Family, like many organizations, have depended on Twitter as their go-to platform for breaking news, Harry and Meghan have opted out of this social media strategy to focus on Instagram instead to highlight the work and issues they both support with their fans and community ("Inside Meghan Markle," 2019).

Social media, like other channels of communication, allows for information to spread almost instantaneously. Breaking and owning the news is no longer limited to the media outlets in today's society. Like Prince Harry and Meghan Markle, more individuals are creating their own media outlets through shared (i.e., social media) and owned media channels (such as websites, blogs, and email newsletters). Because of this, their media relations professionals have to create a balance between being the first to break news while at the same time being sure they are agile and responsive if new developments happen across different platforms at the same time. Owning a digital presence can also generate news in itself as did the Duke and Duchess's Instagram when it broke the world record for getting a million followers in the shortest time ("Meghan Markle and Prince Harry," 2019). News that emerges on social media channels could result in coverage in traditional media outlets, which is an important element to keep in mind for modern media relations practices.

References

Chapman, E. (2019, January 9). What you should learn for your PR strategy from social media influencers. Retrieved May 6, 2019, from Institute for Public Relations website: https://instituteforpr.org/what-you-should-learn-for-your-pr-strategy-from-social-media-influencers/

(Continued)

Furness, H. (2019, April 2). Harry and Meghan launch their own Instagram account as Brand Sussex is born. *The Telegraph*. Retrieved from https://www.telegraph.co.uk/royal-family/2019/04/02/harry-meghan-launch-instagram-account-brand-sussex-born/

Inside Meghan Markle and Prince Harry's new social media strategy. (2019, April). Retrieved May 13, 2019, from *Vanity Fair* website: https://www.vanityfair.com/style/2019/04/meghan-markle-prince-harry-social-media-strategy

Meghan Markle & Prince Harry just broke a huge social media record. (2019, April 3). Retrieved May 13, 2019, from MSN website: https://www.msn.com/en-us/lifestyle/royals/meghan-markle-and-prince-harry-just-broke-a-huge-social-media-record/ar-BBVzogn

Meghan Markle, Prince Harry baby boy birth breaks with royal tradition. (2019, May 6). Retrieved May 6, 2019, from https://www.usatoday.com/story/life/2019/05/06/meghan-markle-prince-harry-baby-boy-birth-breaks-royal-tradition/1118649001/

Karen Freberg, PhD Biography

Karen Freberg (@kfreberg) is an Associate Professor in Strategic Communications at the University of Louisville, where she teaches, researches, and consults in social media strategy, public relations, and crisis communication. Freberg has written several books including *The Roadmap in Teaching Social Media* (Amazon, self-published), *Digital Media Writing for Strategic Communication* (TopHat with Emily Kinsky and Amber Hutchins), and *Social Media for Strategic Communications: Creative Strategies and Research-Based* Applications (SAGE).

Overall, while media relations in the entertainment industry has different aspects than other facets of media relations practice—there are many similarities as well. As a whole, the entertainment industry is one of the few places where publicity is still practiced—and accepted—by both journalists and the public. This allows practitioners greater leeway in terms of the types of tactics they can use, but it also means that they must constantly be putting their clients in front of the media, simultaneously managing journalistic expectations and acting as a gatekeeper for the flow of information. Working in the entertainment industry, a goal for many young practitioners, carries with it unique challenges. While working in entertainment is not—and should not—always be considered media relations, there are substantial similarities in skills, most notably a deep understanding of all facets of media.

Crisis Media Relations

Inevitably, every organization will go through a crisis. A CEO will be fired, a product will need to be recalled, or an employee will have a bad interaction with a customer. Many crises are fairly simple to manage as long as you have built strong relationships with journalists and are transparent. Transparency with reporters with whom you work well and often may be the best defense an organization can provide to handle a crisis successfully in the media. This is not to say that your connections will prevent a crisis from being covered in the media. But, if you've developed a good rapport with those covering your organization, they will at least be more likely to seek out a response from you before disseminating news of the crisis via their media outlets.

However, no matter how often you work successfully with various reporters, there are some organizational crises that will transcend those relationships and will put your organization under a microscope of journalistic investigation. Major environmental disasters—think BP or Exxon; corporate malfeasance—Enron or Theranos; or CEO fraud—Bernie Madoff or Martha Stewart, will usually result in a windfall of negative coverage from nearly every media outlet, blogger, or social media influencer.

We all can hope you will never have to deal with this situation. But if your organization does encounter a crisis of this type, your role is not to mitigate the crisis but to manage the media relations response. It is likely that other parts of the organization will be heavily involved, including corporate executives, the legal department, outside crisis specialty firms, accountants, the list goes on. In a crisis situation, organizations will often "circle the wagons," a cliché that refers to using all available resources to mount a defense. Your role will likely be relegated to planning news conferences and handling calls from journalists.

In an ideal world, the relationships you have developed with journalists will make you an integral part of the advisory team in a crisis. But also remember that in a crisis, journalists who would not normally cover your organization may be the ones attending the press conferences and asking for interviews. Your responsibility will likely be to ensure that these journalists are getting what they need in a timely fashion.

The tactic of many organizations going through major crises is to only release limited amounts of information, to scale back the availability of organizational leaders, and to attempt to limit the potential financial losses. But journalists have a duty to report information that impacts the public, and if they cannot get the information from the organizational leadership, they will get it from other sources. Journalists will seek out employees, volunteers, investors, neighbors or anyone else who might be able to provide some perspective. At the same time, social media will be sharing information, rumors, memes, and fake accounts to further complicate the matter. The result? The crisis will continue to grow in its breadth until your organization is severely threatened.

Most media relations practitioners welcome earned media—but earning media through organizational crisis is not a good tactic. Some crises will bring about an end to an organization, most will not. Keep in mind that after the crisis is over, you will again need to work with journalists to garner earned media coverage. But depending on the nature of the crisis, you will likely not be able to pitch the same types of stories that you did before the crisis. A major food organization that has just gone through an *E. coli* outbreak will likely not be the place that food writers or bloggers will want to visit. But perhaps there would be an opportunity to engage with science journalists to talk about food safety and decontamination procedures. Not every crisis will be an opportunity, but every crisis will probably change the nature of the relationship with journalists, and you will need to be able to adapt to that change.

Government Media Relations

No matter whether you are in federal, state, or local government, the media will be interested in what you have to say. Nearly every announcement, press release, or event will be covered to some extent. Journalists must fulfill their obligation to the public, and when government offices release information, it is generally important to the public. This makes working in the government slightly different from other areas of media relations in that you do not necessarily need to build relationships with journalists to have them use the information you send to them; most of the time the journalist has an "obligation" to disseminate it, for the benefit of the public.

But with this ability comes a great responsibility to be transparent and honest with journalists. Of course, all media relations practitioners should be transparent and honest, but sometimes in an organization you may not reveal all of the information about something. For example, if you are launching a new product, you may know all the details about its release date and the features of the product, but you may choose to release them slowly over time to build public anticipation for the product. In government public relations, such tactics are not an option. Depending on the jurisdiction, the public—including the media—have a right to access all information. This changes the dynamic of the relationship between the media relations practitioner and the journalist.

Although journalists have an obligation to report on information disseminated by the government, they also have a duty to question officials, processes, and procedures. In this case, the journalists act as the "voice of the people." Citizens have a right to ask questions of their elected leaders, and journalists often fill that role. This also potentially alters the dynamic of the relationship between media relations practitioners and journalists, and requires that you, as a practitioner, must fill both the role of the information disseminator and policy defender. If you are working in a large government organization, you are likely part of a team that has developed and trained with key messages. At more-local levels, you may be a sole practitioner, and it will be your job to work with elected officials to develop your message strategy.

Keeping in mind the dual role that you may play when working in government media relations is very important, and like every other area of media relations, developing strong working relationships with journalists is an effective proactive strategy for ensuring your "client" is treated fairly in the media.

Being Adaptable in the Modern Environment

One of the key tenets of media relations is that, at its core, it doesn't change. Establishing relationships with journalists, exchanging information, and helping to convey your organization's key messages and stories will always remain the heart of media relations. However, the tools we use, the journalists with whom we are establishing relationships—including their outlets—are in a constant state of flux. Additionally, organizational structures, including who we as media relations people report to, are also subject to change.

While these changes do not necessarily impact what media relations professionals do on a day-to-day basis, they do have the potential to impact overall strategy for the media relations function of an organization, and ultimately cause a change in how organizations view their relationships with journalists. The next section examines key areas where media relations professionals can be affected by changes from internal and external forces.

The Impact of Integration

We hear a lot about the integration of the communication function within organizations. This is a way of streamlining organizational budgets, ensuring that organizational messaging is consistent across all departments, and—sometimes—reducing the overall staff needed to execute communication campaigns. For you as a media relations practitioner, this may mean that you will need to clear your communication to journalists through multiple people, including marketing and advertising, to ensure message consistency. Ideally, if your organization has integrated its communication function, you will meet often with other areas of the organization's communications team. It may also mean that your messages will be used to support theirs, and vice versa.

In theory, integration should align the multiple communications functions within an organization, and in many organizations it works well. However, it may also add a layer of complexity when getting approvals, and it could potentially limit your creative control. There certainly is nothing wrong with organizations that practice integrated communication, and it doesn't change the purpose of media relations in terms of garnering earned coverage, but it does require that you be adaptable and able to work with people from a variety of communication backgrounds.

Content Marketing

Content marketing is the creation and distribution of content about an organization that is generally intended for an online audience. It is commonly designed to be targeted to a particular audience, but often, because it is usually shared through social media, has a broader audience that includes journalists. Content that is created can be as simple as a chart or infographic, or it could be a fully produced short film. Content marketing often goes hand in hand with integrated organizational communications, because the content that is created is frequently meant to be used in conjunction with advertising and with media relations.

Content marketing is a way of telling organizational stories directly to the public. It is not media relations, but often the product created as part of a content marketing program is used by journalists as an information subsidy. Here, then, is both the challenge and the opportunity. If your organization is actively engaged in content marketing—and many are—then you, as the media relations professional, need to be involved to ensure that the messages being produced are aligned with your information subsidies. The second challenge is that by acting as the media outlet, your organization may be cutting out the journalist and communicating directly with the public. As such, if your organization wants to maintain good relationships with journalists and also plans to continue utilizing earned media, then you need to be strategic about what content is produced by your organization, and what is better left for journalists to report. An organization that forgoes earned media in favor of content marketing may lose out on the advantages that strong relationships with the media can have.

Content marketing is not a bad thing, but from a media relations perspective, it should be managed and made a part of the overall media relations program. As the media relations professional, you can certainly take advantage of high quality content marketing and use it as a way to create interest among journalists. Some journalists may even include links to your content in their online stories or social media posts, which would greatly enhance the reach of your organization's content. However, without a strong relationship as a foundation, they are unlikely to do so, and therefore a strong media relations presence may be an effective strategy for elevating your organization's content marketing efforts.

The Next Generation of Communication Technologies

While we have, for the past several years, seen some stability in social media platforms, new technologies in communication and new platforms for information dissemination are constantly in a state of development. Augmented reality, virtual reality, wearable devices, holographic projections, even implanted communication devices are all on the not-so-distant horizon—in some cases, already being used—for media relations. Any new tool or platform for communication is potentially a way to build relationships with journalists. As a media relations professional in the age of information, you will need to be ready to use any and all tools at your disposal, recognizing that new platforms may mean new outlets and new journalists. This is an exciting time for communications—but also a challenge for media relations practitioners. We must constantly scan for what's next, yet remember that the basic nature of media relations doesn't change. The increased proliferation of information also means that reaching journalists through the channels they are using is more important than ever.

Key Concepts

The overall purpose of media relations remains consistent across all fields, but the execution of media relations may vary from field to field. Understanding the rules, roles, and routines for the relationship between media relations practitioners and journalists in your industry is of vital importance.

Changes in the organizational communications landscape may mean that your organization places less value on media relations than it may have in the past. It is your job as a media relations professional to show how strong relationships with journalists can contribute to aiding your organizational communications goals.

Adaptability is one of the key characteristics of media relations. Keep in mind that the tenets of strong relationships and qualities for media relations professionals will guide you through most new and challenging situations.

Challenge Case

The challenge case for this chapter is more an exercise in reflection and analysis than a particular challenge to solve. However, it is designed to help you think about the adaptability you will need as a media relations practitioner.

Think about the variety of relationships that you have in your life. You likely have very different relationships with your family as compared to your friends as compared to your coworkers. Think about how you communicate with each of these different groups, the tools and channels that you use. Now, come up with the number of different groups you have been considering in terms of your interpersonal communication. Most people would probably list about a half-dozen different groups of people, and then say that they can easily adapt to the different dynamics needed to communicate with each of those groups.

Now think about the number of journalists, outlets, blogs, and influencers out there. There are over 1,200 daily newspapers in the United States alone. The

Bureau of Labor Statistics estimates that there are more than 30,000 reporters and correspondents currently working in the United States, and that number does not include bloggers, which are estimated to be reaching numbers of nearly 30 million—though obviously not all are going to be relevant.

The number of information disseminators is mind-boggling. You may consider yourself adaptable to one or two dozen different people in your daily life, but as a media relations professional, how many more might you need to add?

REFERENCE

1. Saxon, A. H. (1989). *P. T. Barnum: The legend and the man*. New York, NY: Columbia University Press.

By this point in the book, we hope that you are aware of the importance of relationships in media relations. Particularly, we hope that you are convinced that an effective media relations program is marked by a series of successful relationships. Your media relations program, then, is the amalgamation of a series of individual relationships with journalists. At times, we have addressed your overall media relations program, mindful that it is a series of one-on-one relationships with journalists. In other words, each of your relationships exists independently.

Given the individual nature of the many relationships media relations practitioners have—or should have—with journalists, it seems odd that we would need a separate chapter when considering diverse audiences. After all, if you are successful in forming a series of relationships with multiple journalists, you've probably already gained some understanding of the diversity of journalistic audiences that you will be working with. This will likely include multiple types of outlets, a variety of journalists—their backgrounds and experiences, and, consequently, a large swath of ultimate audiences. The general guidelines we've already discussed for establishing and sustaining relationships with journalists don't necessarily change—aside from the fact that each relationship will be unique. However, you may encounter some journalists—and their audiences—which fall outside of what we might traditionally think about. We will address these now.

Diversity has many definitions. In popular usage, it generally refers to the categorical distinctions made about people, such as age, race, gender, ethnicity, and religion. Taken more broadly, diversity refers to variety, and the range of differences that exist. In the context of this chapter, we will look at diversity from both perspectives, as each is important to better media relations practice.

The Diversity of Journalists as an Audience

In several chapters we have addressed some of the challenges that arise for media relations practitioners when working with journalists of varying backgrounds. In this section, we will bring together some of that information from earlier in the book as we begin to look at how media relations practitioners deal with the many journalistic audiences they may want to reach. To begin, we will look at some of the differentiators among journalists and what practitioners should remember about those differences.

Characteristics of Journalists

Media relations practitioners need to keep in mind that each journalist is an individual. Your authors looked at some of the demographic characteristics of journalists while developing the theory of expectations management, including gender, years in practice, their geographic location, and their role within an organization. However, these characteristics are just the beginning when it comes to understanding all the potentially distinct—and shared—attributes of journalists. Unfortunately, there is no list that can tell you the ways different characteristics will impact how journalists will work with media relations practitioners. Our research in this area is ongoing. Eventually, we hope to identify how specific characteristics of journalists *might* impact their relationship with media relations practitioners. To date, we have not yet discovered a definitive solution, though there seems to be some hope that such a solution is possible.

In Chapter 7, we introduced the concept of newsworthiness and discussed how journalists and media relations practitioners share common views of what is newsworthy. Yet each group values different aspects of the information and what is newsworthy within those parameters. Initial research has also shown that male and female journalists differ on which news values are most important; specifically, female journalists ranked breaking, timely, and local news as being significantly more important than did male journalists.[1] And while further exploration is needed to see if the findings of this research would hold up if more journalists are studied, the initial findings do show that different characteristics might play a role in how journalists and media relations practitioners interact. Therefore, media relations practitioners should be mindful of these potential differences.

Differences in Media Type

Several chapters throughout the book have discussed the need to be adaptable in your media relations practices. Newspapers, radio, television, blogs, Internet-only, podcasts, and social media are all appropriate potential outlets for information provided by media relations practitioners. Journalists working within each *type* of outlet may have similarities in terms of their needs—for example, television and streaming outlets will be interested in visuals; radio will want information that can be presented succinctly to work within their time allotments. But each may also have unique elements that will only be important to their *specific* outlet. Newspapers in the United States, for the most part, follow the *Associated Press* in their approach to style, but other newspapers may have their own style guides that should be followed. One broadcast television outlet might accept video, others may always want to produce their own.

So, aside from needing to know the differences in types of outlets, and the information that will be most useful in establishing a relationship with their journalists, we must also be mindful that we cannot generalize based on outlet type.

Differences in Experience

While years of experience has already been discussed as a characteristic that needs to be kept in mind—we must also consider the differences in experience. Throughout the book, we have tried to show that media relations practitioners must be mindful of many types of journalists, including those who are trained in newspapers and other traditional media outlets. These reporters have likely either been trained in their profession via *formal*—specific coursework in an educational setting—or *informal*—on the job—methods. Also, media relations practitioners must keep in mind that not all journalists work in traditional media settings. Some of them may not have received any sort of training outside of working for their specific outlet. These journalists also may not work as professionals—people who are primarily paid for their journalistic work—and may derive their primary income from another occupation. Another group of writers may, in fact, derive their primary income from journalistic work, though they engage as freelancers, working for multiple outlets.

Each of these types of journalists may have different experiences that impact their relationships with media relations practitioners; we need to be aware of these potential differences when we reach out to them and establish relationships. For example, if a journalist has been trained in a formal setting, they will likely have been exposed to public relations, and media relations, in some way; whereas a journalist without formal training may not be familiar with the role of media relations in an organization. A journalist who works for multiple media outlets may be the right person to reach out to, depending on the story and the outlet they are working with at the time. With freelancers, this can change from week to week, or even more often.

You will need to remember that each journalist has unique experiences that will impact your relationship. Just as you likely have different types of relationships—based on past experiences—in your personal life, you will also have different types of relationships with journalists.

Multiple Approaches to Storytelling

Earlier, we discussed different media types and how media relations practitioners must adapt to present information in a way that will work for each journalistic audience. Another aspect that is important across both media outlets and journalists is how stories are told. As we learned in Chapter 10, each outlet, and journalist, has their own *voice*, their way of sharing information. There are some generalizations that can be made. Newspapers and their accompanying websites and daily television news broadcasts most commonly will want to tell the news of the day—or the hour—in a fairly succinct and primarily factual format. Magazines will be less concerned with presenting a facts-only approach and will usually attempt to contextualize information, depending on how frequently they are published.

Some journalists primarily work in long-form narrative, meaning their work might appear over a period of time in multiple columns or video stories, or that they might produce an extended piece that appears in an outlet. Others may produce shorter pieces that are meant to provide information in a quick-to-read or -view format that their audiences can rapidly digest. Knowing a journalist's approach to storytelling is an important part of developing a relationship. The manner in which you provide information to them should be consistent with both their outlet and their individual storytelling style.

Engagement With Audiences

As we discussed in Chapter 10, each outlet's and each journalist's voice can have an impact on the relationship with their audiences. Understanding the relationship between a journalist and their audience can be an important factor in your media relations efforts. For example, some journalists will directly engage with their audience via social media, comments on websites, or in some other way. Others will engage with their audiences in less public settings, or only through the information they present. Likewise, some outlets will encourage their audiences to engage with it directly, such as asking for community members to send in cell-phone videos, or to engage via social media.

Today, increasingly more outlets and journalists are relying on building communities around their information. This is due, in no small part, to the plethora of choices audiences face in deciding where to get their information. As more consumers seek convenience in their information gathering,[2] they are turning to outlets where they are already spending time. This may be one of the main reasons that traditional media outlets are among the most followed accounts on social media. But it also presents a challenge to media relations practitioners. We need to understand how audiences are engaging with reporters and outlets and where they are engaging, to be able to provide information that supports the journalists' efforts. In this way, we can be seen as partners in their attempts to provide information to their audiences.

Diversity of Audiences

While we have spent much of this book focusing on journalists who, as part of their work, construct and share information with general audiences—the public at large—they are not the only journalistic audiences that media relations practitioners will need to consider. In Chapter 1, we discussed that one of the first things an effective media relations practitioner does is "find the audience." Sometimes, those audiences are journalists and outlets that have the public as their main consumers. And sometimes, we need to think more about where our stories should go to reach a more targeted group of people, in terms of journalists and your ultimate audience. In this section, we will explore opportunities for media relations practitioners that take a more direct approach to the audience we are targeting.

Nontraditional Audiences

In thinking about nontraditional audiences for media relations, we start focusing on audiences that may, or may not, be journalists, at least in the sense that we would normally consider. Earlier in this chapter, we looked at diversity in terms of a journalist's experiences. When it comes to working with nontraditional audiences, this diversity becomes even more important. Many of these audiences are "journalists" in the sense that they disseminate information, but it is likely they would not consider themselves as such. Because of this, they are less likely to have experiences dealing with media relations practitioners. Establishing relationships with these audiences, therefore, often takes additional time in order to build trust, and in some cases, to convince them that you are indeed trying to help them in their work. Whereas more traditional journalistic audiences understand the function of media relations, with nontraditional audiences you may need to be more patient; and may also have to serve as an educator while building your relationships.

However, the time you put into building relationships with these information disseminators may allow you to access your ultimate audiences more directly. Because you are likely dealing with sources of information—outlets—that your ultimate audience is paying attention to, and trusts, the dividends your efforts pay can be worth the time needed to develop these relationships.

Business-to-Business outlets are also sometimes referred to as **trade publications** or **B2B**. Of all your nontraditional audiences, the reporters working within these outlets are the most likely to be similar to traditional journalists. The purpose of trade publications is to provide information of interest to those working in specific industries. Most often, B2B outlets are in the form of a magazine—either traditional print or online—or a news website. The information is usually related to organizations that provide products or services to other organizations rather than to the general public. One example of a B2B organization would be a company that produces air conditioners for automobile manufacturers, another example would be an organization that manufactures steel beams for building companies and contractors. And though it may, or may not, come as a surprise, there is a trade publication or outlet for nearly every industry. In fact, there are even several membership organizations that operate within the trade publication world, including the American Society of Business Publication Editors and the Trade Association Business Publications International.

With titles like *Foodservice Equipment Reports, Water & Wastes Digest,* and *Elevator World,* you are unlikely to stumble upon these publications at the newsstand, but their audiences may include key ultimate audiences for your organization's information. For example, if you are working in media relations on behalf of a city government and the police department is adopting innovative techniques in community policing, then the *Police Journal* might be interested in doing a story. If they do pick up your story, then you can probably share that article via social media and with traditional journalists as a third-party endorsement that what your department is doing is of interest. These outlets can be valuable for your media relations efforts, and you will want to take the time to research the opportunities that exist for your organization.

Trade groups and associations can be another source for you to reach your ultimate audience. Larger trade groups may have publications that fall into the B2B category, while others will rely primarily on newsletters or email updates to share with their membership. These trade groups and foundations are most often narrowly focused, so if you hope to engage with the people who are putting these newsletters together, you will need to make sure that your story idea fits into that focus. For example, the Midwest Global Trade Association "focuses on business people from Minnesota and neighboring states who share an interest in international business opportunities,"[3] while the International Caterer's Association is dedicated to "providing education, mentoring and resources for professional caterers and promoting the profession of catering to clients, industry members, vendors and the public."[4]

Many of these trade groups or associations are staffed by volunteers from the industry they cover. The larger ones will also have limited professional staff who work to support the association. Often, the media relations practitioner will learn of these associations because the organizations for which they work have members who belong to the association. Therefore, one of the easiest ways to access the information these associations share is to ask your clients—if you are working in an agency, or people within your organization—if they belong to any of these groups. If so, then there may be an opportunity for you to be introduced to the people who are putting these newsletters together. While these examples represent what are obviously niche audiences, media relations practitioners should seek to communicate with their ultimate audiences at every opportunity.

Internal audiences are also an important targeted public that media relations practitioners may not think of when it comes to audience engagement. Let's face it, media relations is primarily concerned with external audiences, but in order to help in those efforts, we need to consider our internal audiences as well. In his book *BrandSimple,* branding expert Allen Adamson indicates that getting employees engaged in the branding of your organization is one of the key components to success.[5] For media relations practitioners, engaging with internal audiences is no less important. Whether they are your employees, volunteers, or sponsors, internal audiences are vital to supporting your external efforts.

While you, as the media relations practitioner, may not be directly responsible for communicating with internal audiences, it is essential to know who is, and what methods are being used for communicating to those audiences. They might come in the form of a newsletter, email update, or intraorganizational website. As the media relations practitioner, you will need to be keenly aware of what information is being shared with internal audiences and ensure that the internal and external messages are consistent. Remember, every internal audience member can act as an ambassador to the broader media for your organization. Imagine if your organization were going to lay off some employees, would you want those employees to hear about it on Facebook or in the local newspaper first? If they do, you can bet that a journalist would love to get their opinion on the pending downsizing. Sharing information with employees and other internal audiences first is not only the best thing to do when it comes to media relations practice, but—especially in the case of negative news—it's also the ethical thing to do.

Social Media

In Chapter 2, we discussed the four types of media: paid, owned, shared, and earned. Social media can occupy all four of these areas at once. And while media relations practitioners are most often concerned with earned media—in fact, it is our primary role—we should not ignore the potential for audiences among other types of media as well. We have discussed the role that journalists often have as influencers on social media, and in various chapters we have addressed the roles of other influencers, such as bloggers. Here, we will discuss the role that the modern influencer can play outside of earned media. Although their audiences and ours can often intersect, these influencers are often outside of earned media and occupy a space that is both shared and paid.

Social influencers are a popular group with many organizations today. These are people—sometimes celebrities, sometimes not—who have massive followings on social media, most often Twitter or Instagram. Celebrities on social media can have followers in the tens of millions, with some celebrities having nearly 200 million. If you want a celebrity to mention your company on their social media, it usually happens through major endorsement contracts. However, celebrities do not have a monopoly on the influencer game. In fact, some of the most famous influencers are not celebrities, but rather people who have built a following around a topic. These trusted influencers are not journalists but are instead people who have found a niche in a particular topic area and have become trusted disseminators of information. However, these influencers have also sought to monetize their influence, and command large sums of money to post about a product or company. What they charge will depend on their number of followers and their engagement with those followers. While there are no hard and fast rules for paying, general industry practices are $1,000 per 100,000 followers on Instagram, $2,000 per 100,000 on YouTube, and similar amounts for other social media platforms.

You may be saying to yourself that this amounts more to marketing than to media relations, and you would be right. Paying for coverage clearly falls into the advertising or marketing realm, so why are we discussing it in a media relations book? Because you cannot ignore it, and many organizations are putting more and more dollars toward influencer marketing, while at the same time potentially scaling back other efforts, including media relations. In fact, influencer marketing today is estimated as being a more than $1.7 billion industry.[6] It has grown so much, with influencers charging so much, that some researchers have suggested an "influencer bubble" is coming, akin to the dot.com bubble of the early 2000s or the real estate bubble of 2008.[7] We are already seeing that bubble starting to burst, particularly as some influencers have been accused of deceptively increasing their audiences in order to charge higher rates.

Media relations practitioners need to pay attention to the other forms of marketing outreach, used by their own organizations and by their competitors. It should be noted that not all influencers only post content for which they are paid. There are numerous examples of "organic" content being shared by influencers on social media. For example, if an influencer enjoys a restaurant or a product and posts about it—without a hashtag indicating it is either sponsored or an advertisement—then it is considered genuine engagement; and this can be priceless for an organization. While media relations practitioners cannot affect these organic engagements, it is your responsibility to monitor social media, particularly influencers who are engaging with your targeted audiences. And while your organization may not be engaging in influencer marketing, that doesn't mean that you should ignore the opportunity to cultivate relationships with those influencers.

Microinfluencers are a subset of social influencers, but instead of having followers numbering in the tens of millions, their audiences may be as small as a few hundred. A defining characteristic of a microinfluencer is that they are leaders in a specific and narrow market. A microinfluencer might only post about something from a specific city, or post about a specific niche topic, such as woodturning, travel, or health food. Microinfluencers are growing in popularity in terms of influencer marketing because their sponsorship costs are usually low or nonexistent, and their level of engagement with their followers is high.

These influencers, for the right organization, may be a fit within the media relations realm. Microinfluencers, like bloggers, often are looking for what's new, what's unique, and ways to share that information with their followers. While some microinfluencers are working their way to become larger, others have followings that remain fairly static but highly engaged. As a media relations practitioner, you should seek to identify these microinfluencers to see if there are opportunities for information collaboration.

A Final Word on the Diversity of Audiences

Your media relations efforts for your organization may not extend beyond traditional media. If it doesn't, you aren't necessarily doing something wrong. However, if you don't consider the diversity of potential audiences and journalists who are out there, then you may not be fully utilizing your skill sets. Remember the second rule of media relations, *find the audience*. Your audience may be traditional journalists working in community newspapers, and if that is your most valuable potential partner, then you certainly should be spending most of your time cultivating those relationships. Remember that each organization, each client, and each story is unique, but your job as a media relations professional is to match up the right story with the right audience, even if it's not the most obvious one.

Diversity of Media

When you saw the title for this chapter, you probably were thinking that "diversity" was likely referring to the more standard use of the term, primarily addressing racial, ethnic, and religious diversity. These are also important audiences, and an effective media relations practitioner needs to consider all potential media audiences with which they might need to develop relationships. This includes the potential audiences we have discussed so far in this chapter and the journalists and outlets who have racially and ethnically diverse audiences. At the risk of repetition, remember that it is your job as the media relations professional to consider *all* your audiences, and not engaging with ethnic or foreign-language outlets may mean that you are missing out on some key audiences.

Traditional "Ethnic" Presses

The two largest, and most historic, ethnic presses—outlets—in the United States have traditionally been the Hispanic and Black media. However, a 2018 Pew Center report[8] indicates that both have shown declines in recent years in terms of readers and viewers. The two largest Spanish-language news broadcasters, Telemundo and Univision, showed a decline of viewership of 6% during the time of the Pew Center study, though both still command viewership of around 1 million for the early evening newscast. However, this decline in viewership is likely related to the overall drop in viewership in broadcast news as much as it is to consumers switching to English-language broadcasts. Similarly, many of the major daily Spanish-language newspapers have experienced a reduction in their circulation, though again, this may be attributed to the overall decline in newspaper circulation numbers. The same report showed weekly and biweekly Spanish-language newspaper circulation had remained consistent over a period of four years. Circulation of Black-oriented publications remained somewhat steady from 2016 to 2017, with the top ten weekly or biweekly publications changing less than 5% either up or down. These numbers, according to Pew's study, show a leveling of circulation following a consistent decade of decline.

However, in another Pew Study[9] it was found that non-White audiences were using Instagram and Snapchat for their news at a significantly higher rate than were White audiences. These shifting numbers might mean that while Spanish-language and Black audiences are changing their media habits—as are all audiences regardless of ethnicity—they are not necessarily seeking out alternative "mainstream" media. In fact, what is more likely is that they are finding information that is of greater interest to them—likely more focused—in the more-directed social media sphere, rather than in traditional media.

However, because the numbers are generally dropping across the traditional ethnic press does not mean that you, as a media relations practitioner, should not seek to build relationships with journalists at these outlets, if appropriate for your organization. And here's a hint: It's probably appropriate. This is true particularly if you want an older demographic to pay attention to your information.

When seeking to build relationships with ethnic media, like all relationships with journalists, you will need to do your homework. Some outlets are very similar to nonethnic media, while some will be decidedly more focused on issues specifically affecting the community they serve. However, building relationships within these journalistic audiences is no different than with any other journalists: Do your research on the outlet and the journalist, frame your stories and subsidies to be useful, and then reach out to them. If you've done your homework, then you are likely to find the same level of success in your efforts with ethnic media as you would with any other nonethnic outlet or journalist.

International Audiences in the United States

There is one issue that we haven't addressed. What happens when you don't speak the language of the reporter? This could be an issue if we are talking about the Spanish-language media. Or the Chinese-language newspapers in your community or, depending on where you live, the Somali-language press, the German-language press, or any number of community newspapers and websites that exist in the United States and are published in a language besides English. It's important to remember that not all international audiences have news outlets in their native language, but many do, and if you want to reach those audiences, it may take some extra work.

Following is a list of suggestions for working with foreign-language media in the United States. While this is generalized, in the end you will need to decide if the goals for your media relations program can be best met by spending the time to work with foreign language media outlets, or if the time would be better spent elsewhere. There is no hard and fast, right or wrong here, except to do what is best for your organization.

1. **Research**. You need to decide what the advantages and disadvantages are for working with foreign-language media outlets. Is the outlet connecting with a specific, targeted public that would otherwise be difficult to reach? Does the outlet have a strong influence over the community it serves? Is that community an important one for your organization's media relations goals? Prior to spending the time to ensure you "get it right" with these outlets, you need to decide if it is going to benefit your organization. If the answer is "yes," move on to step two.
2. **More research**. You will need to determine who the journalists are. Do they speak the same language as you do in daily life, but produce news articles in a different language? Are they trained journalists from another country, or are they Americans who happen to speak a second language? This can be an important distinction as we will see in the next section.
3. **Language**. How often do you envision working with non-English language outlets? If you live in an area where there are large numbers of Spanish speakers, and they are a key audience for your organization, have you started to learn to speak and write Spanish? If you're not planning

to work with these outlets on a regular basis but you have information that should be in these outlets, you may need to hire a translator. Keep in mind, the English language is extremely complicated. You will likely want to hire one person to do the initial translation, and a second translator to back-translate that work. There are many examples of an idea being lost in translation. If you are trying to share information in a language that you don't personally speak or understand, you will want to be sure you get it right.

4. **A plan for interaction**. If the journalist has questions, or if your goal is to build a relationship with the journalist, what is your plan for the back-and-forth conversation that will be needed? If you don't speak the same language, and you don't have a translator on your team, it's going to be tough . . . and quite possibly, expensive.

5. **Avoiding common pitfalls**. This is the polite way of telling you to check your implicit biases at the door. Are you using slang that doesn't translate? If you are speaking directly to the journalist, are you speaking louder in the hopes that volume will increase understanding? Does your body language mirror what you are saying? Conversely, are you using offensive body language? Also, while you don't want to speak so slowly as to indicate you think the journalist is unintelligent, if you are a fast talker, you might want to pace yourself a little bit. Finally, don't act as though it doesn't really matter if the journalist uses the information or not. If you've gotten this far in the process, you've decided that they are an important audience. Don't treat a foreign-language journalist as any less of a journalist than an English-speaking one.

Overall, you will want to remember that journalists, no matter what language they speak, are people. If your news is of genuine interest to the community they serve, and you have determined that it is important to establish a relationship with the journalist, take your time, do your homework, and you will likely be rewarded. Most media relations practitioners will probably not put in the same effort, which should make you stand out and provide an opportunity to become a valued partner in news dissemination.

International Audiences Abroad

So what if your organization wants to garner international media attention? In the global economy, international journalists could be a key audience for you. But stretching yourself to international media will come with challenges. Andrew Blum, in a post for *PR News*,[10] highlights some of those challenges, from the structural to the cultural.

Professional Commentary

Global Media Relations: A Brave New World

Michael Fernandez
U.S. CEO of LLYC

In the 16th century, Hapsburg King Charles V assembled much of modern-day Europe under his reign as well as some lands in the Americas acquired by Spain and Germany. It was said in his day that his was "an empire on which the sun never set."

Geographically this was never true for Charles, but it is true for an increasing number of companies that have truly gone global. Indeed, more than 1.3 million U.S. citizens are working abroad for multinationals today according to the U.S. Census Bureau. While one might expect they are employees of mostly large companies like Apple, Chevron, Citigroup, ExxonMobil, Ford, GE, General Motors, Google, IBM, Johnson & Johnson, Mars, Microsoft, and Walmart, the scope is much broader. More than 300,000 U.S. companies export goods, and 98% of them are small- and medium-sized companies that account for one third of the U.S. merchandise trade, according to the U.S. Department of Commerce.

So What Does This Mean for Media Relations and Communication Professionals?

It means that now more than ever you must be prepared to operate in an increasingly global and online profession. Even if your company has few offices or plants in other countries, it is likely that it sells products or services abroad, finances parts of its operations from investments from overseas, or sources ingredients and components from other parts of the world.

At first blush, it may seem to you that there is little difference from how your organization operates in the U.S., and interacts with American media. Major markets around the globe now have Al Jazeera, BBC, Bloomberg, CGTN, CNBC, CNN, France 24, NewsAsia, NHK, RT, and Sky News stations. The array of media—print, broadcast, and a multiplicity of online sites and channels— may even seem somewhat familiar, except that they use different languages in difference countries.

(Continued)

Because there are so many major outlets, it is important to realize that your brand and product brands can be mentioned or become the subject of controversy anywhere and anytime. To navigate these pathways safely while boosting your organization's reputation and blunting competitive and other attacks to your enterprise, you must acquire skills beyond the basic media relations capabilities that you need to master in your own country. There are a host of additional topics, challenges, and adjustments to be aware of. These range from cultural to language differences, location and time zone obstacles, differing media customs and expectations, the need for an understanding of the local market for skilled talent, cultural differences in the use of technology and social media, and media tracking and measurement.

Culture Norms, Higher Standards

Being sensitive to other cultures and business practices is important, as is being clear about how your business will organize, operate, and communicate in various markets. Not understanding these issues can cost your organization money and its reputation.

As a starting point, professionals interacting with colleagues in other countries might want to not only learn a bit about the history, culture, and language of their workmates but also familiarize themselves with Geert Hofstede's analysis of six cultural value dimensions. While this may not say a lot about the specific orientation of the individuals they are working with, it can provide a general reference for navigating the proclivities of cultures along a spectrum. These six cultural dimensions you need to be aware of are (1) individualism versus collectivism, (2) uncertainty avoidance, (3) reaction to hierarchy, (4) task versus person orientation, (5) long-term orientation, and (6) indulgence versus restraint. While this provides a thumbnail of cultural tendencies, it is important to acknowledge that countries are not homogenous, they have regional differences, and they are always evolving. The ethnic and racial composition of the populations of Europe and North America have become increasingly diverse in recent decades.

One of the basic decisions organizational leaders have to make is whether the organization will adhere to local standards or to a higher global company standard. There can be monetary costs in deciding to manufacture products in line with a worldwide standard. There can be reputation risks if adhering to minimal local standards has any negative impact on the environment, health, or safety in the production. If issues arise, communicators have to be at the ready to determine how best to communicate their company's choices.

In the 1970s, European and U.S. companies, after successfully introducing baby formula in the developed world as an alternative or supplement to breast milk, decided to introduce the product on the African continent. These companies were convinced the combination of child malnutrition and the desire for Western modernity would drive the demand for baby formula. It did, but the cost of the product in places with lower disposable income prompted mothers to dilute the recipe and thereby dilute the product's nutritional value. Worse, in some markets, the formula was mixed with contaminated local waters resulting in formula that was toxic to many babies. Worse still, initial company reactions exhibited defensiveness and denial, as opposed to showing empathy and listening to local concerns. The controversy led to consumer outrage, boycotts, and ultimately regulation including implementation of the International Code of Marketing Breast-Milk Substitutes in 1981.

Fast forward to April 2015 when Indian regulators said they had found lead in packages of Maggi instant authentic Indian noodles. Nestlé, a Swiss company, was required to remove 35,000 tons of this product from store shelves. The company's initial response was to argue on technical grounds that its tests were better than the Indian government's. The "we-know-better-than-you" attitude did not sit well with consumers in a country with a history of colonialism and occupation by others. A 2018 court ruling overturned the product recall in Nestlé's favor, but reputation damage due to a lack of consumer engagement and media relations was palpable.

Depending on an organization's specific communication demands, one needs to determine whether media relations is to be managed in-house in other countries or outsourced to an agency with developed media relationships as well as a keen sense of the marketplace, public policy, regulatory issues, and influencers. Most companies operating internationally use a blend of internal and external talent in their media relations activities. Budgetary pressures, the skills of individuals at the locale, and the relative importance of the marketplace prompt some companies to use company lawyers, human resource or government relations professionals, plant managers, or others to take on the task of company communicator at a specific site. In these instances, those wearing multiple hats should be appropriately trained by the communication team. That said, it is a huge risk to under-resource media relations in today's world and there is no doubt you will need someone familiar with the local language and business customs.

In managing a globally integrated team that is flexible enough to accommodate to local markets, one has to be careful not to communicate from a headquarters-centric mindset and to smartly collaborate to get things done efficiently. As the bumper sticker from the 1960s proclaimed: "Think Globally, Act Locally." Companies like Cargill, Coca-Cola, and IBM have focused on developing close ties and community projects in the locales where they operate, listening and interacting with key stakeholders in those communities and adapting even in the midst of crises.

Some companies adapt well from location to location. The Austrian company Red Bull is viewed often as a local company in the U.S. and elsewhere due to its sponsorships and hosting of local extreme sports events and advertising that connects culturally. McDonald's, while maintaining brand consistency, has successfully developed new menu items that align with local tastes: from flatbread sandwiches in the Middle East to shrimp burgers in Asia.

As you have global aims, you need to develop local media plans that are aligned to culture, differing communication styles, and professional norms.

(Continued)

Consistent messaging is key, but slavishly delivering the same exact message globally is a mistake.

Lost in Translation (Language)

When it comes to translating information into the local language, communicators, encouraged by global marketers and sometimes lawyers, might translate copy word-for-word. That could be a mistake. Word-for-word translations do not always create the same understanding. Even the differences in British English and American English can lead to consternation. When Nintendo rolled out its new Wii game platform, Brits could not get past the fact that the product name sounded exactly like the word many used for urine.

Mercedes entered the Chinese market with the brand name "Bensi," which in Chinese means "rush to die," and in a misunderstanding of culture and custom an online Mercedes post intended for the Chinese marketplace quoted the Dalai Lama, with whom the government of the People's Republic of China has been at odds for decades. Upon entering China, KFC performed a literal translation of its popular U.S. tagline "Finger lickin' good" which came across in Mandarin as "Eat your fingers off."

To underscore that these missteps are not simply associated with one continent or nation, Perdue marketed its chicken some years ago globally with its well-known U.S. tagline "It takes a tough man to make a tender chicken." In Spanish that became "It takes a hard man to arouse a chicken."

The key with language translations is not to slavishly translate word-for-word. Increasingly professionals are using the term "transcreate" to describe a process where word choice focuses on how the words will be understood in local markets rather than their literal meaning.

The Media Is the Message (Differing Media, Differing Challenges, and Technology)

Throughout the world's markets, online and social media are very much on the rise as is the use of mobile apps; yet broadcast remains important even as it is challenged by online video content. In India, Indonesia, and parts of Africa and Asia, print is even growing.

Coca-Cola's lead communications executive in India, Ishteyaque Amjad, who also has worked throughout South Asia says, "To stay relevant and connected with our consumers, our communications strategy gives equal importance to new age media platforms while continuing to engage with traditional media including print, television, radio and wire agencies."

While Facebook with 2.4 billion monthly active users is the world's largest social network and WhatsApp with 1.5 billion users in over 180 countries is second, other platforms proliferate. In China, Baidu is the most popular search engine and WeChat is the largest social media app. Reddit has become among the most popular sites in Canada and Australia, and TikTok with its easy-to-use app for sharing short-form mobile videos has become particularly popular in Asia. Line has become the most popular instant communications app in Japan and is growing in popularity in Indonesia, Thailand, and Taiwan. As technologies change and new channels emerge, the key for communicators will be to understand where consumers, influencers, and other key stakeholders are having their conversations in the marketplace for ideas and products. Companies are not only interested in discovering who is having conversations about their, and competitors', products and services, they are also interested in topics and ideas that have implications for public policy, marketing trends, or product and service features and benefits.

Years ago when I worked for a telecom company, we found a number of online conversations where people mentioned it would be ideal if people could dial one number and "get me at home or on my mobile phone." Our company then developed and successfully marketed that idea with the brand name AccessOne. What can companies do by monitoring these conversations? It can provide an early warning system about a problem with a product, service, or marketing idea. It can indicate who might be a willing prospective advocate for a product or ally for a public policy idea. It can lead to direct engagement with the consumer, influencer, or stakeholder or to the development of a specific communication or media relations effort.

In countries where state-owned media exists or where governments exert a lot of influence, the Internet and social media have become de facto news media outlets. We saw that with the so-called Arab Spring, a series of protests and uprisings that spread across North Africa and the Middle East between 2010 and 2011 and toppled a number of governments. Most of the news was gathered and shared by individuals outside of the normal media channels.

On July 23, 2011, two high-speed trains collided near Wenzhou, China. Thirty-nine people died and 192 were seriously injured. If you were in the People's Republic of China, you would not have learned this from government-run media outlets, but about 140 million Chinese became aware of it through Weibo, a Chinese Twitter-like platform.

Traditional Chinese media have become more sophisticated since then. Given the history, Chinese social media is viewed as a much more important source of news than in many other countries. Bruce Blakeman, Cargill's vice president of corporate affairs in the Asia Pacific, points to additional cultural differences when it comes to managing media relations in Asia. He said, "Reporters tend to not call you for comment if there is an allegation against your company. And as a foreign company, you have a higher bar to clear to be credible and considered as trustworthy than local companies, and especially state-owned enterprises."

In 2013, as a smoggy haze made its way through southern Asia, a number of media outlets and a few politicians blamed Cargill and others for burning fires to open up more land for palm oil production. Cargill quickly decided to use drones to take video footage of the sources to prove that it and its suppliers were not the culprits and shared the video on social media to quell the misinformation.

(Continued)

Around the globe, after a relationship is forged, reporters seem to be increasingly comfortable receiving pitch ideas over social media and online platforms. In fact, in much of Asia it is nearly impossible to move forward with a reporter unless you are already known to them. Where relationships are not in place, reporters prefer more traditional methods when receiving information from a PR person for the first time. Industry and trade events seemingly play a larger role outside of Western Europe, Canada, and the U.S. as places to forge and develop media relationships. Blind pitches are also frowned upon in some markets. Therefore in many parts of the non-Western world, trade shows and industry conferences serve as good places to meet media, as does scheduling short meetings with media prior to seeking coverage.

Increasingly, countries outside Europe and the U.S. are using social media to share, and the Internet to launch and demonstrate, products and capabilities. Carola Schaub Rapp,[1] an IBM communications vice president who has worked in various roles throughout Latin America and now leads communications for IBM in Europe, has indicated that while the digital world can never replace media relations, more and more social is being moved to the forefront.

As Xiaomi, the Chinese smartphone company, entered the Mexican market, it took special care to use cultural images and elements that were both relevant and hip. Its "Mi" logo was used in a way that played into the Spanish word *mi* (which means "my") with efforts and hashtags labeled *Mi Communicad* ("my community") and *Mi México Lindo* ("My beautiful Mexico"). And it identified and reached out to Mexican online influencers to trial and demo its products online.

To demonstrate its artificial intelligence capabilities, in 2017 and 2018 IBM developed an app that could be used in museums. It not only gave background on various works of art and artifacts but permitted visitors and journalists to ask questions orally and get verbal responses from IBM's Watson, its computer system capable of answering questions posed in natural language. The Voice of Art, with Watson interactive AI audio-guided demonstrations, made art and its context more approachable for casual visitors at the Pinacoteca de São Paulo (Brazil) and Museo Nacional de Antropología de México, many of whom had never toured a museum.

Getting It Done, Taking Action, Navigating Reputation

Technology is playing a larger role in how global media relations and public relations functions are managed as well. Digital analytics are used to identify key influencers, channels, and sites where a company's messages will resonate. Many online databases provide the backgrounds and contact information for journalists and bloggers specific to various markets and globally. Online media tracking in multiple languages is used to provide real-time reconnaissance as to what is happening to a brand or company in key markets and whether a potential crisis is brewing.

While I was the chief communications officer at Cargill, my team developed what we termed the "Global News Desk." It was not a physical space, but a virtual one. We live in a world today that is always on, hyper-social and highly contentious. Consequently, we saw it as vitally important to manage our reputation 24/7. To do that, we created an online tool that provided colleagues across the globe with the most up-to-date information on fast moving issues in ways that would permit them to respond to media inquiries and Internet rumors while we were asleep. At the close of business, we would hand the baton to our colleagues in Asia, and at the close of their day they would hand off the baton to our colleagues in Europe.

Other organizations have used their expanded geographies to identify less expensive or more-talented professionals to do the work. Just as some companies have moved call centers to India, communication shops are finding multilingual talent in places like Bulgaria and Costa Rica, and hire workers from these remote locales to work for them online to decrease the company costs for web designers and communication planners. There are places, like China, and other parts of Asia, Africa, and Latin America where the supply of media relations and communication professionals has not adequately met demand, and companies have found themselves in bidding wars for the limited supply. That is changing somewhat, as more Chinese, Indian, and other nationalities are attending undergraduate and graduate public relations programs in Europe, Canada, and the United States. Some companies in the interim have resorted to retraining talent from other disciplines.

What is certain is that the need for media relations talent is not ebbing. In September 2018, the Brookings Institution published a report that announced a global tipping point had been reached: Half the world's population for the first time is now middle class or wealthier. That means more of the world's 7.7 billion people are able to purchase goods and services and are more comfortable competing in the marketplace of ideas.

Navigating reputations in this brave new world will require that more organizations think globally about their media relations and consider it from both a traditional and online media vantage. At the same time they will need to use technology to act in an integrated fashion, engage multiple stakeholders, and build advocacy that is smart, quick, and at scale. This will require communicators who understand other cultures, customs, and languages. It will also mean those who are comfortable with engaging consumers and multiple stakeholders where they are, and in ways that enable not only their company's success, but also enable the communities they come into contact with, to thrive.

Reference

1. Carol Schaub Rapp, personal communication, 2018.

(Continued)

Mike Fernandez Biography

Mike Fernandez is U.S. CEO of LLYC, the leading public relations and strategic communication consultancy in Latin America, Spain, and Portugal. He oversees three U.S. offices, helping U.S.-based clients navigate Latin America and serve diverse populations in the U.S. market. He is also a professor of the practice in strategic communication at Boston University.

Formerly, Fernandez served as U.S. chief executive officer of Burson-Marsteller, corporate VP/chief communications officer at Cargill, and VP of public affairs and chief communication officer for State Farm. He started his career as press secretary for Senator "Fritz" Hollings of South Carolina. At the time he was the youngest press secretary in the history of the U.S. Senate as well as the second Hispanic to hold that role.

Fernandez is the first recipient of the Pioneer Award from the Hispanic Public Relations Association (HPRA). He has also been honored with the Paladin Award from the PRSA Foundation, and the Alexander Hamilton Award, for contributions to public relations from the Institute for Public Relations. He is a member of *PRWeek's* PR Hall of Fame.

The first challenge is **time zones**. Blum indicates that while working with national media, you might have a time difference of one to three hours, but with international media, you could be as many as 12 hours off. This means that if you want to make sure your releases are timed for a specific launch, you potentially will find yourself in the office at 2:00 a.m.

We've talked about **language**, but it's important to keep in mind that not every country has a homogenous language population. For example, it is common in Europe or some Asian countries to have a population that speaks several languages, or variations of the same language. You will need to do your research to make sure you are producing materials in the right language and dialect.

The **culture of media** varies greatly from country to country, as does the culture of public relations. In Brazil, if you want to call yourself a public relations practitioner, you will need a license to do so. In some countries, paying for placement is still commonly practiced—though this is becoming less common—or the media is tightly regulated. Understanding the media environment of a country is important if your media relations efforts will take you abroad.

Ultimately, Blum suggests that if you are planning to work with international media, then it would be in your best interest to engage with a local media relations person who understands both the language and culture of the country. Many large American agencies exist throughout the world, so it might be simple to approach one of these potential partners to see if they could provide the service for you. Alternatively, if you are in a large organization, it is possible your company already has a presence in the international location.

Much like working with foreign-language media, you will need to determine whether engaging with international media is worth the time and expense. However, if you determine that a key audience is in a different part of the world, then it will likely be worth it for you to build those relationships, even if it's through a local practitioner living in that country.

Key Concepts

Understanding the diversity of journalists, audiences, and media is integral to becoming an effective media relations practitioner. Keeping in mind the breadth of audiences that exist will heighten your opportunities for success.

Nontraditional media may provide you with an opportunity to reach out directly to the ultimate audience; forming relationships with nontraditional journalists, and those who we normally don't identify as journalists, will likely enrich your stories.

Working with ethnic, foreign-language, and international media might help you realize some potential audiences. But, particularly in the case of foreign-language and international journalists, you will want to be sure that the time and effort required are worth it for your organization's media relations goals.

Challenge Case

In this chapter, we've discussed diversity from a number of perspectives for media relations practitioners. However, we've operated under the assumption that some form of media can still achieve our goals. Here's a challenge pulled from a real-world example where the media relations team had to look beyond the media. How might you solve the issue?

A local health organization has approached your firm to promote the idea of health screenings, specifically, diabetes testing, in a primarily African American, urban, and socioeconomically depressed neighborhood. You have reached out to journalists in the community media and have garnered placements in both the mainstream—large daily newspaper, local television and top radio stations—and weekly community publications. You have also received significant mention on social media outlets, with several thousand unique shares. By all accounts, you have had a successful media relations campaign.

The problem is, community health advocates report no change in people coming in for diabetes screening. It turns out, that even though you have generated significant media interest, the targeted audiences have not paid attention. Through some research, you determine that this particular community does not trust health messages in the media.

You're going to need to engage in other types of public relations, but you don't want to set aside your successes in media relations. How will you leverage your strong media coverage to generate a community campaign? What steps will you need to take in order to get this audience to change its behavior?

REFERENCES

1. Supa, D. W., & Zoch, L. M. (2013). *Bridging the journalist–public relations practitioner gap: Toward an "expectations management" theory of media relations.* Paper presented at Association for Education in Journalism and Mass Communication (AEJMC) Annual Conference, Washington, D.C.

2. Matsa, K. E., & Shearer, E. (September 10, 2018). News use across social media platforms 2018. Pew Research Center. Retrieved from https://www.journalism. org/2018/09/10/news-use-across-social-media-platforms-2018/

3. Midwest Global Trade Association history. Retrieved from https://www.mgta. org/page/MGTA_History.

4. International Caterers Association mission statement. Retrieved from https:// www.internationalcaterers.org/our-values

5. Adamson, A. (2007). *BrandSimple: How the best brands keep it simple and succeed.* New York, NY: St. Martin's Griffin.

6. The remarkable rise of influencer marketing. (March 19, 2019). *Influencer Marketing Hub.* Retrieved from https://influencermarketinghub.com/the-rise-of-influencer-marketing/

7. Kelly, M., Dodd, M. D., & Supa, D. W. (2018). *Social media influencers: A multi-billion dollar bubble.* Paper presented at International Public Relations Research Conference, Orlando, Florida. March.

8. Hispanic and African American news media fact sheet. (July 25, 2018). Pew Research Center. Retrieved from https://www.journalism.org/fact-sheet/hispanic-and-black-news-media/

9. News use across social media platforms. (September 10, 2018). Pew Research Center. Retrieved from https://www.journalism.org/2018/09/10/news-use-across-social-media-platforms-2018/

10. Blum, A. (September 16, 2016). Dealing with international media: Time zones, language, culture and other factors. PR News. Retrieved from https://www.prnewsonline.com/international-media

14 CASE STUDIES FOR DISCUSSION

Introduction and Acknowledgments

This final chapter of the text includes four case studies of various lengths. Each one started as a business case provided to us by the Mendoza College of Business at the University of Notre Dame. Professor James S. O'Rourke, teaching professor of management at the Eugene D. Fanning Center for Business Communication, has cooperated with us as we turn these business cases, which he and his students wrote, into communication case studies with a media relations slant. We thank him and the Fanning Center for their assistance.

We have updated several of the cases, and in each case have added information that will help you think from a communication rather than an administrative perspective. We also focus the questions for discussion on areas of interest to you, communication students and professionals, who have read this book to learn about using media relations strategically.

Using These Case Studies

Before we present these studies, we'd like to mention a few things. The Buon Giorno Foods and O'Brien Paints case studies place you, the reader, in the role of a public relations professional tasked with communicating to the media about the circumstances of the case. Although these two cases are based on actual events, they each hide the real name of the organization and the geographic location in which the events took place. Each case is followed with "Questions for Discussion" to help place you in the role of the practitioner involved.

The other two cases, "Amazon Go" and "In-N-Out Burger," are lengthier and present more-complex issues facing the organizations involved. These cases discuss recent organizational events about which you can easily do additional research to find out what has happened with the organization since the cases were originally written. They also are not clearly or directly related to media relations, so in neither case does using media relations as a potential solution seem the obvious choice. These cases, too, end with "Questions for Discussion." For these case studies, the questions are a place to start discussion.

Although we ask you to answer specific questions, there are many directions you can take these cases. How might you have handled things differently, right from the beginning, from the way the case situation actually played out? As a public relations practitioner, at what point, or points, could you have stepped in to change the way the case was progressing? How might you have done that? What mistakes did people make as the situation progressed? How you proceed is up to you and your course instructor.

You can also conduct research about what is currently happening with the organizations at the time you are reading the cases, which will help to better decide how well the companies actually handled the situations discussed.

O'Brien Paint Company

Dealing With the Media in an Inflammable Situation

The Facts of the Case

A fire broke out early this morning in the Western Avenue plant of the O'Brien Paint Company in South Bend, Indiana. A night security officer smelled smoke in one of the bulk storage facilities and called South Bend fire officials on the 911 emergency line. When the officer returned from the telephone to the scene of the fire, he saw flames and immediately recognized the danger to various paints and chemicals stored in the area. He removed a hand-held fire extinguisher from the wall unit in the storage facility and attempted to extinguish the flames himself; he was largely unsuccessful.

A pumper unit, a hook-and-ladder unit, one rescue unit, and a command vehicle responded to the fire call from the South Bend Fire Department's #7 Station, located at 1616 Portage Avenue. Those units were under the command of Fire Captain Cazimir Pelazinski and arrived on scene 4 minutes and 30 seconds after the emergency call was received, at approximately 3:25 a.m.

By the time the fire units arrived, flames had spread from the bulk storage area to a production unit, a packaging room, and a box and dry-storage facility. Because of the spreading flames, Captain Pelazinski upgraded the fire designation from one alarm to three and called for two backup pumper units from Fire Station #6 at 4302 West Western Avenue; those units were on scene by 3:41 a.m.

Fire officials briefly considered evacuating the surrounding neighborhood, mostly low-income, single-family dwellings and a few low-rise apartment buildings, because of the toxic nature of smoke and fumes from the fire. A significant danger of explosion from paint, chemicals, varnish, turpentine and other products also existed at the time.

The Occupational Safety and Health Administration, an agency of the U.S. Department of Labor, requires that Material Safety Data Sheets (MSDS) be available to employees for potentially harmful substances handled in the workplace under the Hazard Communication regulation.

Section 311 of the Emergency Planning and Community Right-to-Know Act requires that MSDS be made available to local fire departments and emergency planning officials. Their purpose is to provide workers and emergency personnel with procedures for handling or working with any potentially dangerous substance in a safe manner. This would include information such as physical data (melting point, boiling point, flash point), toxicity, health effects, first aid, reactivity, storage, disposal, protective equipment, and spill handling procedures.

For a variety of reasons, fire officials elected not to evacuate the neighborhood. The fire was eventually brought under control by approximately 7:20 a.m. but has not yet been declared fully extinguished.

The security officer, Rupert J. Watson, 57, of 819 Christiana Street, Elkhart, Indiana, was unhurt in the incident. He has been employed by O'Brien Paints, Inc. since October 14, 2009, as a security specialist. Mr. Watson is a native of Elkhart, Indiana, and a veteran of the U.S. Army; he served as a combat infantryman in Operation Enduring Freedom in Afghanistan.

Your supervisor, Mr. Fredrick J. McQuethy, who is the Plant Manager at the South Bend Plant, spoke with you by telephone this morning for several minutes. At this point, apparently, no cause for the fire can be specified, though both you and Mr. McQuethy are aware that several small fires have broken out in the Western Avenue Plant in recent months, none of them causing extensive damage.

Mr. McQuethy is personally convinced that militant trade unionists in the plant set the fire. The collective bargaining agreement with members of the International Brotherhood of Oil, Atomic and Chemical Workers, local 326, is set to expire in less than 30 days. The union is adamant about renegotiating elements of the contract dealing with compensation, job security, and working conditions in the Western Avenue plant.

The building was last inspected 11 months ago by a South Bend fire marshal and was due for inspection in about 30 days. Several minor fire safety discrepancies were noted in the previous inspection but were corrected in a matter of weeks. The production area was equipped with a fire suppression system that functioned satisfactorily. The storage units were equipped with a sprinkler system that apparently failed, permitting a substantial amount of damage to occur. All areas were in compliance with state and local fire ordinances.

One last item: South Bend police have been called in by the fire department within the past hour to investigate the charred remains of an individual found in the fire rubble. As far as you know, that individual is not an employee of the firm. The security officer, Mr. Watson, claims no knowledge of anyone on the plant grounds last evening and has told investigators he has no idea how someone could have gotten in the building without his knowledge or permission. At the moment, police are silent on this matter.

Damage to portions of the plant is extensive, but production could probably resume within a week to ten days, depending on the findings of the fire investigators. Most short-term orders could be filled by the O'Brien Paint plants in Alameda, California, and Linden, New Jersey, until that time.

The Media Relations Challenge

You are the director of communications for the South Bend plant. You have successful working relationships with the local media, both print and broadcast, primarily because not much happens at the plant. Most of the big news comes out of the corporate headquarters in San Francisco. When news does occur, it is usually an announcement of interest to the city and region. Thus far, your main activities have been to send out media releases, and cheerfully and professionally answer reporters' questions when asked. You keep your online newsroom updated with information about the company and the plant. The plant manager prefers to act as the spokesperson in the unlikely event someone in the media asks for an interview or you hold a plant open house for the community.

This time things are different. Because of your communication background, Mr. McQuethy has asked *you* to explain the information about the fire to the media and, through them, to the public.

Questions for Discussion

1. Now that you've read the case, go back and reread it. Make some notes about the series of events that occurred from the time Watson, the security guard, smelled smoke. Also consider the additional information you are aware of about safety regulations, as well as your boss's thoughts about the cause of the fire.
2. Are there any items of information that you think you should *not* talk about with the media? What are they, and why shouldn't you bring them up?
3. Is there any information you prefer *not* to communicate to the media but believe you should anyway? Why do you feel that way?
4. Based on what you've read in this book, what do you think is the best way to communicate this information to the media? Why?
5. How do ethics and transparency play into this situation?
6. How quickly should you contact the media? Do you think this situation will be a case of proactive or reactive media relations?
7. What do you think will happen once you answer local journalists' questions?

8. What are the most important audiences for you to reach through media relations in this situation? What would be the best ways to reach them?

9. For which stakeholders will media relations *not* be the best way to communicate?

This case was originally prepared from public sources by James S. O'Rourke, Teaching Professor of Management, as the basis for class discussion rather than to illustrate either effective or ineffective handling of an administrative situation. Personal identities have been disguised.

Additional details related to the media relations portion of the case, and your role as a company communicator, have been added by the authors of this text with the express permission of James S. O'Rourke and the Eugene D. Fanning Center for Business Communication.

Buon Giorno Italian Foods, Inc.

Background to the Case

Buon Giorno Italian Foods has just one plant in Mishawaka, Indiana, but grosses nearly $3,000,000 per year, producing specialty Italian food items for wholesale distribution through food brokers to restaurants. The company has recently launched a highly successful line of similar food items under the Buon Giorno label that are designed for retail sale through supermarkets and specialty food shops.

A new line of specialty Italian soups has proven particularly success-ful throughout the Midwestern United States. The Mishawaka plant now produces more than 2,000 cases a month of the soups, including pasta e'fagiole, minestrone, and rigatoni arrabbiata. Retail sales of these soups have tripled in the past six months and now account for 15% of sales. The national and North American markets appear virtually unlimited.

Buon Giorno purchases ingredients for its specialty food line from a number of different importers, most of them in New York and New Jersey. Its largest supplier of pasta is Dellafina Imports of Secaucus, New Jersey. Many of the fresh produce, including beans, onions, and other vegetables come from local and regional green grocers. Specialty items, such as anchovies, roasted red peppers, oregano and other ingredients come from literally dozens of small food brokers in the Midwest and along the east coast. Such items are price sensitive and the company shops for the best bargains wherever they may be found.

The Facts of the Case and Your Involvement

You are the Director of Communications for Buon Giorno Italian Foods and are based at the Mishawaka plant. Your job involves overseeing all internal and external public relations for the firm, including media relations. In the media relations role, you also work with the director of marketing to help with media outreach for company products.

Your supervisor, Mr. Anthony Delgado, vice president of marketing and communication, called you this morning and told you that the company president, Mr. Carmine Matuso, was notified by the Michigan Public Health commissioner that your company's food products have been implicated in a series of mysterious deaths in the Midwest. The Michigan Public Health Service and several Michigan county coroners have quickly begun gathering data and reviewing autopsies dating back several months.

The link, according to Michigan Public Health commissioner, Dr. Viola Nelson, was established tentatively over the weekend in Detroit when three people became seriously ill after eating what they claim were cans of your company's soup. Dr. Nelson notified the FDA and regional public health officials and contacted your CEO, Mr. Matuso, three days ago. Since that time, one additional death has been recorded under similarly suspicious circumstances in the Birmingham, Michigan, area. For reasons known only to him, your boss has delayed telling you about this until today.

Health officials now suspect the culprit may be a deadly botulism bacterium in one or more batches of your Minestrone Milano. You make a quick series of telephone calls to production supervisors in the Mishawaka plant that reveal employees had heard rumors over the weekend and, in fact, the plant had received several phone calls from Detroit area hospitals.

The Executive Committee Decision

Following an executive committee meeting this morning at Buon Giorno Foods, the company has decided to begin an immediate recall of all Minestrone Milano. Some 6,000 cans of the soup are thought to be on supermarket shelves and in consumer cupboards throughout a seven-state area. The Minestrone Milano in question has a "Sell by" date of March 2022 and bears the lot number G-7114-AB9. The Sell by date and that number are stamped on the bottom of the cans.

The committee has decided not to recall any other soup lines or any of the company's other products. Supermarkets are being asked to pull their shelf stocks and return them to the broker who supplied them. Consumers have already been notified and are being asked to return the soups to the stores where they were purchased. Above all, the committee feels, no one should panic over this matter. After all, no definitive link has yet been established between your products and the illnesses and deaths in Michigan.

The company has retained the service of Blank, Hobbes, Harter, and Freeman, a Chicago law firm specializing in product liability. Your firm has also contracted the services of an epidemiologist and a pathologist from St. Joseph Hospital, South Bend, Indiana. They're planning to examine your production and processing equipment and packaging facilities, perhaps as early as tomorrow.

Your task is to explain this to the media and the public.

Questions for Discussion

1. Do you need to follow a proactive or a reactive media strategy in this situation?
2. What is the first thing you will do relating to the media? The second thing?
3. What kind of information about the recall will you post on your company's media website?
4. Is the fact your company has retained a law firm specializing in product liability something you would share with the media? Why or why not?
5. Would you want to discuss with the media the fact Buon Giorno has engaged an epidemiologist and a pathologist to examine your processing equipment and packaging facilities? Why or why not? If asked the question, how would you *frame* for the media the decision to hire inspectors in terms of the allegations that people got sick from eating your product?
6. Think about, and list, all the important pieces of information leading up to the recall. How might you frame the entire situation to help build the media's agenda in this food poisoning case?
7. After your initial contact with the media, when will you be in touch with them again? Why did you make the decision you made?

This case was prepared from public sources by James S. O'Rourke, Teaching Professor of Management, as the basis for class discussion rather than to illustrate either effective or ineffective handling of an administrative situation. Personal identities have been disguised.

Additional details related to the media relations portion of the case, and your role as a company communicator, have been added by the authors of this text with the express permission of James S. O'Rourke and the Eugene D. Fanning Center for Business Communication.

Amazon.com, Inc.: Going Shopping With AI

Introduction

On a wintry morning in Seattle, more than a hundred people gathered outside a grocery store. January 22, 2018, was a milestone. Although the store was more than a year old, at last it was open to the public. Inside, the unusual layout immediately distinguished it from the standard supermarket. Where were the checkout lines? Where were the cashiers?

Amazon Go, the first cashierless convenience store, was open for business. Before shopping, customers downloaded the Amazon Go app and connected it to their Amazon account. They entered the store, took the products they wanted from shelves, and left, bypassing the normal checkout process.[1] The store offered a wide variety of food and drinks, including snacks, ready-made meals prepared by professional chefs, pastries from local bakeries, and alcoholic beverages.

Employing the same technology applied to self-driving cars, Amazon's "Just Walk Out" system detects when a customer removes a product from a shelf, adding it to a virtual shopping cart.[2] If the customer then decides not to buy the item and returns it to the shelf, it disappears from the virtual cart. Once the customer has finished shopping, he or she may walk out of the store. Minutes later, Amazon bills the customer's account and sends an email confirming the purchase.

Amazon's technology is an innovative application of artificial intelligence. Critics see a downside, however, to encouraging too much automation in labor-driven industries.

Company Background

CEO Jeff Bezos founded Amazon.com in 1994, determined to catch the e-commerce wave of the 1990s. Amazon started as an online bookseller. During the dot-com bubble, it expanded through partnerships and acquisitions into other areas of retail. Unlike several competitors, it survived the Internet crash. After nearly 25 years in operation, it has become one of the largest online retailers in the world, ranked alongside Chinese web giant Alibaba. Some industry analysts predict that Amazon will be one of the few companies to achieve a trillion-dollar market cap.[3]

Amazon has expanded into selling cloud computing and subscription-based services such as Amazon Prime, but the majority of its revenue still comes from retail. Amazon claims that improving customers' shopping experience is its primary objective. "We seek to be Earth's most customer-centric company," states the company's 2017 Form 10-K.[4] Since its founding, Amazon has continuously re-envisioned how customers interact with online sales platforms.

Launching the Amazon Go store is the third move Amazon has recently made in the grocery space. In 2017, Amazon announced AmazonFresh, a fresh produce delivery service available in select major cities in the U.S. and abroad. The second development later in the year was the acquisition of Whole Foods, which gave Amazon brick-and-mortar sites and access to supply chain expertise.[5] Jeffrey Wilke, CEO of Amazon's Worldwide Consumer business, is leading the transition. The Amazon Go initiative, headed by Amazon VP Gianni Puerini, could be seen as a continuation of Amazon's expansion strategy, as well as an affirmation of its commitment to revolutionizing the shopping experience.

Innovations in the Grocery Industry

Amazon Go bridges two competing retail models: the emerging online grocery industry and the traditional supermarket and grocery store space.

Prior to the Great Depression, independent grocers ran local mom-and-pop, full-service businesses, attended by store clerks who would take a list from the customer and personally collect items from the shelves. Specialized stores such as butcher shops and bakeries were far more common than the one-stop, supermarket setup. In 1916, Clarence Saunders founded Piggly Wiggly in Memphis, Tennessee. Piggly Wiggly chain stores were unique because they were self-service. Customers picked up wooden baskets at the front of the store and then shopped for items themselves. Furthermore, the store labeled each item with a price and carried multiple food categories in one location.[6] By eliminating the need for store clerks, Piggly Wiggly lowered costs enough to compete with independent grocers. By the 1930s, the self-service concept had spread to the East Coast. Chains such as King Kullen, Safeway, Kroger, and A&P became major players. The outbreak of World War II further solidified their position, as independent grocers lost employees to the war. In the mid-1950s, although grocery chains operated 5% of outlets, they accounted for 50% of the sales volume in the industry.[7]

As inflation rose in the 1970s, price competition intensified and supermarkets began to offer coupon discounts and supply cheaper, generic goods in addition to the traditional brand products. The industry consolidated when the economy recovered in the 1980s. A decade later, chains dominated the industry, offering fourteen different store formats. *Ad Age* identified the following notable types: supermarkets, which carried around 9,000 items and often had a service deli and bakery section, and their larger counterpart, the superstore; supercenters, such as Walmart, that combined food and pharmacy departments and spanned an average of 150,000 square feet; and the wholesale club, like Costco, a membership-based, retail-wholesale hybrid.

According to IBISWorld industry reports, supermarket-style grocery stores are now the largest food retail channel in the U.S.[8] At the peak of a mature industry, they face severe price competition from mass merchandisers, particularly Costco and Walmart. Furthermore, consumer demand, driven by

millennials, has shifted away from traditional supermarkets to limited assort-
ment stores such as Aldi and Trader Joe's, as well as fresh format stores like
Whole Foods and Fresh Market that carry high-quality but small selections of
organic healthy foods. Supermarkets have struggled to adapt, because they
are already heavily invested in their current infrastructure.

Online grocery retail takes advantage of consumers' increasing internet
presence. The industry is still developing and is more adaptable than
supermarkets. The use of technology, especially secure payment and tracking
systems, increases margins by reducing the reliance on labor. Market penetration remains low, however, due to irregular sales volume. Online grocers
struggle to compete with brick-and-mortar stores because consumers find it
too expensive to pay for shipping. Also, consumers prefer to personally select
perishable produce, to guarantee quality. Despite the challenges, online
grocers expect that sales will improve once consumers adapt to the new way
of buying groceries.

Artificial Intelligence in Retail

Artificial intelligence (AI) enables machines to perform tasks and make
decisions in an increasingly human way. Implementing AI often reduces the
reliance on human labor. Although delegating tasks to machines benefits
humans by freeing up time for other activities, the risk is that machines will
make certain jobs unnecessary. Most of the developments in AI are task-
oriented, but researchers studying generalized AI aim to create a machine,
such as IBM's Watson, that can handle any kind of task.[9]

AI replacing human workers is a significant concern for the future.
Currently, less than 5% of occupations are entirely automated, and about
60% of occupations have at least 30% of tasks that can be automated.[10]
Businesses have the incentive to find lower cost alternatives to human labor,
especially in tight-margin industries like grocery retail. If automation becomes
more widespread, other supermarkets may also invest in updated infrastructure, and new players such as online retailers may emerge that can invest in
AI technology, reducing demand for labor in the industry.

The potential impact on low-wage employees poses an ethical issue for
companies that wish to implement AI on a wider scale. Cashiers have the
second most common job in the U.S., and the concern is whether or not this
position will become obsolete. The United Food and Commercial Workers
International Union (UFCW), the largest private sector union in the U.S.,
criticized Amazon and the Amazon Go store. It stated, "Amazon is masking
its blind greed as progress," and, "This is not about improving the customer
experience: It is about destroying good jobs, with no regard to the families
and communities impacted."[11]

Amazon's "Just Walk Out" technology may threaten existing competitors.
According to a study by research and consulting firm Magid, the same shop-
per who frequents stores such as BJ's Wholesale, Trader Joe's, and Sam's

Club would choose to instead visit a cashierless, cashless convenience store. The study also reported that over half of Target and Kroger customers surveyed, as well as 44% of Costco shoppers, said they would consider shopping at an Amazon Go-style store.[12] Thus, competitors may be forced to adapt to a similar model or lose customers, if Amazon Go proves successful.

Promotion of Amazon Go

Amazon promoted Amazon Go through its website and YouTube, but did not prominently advertise the opening day. A press release from February 1, 2018, highlighted the store's novelty and technological innovation: "Amazon Go, a new kind of store with no checkout required, is now open to the public in Seattle. The checkout-free shopping experience is made possible by the same types of technologies used in self-driving cars: computer vision, machine learning, and sensor fusion."[13] The statement was repeated in a Form 8-K disclosure. Amazon has given no clear indication about its future vision for Amazon Go technology.

Initial Reactions

For the most part, reactions to the Amazon Go store have been positive and cautiously optimistic. Few problems were reported, except for some rare instances, such as when an individual was able to walk out with a yogurt, undetected.[14] Thus far, shoppers are impressed with the store's technology and its smooth operation; however, whether or not the store will be able to maintain its appeal long-term is still uncertain.

While many customers are satisfied with the technology, it has sparked a discussion about the store's use of AI and Amazon's commitment to automation. Five days after the Amazon Go store opened, the *Seattle Times* posed the following question: "What will automation, robots, and artificial intelligence mean for the labor market of the future, beyond retailing?"[15] The article opens with the story of Zanadu, a comic-book store that closed its store after 42 years in business to operate solely online. It also discusses how Amazon Go is a radical leap in automation but comes across as soulless.

Some people doubt that Amazon Go has the power to disrupt the industry and view the store solely as a novelty. Carol Leaman, CEO of Axonify, argues that many shoppers "still appreciate the human factor and personalized, one-to-one interactions with store associates."[16] Other customers had mixed experiences using the cashierless system. The UK *The Sun's* James Beal commented that the "checkout-free shop is good—but it makes you feel like a criminal."[17] One couple was so worried about leaving without being charged that they waited in the store until they received their e-mail receipt.

Finally, because the technology gathers data and tracks customers as they move around the store, privacy and security are two major concerns. Rebekah Denn of the *Washington Post* went with her son into Amazon Go, and although Rebekah thought it was "creepy" how the AI worked, her son did not care, indicating a generational difference.[18] Data collection and tracking may seem less significant to millennials, who are more accustomed to publishing personal information on social media and participating in shared economy businesses such as Airbnb and Uber. For others, however, the privacy risk may deter them from ever accepting a "Just Walk Out" checkout system.

Discrimination GOing Forward? When You Can't "Just Walk Out."

Within a year of the first store opening, another issue had arisen with the AI–connect to your Amazon account–"Just Walk Out" payment system. It was facing backlash from consumer advocates who said the cash free stores discriminated against the increasing number of Americans who didn't have bank accounts or credit cards. In an April 2019 meeting Amazon's senior vice president of physical stores announced to employees that Amazon planned to add "additional payment mechanisms ... including a pilot that accepts government subsidized SNAP benefits and a new program called Amazon Cash, which lets users add cash to their digital accounts by bringing money to a local store like 7-Eleven or CVS."[19]

When the twelfth Amazon Go store opened in New York City in May 2019 it accepted cash. The question still remains, however, whether cash only customers will feel no discrimination. CNBC reported, "while there still won't be cash registers in the store, shoppers will have the option to use paper money or coins by having a store employee come to them with a mobile device to help them check out and pay, the company said. Otherwise, Amazon Go shoppers are able to simply walk in and out of the store's turnstiles, scanning the Amazon app, to purchase items."[20]

Questions for Discussion

1. What signal has Amazon sent to its constituents by opening the Amazon Go store?
2. Why do you think Amazon used only its website and YouTube to reach out to its potential customers? Could media relations have been a good addition to the initial rollout of the stores?
3. This case sets out a number of issues that Amazon is facing with its new stores. What are those issues? Of the problems you've identified, which ones might be helped through a strategic media relations plan? Why did you pick those topics and not others?
4. What media relations strategies can Amazon use to help consumers adapt to the new shopping experience?
5. Which communication theories would be applicable and useful in putting together a media relations plan for Amazon Go?
6. What media relations output objectives would you set for each of the strategies you are planning to use?

This case was prepared by research assistants Emily Campagna and Billy Munch under the direction of Amanda McKendree, Teaching Professor of Management, as the basis for class discussion rather than to illustrate either effective or ineffective handling of an administrative situation. Information was gathered from corporate as well as public sources.

Additional details that update the situation, and relate to the media relations portion of the case, have been added by the authors of this text with the express permission of James S. O'Rourke and the Eugene D. Fanning Center for Business Communication.

In-N-Out Burger: The Perils of Political Contribution

Twitter Scandal: Party Donation Exposed

On Wednesday, August 29, 2018, at 11:49 p.m. (PDT) Chairman of the California Democratic Party, Eric Bauman, posted a tweet:

> @EricBauman: *Et tu In-N-Out? Tens of thousands of dollars donated to the California Republican Party . . . it's time to #BoycottInNOut—let Trump and his cronies support these creeps . . . perhaps animal style!*

That tweet can be seen as Exhibit 14.1.

By the next morning, the call to action had gone viral. Social media sites, blogs, and Twitter accounts responded with passionate but mixed reviews. Some called for an outright boycott of the In-N-Out chain, while others found humor in the outrageous notion of shunning their beloved burger joint. News outlets were also quick to pick up on Bauman's call to action and the Twitter debate spread rapidly across the nation.

EricBauman ✓
@EricBauman

Et tu In-N-Out? Tens of thousands of dollars donated to the California Republican Party... it's time to #BoycottInNOut - let Trump and his cronies support these creeps... perhaps animal style!lamag.com/digestblog/in-...

11:49 PM · Aug 29, 2018 · Los Angeles, CA

Your Favorite Burger Chain Just Donated a Bunch of Money t...
In-n-Out just dropped $25,000 into the GOP's coffers
lamag.com

♡ 775   ◯ 3,615 people are talking about this

The Republican Party was swift to respond to the trending movement and took to social media to express their gratitude. Republican Senator Jim Nielsen, and the Republican candidate for Governor of California, John H. Cox, posted unabashed photos of their In-N-Out meals and thanked the restaurant for their generous support. By the afternoon of August 30th, both the Democratic and Republican parties had thrown their hats in the ring.[20, 21]

The exposed contribution had been made on Monday, August 28, 2018, just two days before Bauman's tweet had gone live. In-N-Out's latest donation of $25,000 was given to the California Republican Party in support of the November 6th California General Election. This wasn't, however, the first time that In-N-Out had donated to the GOP. In August of 2017, the burger chain contributed $30,000 to party initiatives and yet another $30,000 in May of 2016. Unknown to most people at the time, In-N-Out had also donated $50,000 in May of 2018 and $30,000 in both 2016 and 2017 to the Democratic PAC known as "Californians for Jobs and a Strong Economy."[22, 23]

As flurries of responses continued to swirl about the social media sphere, In-N-Out found itself isolated in the middle of a blue state, amidst a polarizing political climate, looking down the barrel of a possible boycott. As word spread across the nation, the famous burger drive-through must decide how to address the midnight Tweet before the boycott becomes a reality.

In-N-Out Burger Corporation

In-N-Out was founded in 1948 by Harry and Esther Snyder in Baldwin Park, California. The restaurant was California's first drive-through hamburger stand with a two-way speaker that allowed customers to place their orders from their vehicle without having to use the traditional carhop. While competitors in the area focused on innovating their menu and increasing speed, In-N-Out stayed true to its humble beginnings. Quality and freshness was the priority; the food was prepared to order, and the ingredients were sourced locally by Harry Snyder himself.[24]

The menu has not changed much since 1948 and includes three different kinds of burgers (the hamburger, the cheeseburger, and the "Double-Double"), French fries, fountain drinks, and milkshakes in three flavors (chocolate, strawberry, and vanilla). Despite the simple menu, In-N-Out offers a famous "Secret Menu" that can be sourced solely through word-of-mouth. Popular items on the mysterious menu include, "Animal Style" burgers and fries, Neapolitan milkshakes, and Protein Style burgers.

Today, In-N-Out boasts 335 locations across California, Nevada, Arizona, Utah, Oregon, and Texas. Despite the tremendous growth, In-N-Out remains a family-run company with Lynsi Snyder, the only grandchild of Harry and Esther, at the helm as President. Headquartered in Irvine, California, the company has remained close to its roots and has nearly 250 locations in California alone.[25] In-N-Out's success on the West Coast stems from their cult-like following that attracts locals, Hollywood celebrities, and tourists alike.[26]

The United States Political Climate

The United States of America was in the midst of a highly polarized political climate in 2018. President Donald J. Trump took office on January 20, 2017, following the aftershock of his victory over Democratic candidate Hillary R. Clinton. By September 30, 2018, Trump's Presidential approval rating had plummeted to 41%, lower than any first-term president in American history.[27] Talks of Russian collusion, election tampering, and impeachment have been circulating vigorously throughout news outlets around the world and the Republican Party reputation has taken a significant hit.[28, 29, 30, 31]

In the weeks leading up to Bauman's tweet, the Republican Party, with Trump at the helm, has been under heavy scrutiny. Michael D. Cohen, President Trump's former personal lawyer, pleaded guilty to eight felonies in August and was interviewed frequently about the Republican presidential campaign and its possible link to Russian operatives.[32]

Democrats, on the other hand, were less active in the news headlines during the month of August. Leading up to the In-N-Out call for boycott, Democrats were slightly favored to win a House majority due to Trump's relatively low approval ratings and poor feedback on major congressional GOP initiatives.[33] This forecast came as no surprise, considering the majority of Millennials lean toward the Democratic Party and less than a third identify as Republicans. Gen-Xers and Boomers, however, demonstrate a more balanced split with only a slight majority leaning Democratic.[34]

Despite the criticism and polarity of the political landscape, leading restaurant chains have continued to show their support. In 2018, the Republican Party received $150,000 in donations from Wendy's Company employees in the form of individual donations; $39,200 in donations from Yum! Brands; and $7,270 in donations from Chick-Fil-A employees.[35, 36, 37] McDonald's Corporation led the pack with generous donations amounting to $368,570 to the Republican Party. These donations all stemmed from company PACs and individual employees.[38]

The Blue State

With an estimated population of 39.78 million in 2018, California is the largest state on the West Coast and is home to one of the most diverse populations in the world.[39] As the most populous state in the U.S., California has a well-earned reputation as a strongly Democratic culture. According to the Public Policy Institute of California, in 2018 Democrats made up 44.4% of California's 19 million registered voters. No-party-preference voters made up 25.5% and leaned predominantly liberal, while Republicans represented 25.1% of California voters. With 83,518 fewer members than the group of voters who reject party labels altogether, the Republican Party saw a significant decrease in party support from a previous poll of 28.4% in 2014.[40]

With the mid-term election just a few months off, voter registration had hit a record high of 75.7% of eligible adults during the In-N-Out

Burger controversy. Some 46% of likely voters were extremely or very enthusiastic about voting in congressional races that year and 52% of likely voters said they would vote for the Democratic candidate in their House of Representatives election.

Republican Response

Republicans quickly seized the call for a boycott as an opportunity to attack the left and show support for In-N-Out. Multiple Republican elected officials took to social media to show their support and appreciation for the burger chain In-N-Out of California. Senator Jim Nielsen posted a picture of himself surrounded by multiple bags of burgers and fries saying:

> *Enjoying our favorite fast food restaurant In-N-Out Burger at the Capitol today. No boycott here!*

Gubernatorial hopeful John Cox took the opportunity to call out his Democratic opponent, Gavin Newsom, tweeting:

> @TheRealJohnHCox: *There's nothing more California than In-N-Out Burger... If @GavinNewsom is nervous about debating me on CA issues— maybe a friendly Double Double vs Caviar joust?* (4:23 p.m., August 20, 2018). See Exhibit 14.2.

Antonio Sabato Jr, a model turned actor, turned aspiring politician, used the platform to show his support for In-N-Out and support for the "Make America Great" movement with his tweet:

> @AntonionSabatoJr: Heading to @inandoutburger, have you heard how good the burgers are? #kag #maga. (4:35 p.m., August 20, 2018)

The official California Republican Party took a more subtle approach, praising the restaurant chain for its ties to California and fair treatment of its employees. Communications director for the California Republican Party, Matt Fleming said:

> *It's disappointing that he's attacking a company that's a California institution and widely regarded as a good employer.* [41]

Other Republicans with large social media followings quickly jumped in on the action, announcing their support. Franklin Graham, Kristy Swanson, and James Woods proudly declared they would be eating at In-N-Out and urged

their followers to do the same.[42] See
Exhibit 14.3.

The call for a boycott also caused
some of the more energized and
extremist MAGA supporters on the
right to publicly pledge their alle-
giance to the California burger giant.
All over Twitter, proud Trump supporters used this opportunity to call
out the delicate nature of liberals and
how intolerant the left really is.

Democratic Response

Democrat Eric Bauman's call for the
boycott was unenthusiastically met
by other Democrats. No other major
elected Democrat chimed in with
support of his boycott suggestion.

If my followers would be so inclined, please buy an IN-N-OUT BURGER every chance you get. #InNOutBurger #ScrewTheLiberals

Most of the left-leaning support for the boycott came from active Twitter
users and grassroots organizers. Twitter user @KatrinaHagen2, whose profile
describes her as "a proud member of the resistance," tweeted that the burger
chain's food had been a staple of their kids and friends but that the boycott
was a no brainer.[43] Another user, @PatClaerySoCal, tweeted:

> Guess I ate my last In-N-Out burger last week. I will write them to let them
> know about my decision, maybe we all should.[44]

However, many within the Democratic Party found the boycott nonsensi-
cal. *The Los Angeles Times* interviewed Anthony Grigore, a self-proclaimed
Democrat, who was on his way to eat at In-N-Out that Thursday. "Eating
at In-N-Out is such a standard thing to do across California," Grigore said,
clearly unimpressed by the boycott idea.[45]

At least one elected Democrat dismissed the boycott by coming to the defense of In-N-Out. Progressive California Assemblywoman Lorena Gonzalez
Fletcher tweeted:

> @LorenaSGonzalez: *For the record, at least In-N-Out pays their workers
> living wage, as employees. More than we can say about countless political
> donors on both sides.* (3:17 PM–Aug 30, 2018)

The negative backlash and swift, overwhelming response from the right led
other California Democratic Party officials to detach themselves from the boycott.
In an interview, John Vigna, Democratic Party Communications Director, said:

> It was his personal tweet and doesn't reflect party policy. That said, he is
> giving force to a sentiment many people feel right now. Which is that, in

this era, with the stakes so high, engaging in things like personal boycotts is a way for people to effect change.[46]

In-N-Out Decision Point

Much like every political news story during that time period, the responses from the left and the right were highly dichotomous. In previous years, a political contribution like this would likely have gone unnoticed, but the political climate in 2018 was more delicate. In-N-Out faced the possibility of alienating its mostly liberal California customers or, perhaps, losing support from Republican-leaning or Independent and unaffiliated customers in other states.

During this time period In-N-Out did not have a strong social media presence, although it does have Twitter, Facebook and LinkedIn accounts. It also still has the most basic of websites, focusing mainly on its locations and food. However, Executive Vice President Arnie Wensinger acted fast to ensure the 24-hour news cycle didn't turn the boycott into a communication professional's worst nightmare. He released a statement that said:

> In 2018, In-N-Out Burger has made equal contributions to both Democratic and Republican Political Action Committees in the State of California. For years, In-N-Out Burger has supported lawmakers who, regardless of political affiliation, promote policies that strengthen California and allow us to continue operating with the values of providing strong pay and great benefits for our Associates.
>
> It is actually far more important to In-N-Out and our Foundations to support our communities by contributing millions of dollars to hundreds of organizations in California to prevent child abuse, human trafficking and substance addiction.
>
> We have been fortunate to do business in this great state for almost 70 years. While it is unfortunate that our contributions to support both political parties in California has caused concern with some groups, we believe that bipartisan support is a fair and consistent approach that best serves the interests of our company and all of our customers.[47]

Questions for Discussion

1. Given your knowledge of communicating with constituents and stakeholders, in addition to Wensinger's statement, how do you believe In-N-Out should have responded to the boycott threat?
2. Is there a mix of earned, owned, and shared media you might have recommended the company use in this situation? Specifically, which media would you have suggested they use to respond? Why did you choose those media?
3. Review the In-N-Out Burger corporate website at www.in-n-out.com. Make some notes about what they could do better to communicate with

their customers and other constituents—particularly journalists interested in the company and what it's doing—on this owned medium. Be prepared to discuss this with your colleagues.

4. Do you see In-N-Out as a company that uses a proactive or a reactive strategy in its communication? Why do you think they do this? How could the type of company and its history play into the decisions it has made about its communication strategies?

5. If you had been in charge of their communication team, would you have suggested reaching out to the media in the situation In-N-Out faced in this case? Why or why not?

This case was originally prepared by Research Assistants Maria Muldoon and Rachel Youdale under the direction of James S. O'Rourke, Teaching Professor of Management, as the basis for class discussion rather than to illustrate either effective or ineffective handling of an administrative situation. Information was gathered from corporate as well as public sources.

Additional details that update the situation and others that relate to the media relations portion of the case have been added by the authors of this text with the express permission of James S. O'Rourke and the Eugene D. Fanning Center for Business Communication.

REFERENCES

1. Amazon, "Welcome to Amazon Go," https://www.amazon.com/b?node=16008589011

2. Ibid.

3. Teresa Rivas, "Amazon Will Join the Trillion Dollar Market Someday," *Barron's Tech Trader Daily*, 1/10/2018, https://www.barrons.com/articles/amazon-will-join-the-trillion-dollar-market-cap-clubsomeday-1515611070; Eugene Kim, "Morgan Stanley makes a bull case for Amazon in 2018, and sees it hitting $1 trillion in market cap," *CNBC Tech*, 1/12/2018, https://www.cnbc.com/2018/01/12/morgan-stanley-is-bullish-on-amazon-and-sees-1-trillion-market-cap.html

4. Amazon, 2017 *Form 10-K* (2/2/2018), 3

5. Laura Stevens, "Jeff Wilke: The Amazon Chief Who Obsesses Over Consumers," *The Wall Street Journal*, 10/11/2017, https://www.wsj.com/articles/jeff-wilke-the-amazon-chief-who-obsesses-over-consumers-1507627802

6. Ashley Ross, "The Surprising Way a Supermarket changed the World," *TIME*, 9/9/2016, http://time.com/4480303/supermarkets-history/

7. Adage, "Grocery and Supermarket," *Adage*, 9/15/2003, http://adage.com/article/adage-encyclopedia/grocery-supermarket/98499/

8. Andrew Alvarez, "IBISWorld Industry Report OD5085: Online Grocery Sales in the U.S." *IBISWorld*, June 2017, accessed 2/12/2018; Meghan Guattery, "IBISWorld Industry Report 44511: Supermarkets & Grocery Stores in the U.S." *IBISWorld*, October 2017, accessed 2/12/2018

9. Bernard Marr, "What Is the Difference Between Artificial Intelligence and Machine Learning," *Forbes*, 12/6/2016, accessed 2/23/2018, https://www.forbes.com/sites/bernardmarr/2016/12/06/what-is-the-difference-between-artificial-intelligence-and-machine-learning/#683d1dc82742

10. Lori G. Kletzer, "The Question with AI Isn't Whether We'll Lose Our Jobs—It's How Much We'll Get Paid," *Harvard Business Review*, 1/31/2018, accessed 2/7/2018, https://hbr.org/2018/01/the-question-with-ai-isnt-whether-well-lose-our-jobs-its-how-much-well-get-paid?utm_medium=email&utm_source=newsletter_daily&utm_campaign=dailyalert&referral=00563&spMailingID=18928771&spUserID=Mzg0MTM0OTQ2S0&spJobID=1200042776&spReportId=MTIwMDA0Mjc3NgS2

11. Marc Perrone, "UFCW Statement on Amazon Go," *UFCW for working America*, 12/7/2016, http://www.ufcw.org/2016/12/07/ufcw-statement-on-amazon-go/

12. Elaine Low, "Amazon Go Threatens This Wal-Mart Chain, Five Others: Expert," *Investor's Business Daily*, 1/22/2018, https://www.investors.com/news/amazon-go-threatens-this-wal-mart-chain-five-others-expert/

13. Amazon Investor Relations, "Amazon.com Announces Fourth Quarter Sales up 38% to $60.5 Billion," Amazon Press Releases, 2/1/2018, http://phx.corporate-ir.net/phoenix.zhtml?c=97664&p=irol-newsArticle&ID=2329885

14. Deirdre Bosa and Sara Salinas, "We accidentally took a yogurt from Amazon's new grocery store without paying, but Amazon told us to keep it," *CNBC*, 1/22/2018, https://www.cnbc.com/2018/01/22/amazon-go-grocery-store-opened-and-we-accidentally-stole-a-yogurt.html

15. Jon Talton, "Seeing a retail future beyond Amazon Go," *Seattle Times*, 1/27/2018, https://www.seattletimes.com/business/economy/seeing-a-retail-future-beyond-amazon-go/

16. Ibid.

17. James Beal, "Shelf Conscious Amazon's checkout-free shop is good—but makes you feel like a criminal," *The Sun*, 1/26/2018, https://www.thesun.co.uk/tech/5427283/amazon-go-seattle-test-review/

18. Rebekah Denn, "I thought Amazon's new cashier-free store was creepy. My teenage son couldn't care less." *The Washington Post*, 1/26/2018, https://www.washingtonpost.com/lifestyle/food/i-thought-amazons-new-cashier-free-store-was-creepy-my-teenage-son-couldnt-care-less/2018/01/25/1f805838-020c-11e8-9d31-d72cf78dbeee_story.html?utm_term=.a0a98eeb10e3

19. Eugene Kim, "Amazon Exec tells employees that Go stores will start accepting cash to address 'discrimination' concerns," CNBC, 4/10/2019, https://www.cnbc.com/2019/04/10/amazon-exec-tells-employees-that-go-stores-will-start-accepting-cash.html.

20. Cox, John (TheRealJohnHCox). "There's nothing more Californian than In-N-Out Burger. Great lunch today in If. @GavinNewsom is nervous debating me on CA issues—maybe a friendly Double Double vs Caviar joust?" 30 August 2018, 1:23PM. Twitter.

21. Nielsen, Jim (CASenatorJim). "End of Session feast from our favorite fast food restaurant https://twitter.com/innoutburger> @innoutburger." 30 August 2018. 1:12PM. Twitter.

22. Daniels, Jeff. "In-N-Out Burger's $25,000 Donation to California GOP Brings Call for Boycott from Democrats." CNBC, 31 Aug. 2018, www.cnbc.com/2018/08/30/in-n-out-burger-faces-boycott-for-california-gop-donation.html

23. Hart, Angela. "'Stop Eating In-N-Out like Yesterday.' California Democrats Call for Boycott." The Sacramento Bee, 30 Aug. 2018, 10:31AM, www.sacbee.com/news/politics-government/capitol-alert/article217577065.html

24. "History-In-N-Out Burger." In-N-Out Burger, 2014, www.in-n-out.com/history.aspx.

25. "California Restaurant Locations-In-N-Out Burger." In-N-Out Burger, 2014, www.in-n-out.com/locations/california

26. People Staff. "25 Times Celebrities Have Hit Up In-N-Out Burger After Awards Shows." People.com, 24 Jan. 2018, people.com/food/celebrities-eating-at-in-n-out-burger-photos-miley-cyrus-anna-kendrick/#aziz-ansari-eric-wareheim

27. Gallup, Inc. "Presidential Approval Ratings—Donald Trump." Gallup.com, 2018, news.gallup.com/poll/203198/presidential-approval-ratings-donald-trump.aspx

28. Haltiwanger, John. "US Reputation Will Take 'Years to Recover' from Trump Presidency, Warn Experts." The Independent, 23 July 2018, www.independent.co.uk/news/world/americas/donald-trump-us-america-reputation-nato-putin-russia-a8459671.html

29. Mayer, Jane. "How Russia Helped Swing the Election for Trump." The New Yorker, 24 Sept. 2018, www.newyorker.com/magazine/2018/10/01/how-russia-helped-to-swing-the-election-for-trump

30. McArdle, Megan. "Opinion | Poll by Sinking Poll, Trump Inches toward Impeachment." The Washington Post, 31 Aug. 2018, www.washingtonpost.com/blogs/post-partisan/wp/2018/08/31/poll-by-sinking-poll-trump-inches-toward-impeachment/?utm_term=.183ac6045581

31. McCarthy, Tom. "Trump and 'Collusion': What We Know so Far about Mueller's Russia Investigation." The Guardian, 15 Sept. 2018, www.theguardian.com/us-news/2018/sep/14/robert-mueller-trump-russia-investigation-what-we-know

32. Haberman, Maggie, et al. "Michael Cohen Has Spoken Repeatedly About Trump With Mueller's Prosecutors." *The New York Times*, 20 Sept. 2018, www.nytimes .com/2018/09/20/us/politics/michael-cohen-mueller-interviews.html

33. Pramuk, Jacob. "'You'd Rather Be the Democrats than the Republicans': How Election Analysts See the Battle for House Control." *CNBC*, 26 Aug. 2018, www .cnbc.com/2018/08/24/democrats-have-edge-over-republicans-in-battle-for-house-majority.html

34. Fingerhut, Hannah. "The Generation Gap in American Politics | Pew Research Center." Pew Research Center for the People and the Press, 7 Mar. 2018, www .people-press.org/2018/03/01/the-generation-gap-in-american-politics/

35. "YUM! Brands Contributions to Federal Candidates, 2018 Cycle." *OpenSecrets.org*, 2018, www.opensecrets.org/pacs/pacgot.php?cycle=2018&cmte=C00329474

36. "Wendy's Co Contributions to Federal Candidates, 2018 Cycle." *OpenSecrets.org*, 2018, www.opensecrets.org/pacs/pacgot.php?cycle=2018&cmte=C00369090

37. "Chick-Fil-A: Summary." *OpenSecrets.org*, 2018, www.opensecrets.org/orgs/ summary.php?id=D000032532

38. "McDonald's Corp: Recipients." *OpenSecrets.org*, 2018, www.opensecrets.org/ orgs/toprecips.php?id=D000000373&cycle=2018

39. "California Population 2018." *Total Population by Country 2018*, worldpopula-tionreview.com/states/california-population/

40. "California Voter and Party Profiles." *Public Policy Institute of California*, Aug. 2018, www.ppic.org/publication/california-voter-and-party-profiles/

41. Mikelionis, Lukas. "As In-N-Out boycott plan flops, Dem party chief dines alone, GOP feasts." Fox News. September 3, 2018. https://www.foxnews.com/politics/ as-in-n-out-boycott-plan-flops-dem-party-chief-dines-alone-gop-feasts

42. Enloe, Chris. "Top California Dem Called for boycott of In-N-Out Burger over GOP donations. It backfires big time." *The Blaze*. Sept 2, 2018 https://www. theblaze.com/news/2018/09/02/top-california-dem-called-for-boycott-of-in-n-out-burger-over-gop-donations-it-backfires-big-time

43. Daniels, Jeff. "In-N-Out Burger's $25,000 donation to California GOP brings call for boycott from Democrats." *CNBC*. Aug 30, 2018. https://www.cnbc. com/2018/08/30/in-n-out-burger-faces-boycott-for-california-gop-donation. html

44. Ibid.

45. Smith, Dakota & Etehad, Melissa. "Democratic Leader's call for In-N-Out Burger boycott meets its own resistance." *LA Times,* August 30, 2018. http://www .latimes.com/local/lanow/la-me-in-and-out-donations-20180830-story.html

46. Heath, Thomas. "California Democrat urges boycott of In-N-Out for donat-ing to the GOP. The burger chain gives to Democrats, too." *The Washington Post,* August 31, 2018. https://www.washingtonpost.com/business/economy/

california-democrat-urges-boycott-of-in-n-out-for-donating-to-gop-the-burger-chain-gives-to-democrats-too/2018/08/31/25c7301e-ad46-11e8-b1da-ff7f-aa680710_story.html?utm_term=.7ea9fa6394b8

47. Morefield, Scott. "In-N-Out refuses to back down, responds to Democratic boycott push with strong statement." *Daily Caller.* August 30, 2018. https://dailycaller.com/2018/08/30/in-n-out-responds-to-democrat/

INDEX

CPSIA information can be obtained
at www.ICGtesting.com
Printed in the USA
LVHW081929030222
710074LV00004B/248

9 780190 844271